FRANKLIN ROOSEVELT AND THE ORIGINS OF THE CANADIAN-AMERICAN SECURITY ALLIANCE, 1933–1945

FRANKLIN ROOSEVELT AND THE ORIGINS OF THE CANADIAN-AMERICAN SECURITY ALLIANCE, 1933–1945

Necessary, but Not Necessary Enough

GALEN ROGER PERRAS

PRAEGER

Westport, Connecticut
London

E
183.8
.C2
P47
1998

Library of Congress Cataloging-in-Publication Data

Perras, Galen R., 1961–
    Franklin Roosevelt and the origins of the Canadian-American
security alliance, 1933–1945 : necessary, but not necessary enough /
Galen Roger Perras.
        p. cm.
    Includes bibliographical references and index.
    ISBN 0–275–95500–1 (alk. paper)
    1. Roosevelt, Franklin D. (Franklin Delano), 1882–1945. 2. United
States—Foreign relations—Canada. 3. Canada—Foreign relations—
United States. 4. United States—Foreign relations—1933–1945.
5. Alliances. 6. Security, International. I. Title.
E183.8.C2P47 1998
327.73071′09′043—DC21   97–39773

British Library Cataloguing in Publication Data is available.

Library of Congress Catalog Card Number: 97–39773
ISBN: 0–275–95500–1

First published in 1998

Praeger Publishers, 88 Post Road West, Westport, CT 06881
An imprint of Greenwood Publishing Group, Inc.

Printed in the United States of America

The paper used in this book complies with the
Permanent Paper Standard issued by the National
Information Standards Organization (Z39.48–1984).

10 9 8 7 6 5 4 3 2 1

Copyright Acknowledgments

The author and publisher gratefully acknowledge permission for use of the following material:

Passages from the Vincent Massey Papers used by permission of Massey College.

Passages from the manuscript material of J. Pierrepont Moffat, shelf mark MS Am 1407, used by
permission of the Houghton Library, Harvard University.

Contents

Acknowledgments

No historical study is the product solely of its author, although the conclusions found herein are mine alone. The following institutions and repositories kindly permitted me access to their valuable collections: the Australian Archives, Canberra; the British Columbia Archives and Records Service, Victoria; the Directorate of History and Heritage, Department of National Defence, Ottawa; the Durham University Archives, Durham; Duke University Archives, Durham; the Herbert Hoover Presidential Library, West Branch; the Houghton Library, Harvard University, Cambridge; the Manuscript Division, Library of Congress, Washington, D.C.; the George C. Marshall Library, Lexington; the Massey Library, Royal Military College of Canada, Kingston; the National Archives of Canada, Ottawa; the National Archives and Records Administration, College Park and Washington, D.C.; the National Defence Headquarters Library, Ottawa; the Naval Historical Center, Washington, D.C.; the Public Record Office, Kew; the Queen's University Archives, Kingston; the Franklin Delano Roosevelt Presidential Library, Hyde Park; Sterling Memorial Library, Yale University, New Haven; the United States Air Force Academy Library, Colorado Springs; the United States Army Military History Institute, Carlisle Barracks; and the University of Toronto Archives, Toronto.

The Social Sciences and Humanities Research Council of Canada graciously provided me with a two-year postdoctoral fellowship, and the Franklin and Eleanor Roosevelt Institute and the Herbert Hoover Presidential Library Association furnished travel grants that enabled me to visit those fine presidential libraries. Jack English is due a special round of applause for convincing Greenwood Press to give me a book contract. Professors John English, R.G. Haycock, and Keith Neilson provided the letters that brought forth the financial aid that made this project possible. Heather Ruland and especially Rebecca Ardwin from Greenwood Press proved especially helpful in shepherding me safely through the publishing process, as did copy editor Henry Lazarek. Charlene Elliott also applied her formidable editing and effective writing skills to my manuscript.

John Fraser, the Master of Massey College, kindly has granted permission to cite from the Vincent Massey Papers held by the University of Toronto Archives. Quotations from the Pierrepont Moffat Papers appear here with the approval of the Curator of Manuscripts, Houghton Library, Harvard University. As always, this book is dedicated to my parents, Roland and Dolores Perras.

Introduction

One approaches a study of Franklin Delano Roosevelt and Canadian-American security relations with some trepidation because perhaps no other American president has attracted so much scholarly attention. Elected at the very height of the Great Depression, Roosevelt won four presidential terms, created the modern American welfare state that lasted almost six decades, led his nation into World War Two only to die of a stroke as victory came into sight, and acquired a reputation as a "protean figure" ranking with his fellow presidents, George Washington and Abraham Lincoln.[1] Dozens of books have sought to illuminate aspects of this enigmatic man's life from his days as a New York assemblyman to his status of liberal New Dealer and wartime commander-in-chief. More than 50 years after Roosevelt's death, many still argue about his foreign policy goals and whether those policies succeeded. Orthodox and some revisionist historians regard Franklin Roosevelt as the ultimate realist who confronted difficult domestic and international conditions, whereas neoconservatives portray him as a naive and idealistic bumbler who misunderstood both the practice of international relations and the Soviet Union. Still others see Roosevelt either as a realist who failed to understand his room to maneuver, a skilled pragmatist operating under a series of misconceptions about the Stalinist regime, or an "idealist-realist" who sacrificed a clear and defensible vision of a reformed international order because of wartime needs and dilemmas.

All such studies suffer from the affliction of getting a handle on Roosevelt's intentions. Characterized by Arthur M. Schlesinger, Jr., as often lazy and superficial in his thought, and intuitive rather than logical,[2] Roosevelt was famously described by the noted American jurist Oliver Wendell Holmes as possessing "[a] second-class intellect but a first-class temperament."[3] Notoriously private and prone to revealing his innermost thoughts only in dribs and drabs when it suited him, Roosevelt proved a mystery even to his closest friends and collaborators. Henry L. Stimson, Roosevelt's secretary of war from 1940 to 1945, frustrated by Roosevelt's sloppy administrative practices, found the president's propensity for using anecdotes and stories to make his points akin to "chasing a vagrant beam of sunshine around a vacant room."[4]

Indeed, there exists considerable evidence that Roosevelt deliberately (and happily) went out of his way to keep his advisers guessing and the administrative pot boiling. There is a story, perhaps apocryphal, that Roosevelt's good mood on the eve of his presidential library's inauguration had been prompted by the his "thinking of all the historians who will come here thinking that they'll find the answers to their questions."[5] According to Schlesinger, "Roosevelt had decided early that he wanted an inventive government rather than an orderly government," and fellow historian Warren Kimball has concluded that the president's "'competitive' administrative style, wherein different officials and agencies had responsibility for the same tasks and policies, often worked to make him the referee and thus concentrate power in the White House."[6] Roosevelt refused to allow notes to be taken at his cabinet meetings and—according to Sumner Welles, his personal friend and under-secretary of state—possessed an "almost invariable unwillingness to dictate any memoranda of his conversations with foreign statesmen."[7] Nor did Roosevelt attempt to hide his love of presidential power and privilege. In May 1942 he told treasury secretary Henry Morgenthau, Jr., that he was "a juggler, and I never let my right hand know what my left hand does. I may have one policy for Europe and one diametrically opposite for North and South America. I may be entirely inconsistent, and furthermore I am perfectly willing to mislead and tell untruths if it will help win the war."[8]

This historian too made the trip to Hyde Park in the hope of finding some answers to questions about the origins of the Canadian-American security alliance. Although studies abound regarding Roosevelt's policies towards the European powers, Japan, China, the Soviet Union, and Latin America, one would be hard-pressed to find much American scholarship about Roosevelt and Canada. Canada has merited just 14 brief mentions in Robert Dallek's exhaustive examination of Roosevelt's foreign policy, and the Permanent Joint Board on Defense (PJBD), created by the president and Canadian Prime Minister William Lyon Mackenzie King in the desperate and dark summer of 1940, is cited but once.[9] Warren Kimball's 1991 study of Roosevelt's wartime career has just five pages dedicated to Canada and almost nothing about the Canadian-American relationship prior to 1939 except that the president seemed to regarded Canada as a natural part of an American-led regional hemispheric system.[10] Even those American studies dealing more directly with Canadian-American military relations leave something to be desired. Colonel Stanley W. Dziuban's dated but still useful account of Canadian-American military relations in World War Two (it suffers from a lack of access to relevant Canadian records) quickly dispenses with the years prior to 1940, and Joseph T. Jockel's account of the origins of North American air defense begins only in 1945.[11]

But this monograph is a study not only of Roosevelt. As Canada's prime minister for most of the 1920s and from 1935 until his 1948 retirement, William Lyon Mackenzie King dominated Canadian political life in a manner few politicians, before or since, have managed. Fiscally and socially conservative, suspicious of imperialists, and appalled by the unity crisis that had afflicted Canada in World War One (King had lost his parliamentary seat in the 1917 election that had decimated his beloved Liberal Party), King sought, above all, to preserve national unity and to increase Canadian foreign policy autonomy from Britain. And though a recent poll of 25 Canadian historians, citing his "great political skills, his devotion to unity, his establishment of Canada's international persona, his crucial steps towards establishment of the social welfare safety net, and the brilliant way he ran Canada's enormous war effort," rated King as Canada's greatest prime minister,[12] Australian politician and diplomat R.G. Casey declared that "no one man can claim credit for having done as much as Mackenzie King to damage what remains of the fabric of the British Empire. His efforts to make political capital out of his domestic nationalism are analogous to a vandal who pulls down a castle in order to build a cottage."[13] To Canadian nationalist historians, the "puppet" King, acting without the knowledge of his cabinet, Parliament, or his advisers, had "effectively bound Canada to a continental system dominated by the United States" that "largely determined Canadian foreign and defence policy for the next thirty years,"[14] thus setting the stage for "the present condition of Canada, in which the country is so irradiated by the American presence that it sickens and threatens to dissolve in cancerous slime."[15]

Canadian accounts of the relationship between Roosevelt and King have their problems too. Many accept, often without question, two basic and inaccurate notions: that King, beset by an "obsequious" relationship with Roosevelt, was all too eager to accept offers of American military aid for Canada regardless of the possible long-term consequences;[16] and that King's knowledge of and interest in martial matters was so limited that he "would have understood those Chinese intellectuals, who, we are told, regard soldiers as an inferior race of beings whose proceedings deserve only the contempt of civilized men."[17] Unfortunately, studies presenting nuanced explanations of Canadian-American relations have their faults as well. Robert Bothwell's otherwise excellent rendition of the Canadian-American partnership emphasizes the post-1945 years at the unhappy expense of the prewar era, and the weakest chapter of Richard A. Preston's seminal monograph on North American war planning deals with the interwar period.[18]

This study hopes to fill these gaps by illuminating Roosevelt's absolutely pivotal role in the formation of the Canadian-American military alliance. As the first president to display a keen understanding of the ways in which modern weaponry and political developments had altered America's geopolitical environment in the twentieth century (Welles termed Roosevelt's grasp of geopolitics as "almost instinctive"[19]), Roosevelt had begun to identify Canada's security with his nation's as early as 1934. And though he never had a concrete blueprint for drawing the two nations together militarily, he consistently pursued, whenever any suitable opportunities presented themselves, two distinct strategies: He encouraged his senior civilian and military advisers, many long accustomed to seeing the Canadian Dominion as part of a British imperial monolithic rival, to regard Canada as a natural ally in hemispheric security efforts; and he used his influence, sometimes in a most unsubtle manner, to compel Canada to pay more attention to North American defense.

The creation of a Canadian-American military alliance in the dark days of the summer of 1940, however, was not a foregone conclusion. Although King proved willing to explore strategic possibilities prior to 1940, at no time before the outbreak of World War Two did he express a desire to firmly ally his Dominion with the United States. In fact, until 1939 both King and the Canadian military resisted Roosevelt's overtures in favor of a policy of modest rearmament so that the Americans could summon no excuse to intervene if Canada remained neutral during an American war with Japan. And as World War Two progressed, King, worried that closer ties with the United States might mean Canada's political absorption into the American union, sought to reverse much of what he agreed to with Roosevelt. Moreover, the American military remained unconvinced until quite late as to the merits of a security pact with Canada, and had Roosevelt not personally intervened to propose the creation of the PJBD in August 1940, the alliance that so many Canadian and Americans have taken for granted for the last 50 years may have had a far more difficult birth. However, Franklin Roosevelt proved a largely disinterested catalyst. After the North American alliance was set in place, his attentions swung towards the much larger issues of war and peace in Europe and the Pacific, and even before America's official entry into the global conflict in December 1941, Canada found itself both unable to get Roosevelt's attention and growing increasingly suspicious of American intentions. The alliance would survive the war's end and Roosevelt's demise, but that was due largely to the emergence of a new and far more dangerous Soviet foe lurking just over the North American horizon.

NOTES

1. William E. Leuchtenburg, *In the Shadow of FDR: From Harry Truman to Ronald Reagan* (Ithaca: Cornell University Press, 1985), xi.

2. Arthur M. Schlesinger, Jr., *The Age of Roosevelt: The Crisis of the Old Order 1919–1933* (Boston: Houghton Mifflin, 1957), 407.

3. Arthur M. Schlesinger, Jr., *The Age of Roosevelt: The Coming of the New Deal* (Boston: Houghton Mifflin, 1959), 14.

4. Henry L. Stimson and McGeorge Bundy, *On Active Service in Peace and War. Volume II* (New York: Harper & Brothers, 1948), 495; and Henry L. Stimson Papers, Diary, 18 December 1940, Sterling Memorial Library, Yale University [YU], New Haven.

5. Quoted in John Charmley, *Churchill's Grand Alliance: The Anglo-American Special Relationship 1940–57* (San Diego: Harcourt Brace & Company, 1995), 11.

6. Schlesinger, *The Coming of the New Deal*, 544; and Warren F. Kimball, *The Juggler: Franklin Roosevelt as Wartime Statesman* (Princeton: Princeton University Press, 1991), 4.

7. Sumner Welles, *Seven Major Decisions* (London: Hamish Hamilton, 1951), 205.

8. Quoted in Kimball, *The Juggler*, 7.

9. Robert Dallek, *Franklin D. Roosevelt and American Foreign Policy, 1932–1945* (New York: Oxford University Press, 1979).

10. Kimball, *The Juggler*, 109–15.

11. Colonel Stanley W. Dziuban, *Military Relations between the United States and Canada 1939–1945* (Washington, D.C.: Department of the Army, 1959); and Joseph T. Jockel, *No Boundaries Upstairs: Canada, the United States and the Origins of North American Air Defence, 1945–1958* (Vancouver: University of British Columbia Press, 1987).

12. Norman Hillmer and J.L. Granatstein, "Historians Rank the Best and Worst Canadian Prime Ministers," *Maclean's*, 110 (21 April 1997), 37.

13. Quoted in W.J. Hudson and Jane North, eds., *My Dear P.M.: Letters to S.M. Bruce, 1924–1929* (Canberra: Australian Government Publishing Service, 1980), 336.

14. Donald Creighton, *The Forked Road: Canada 1939–1957* (Toronto: McClelland and Stewart, 1976), 43–44.

15. W.L. Morton, "Review of *William Lyon Mackenzie King. II. The Lonely Heights, 1924–1932*," *Canadian Historical Review*, 45 (December 1964), 320–21.

16. Denis Smith, *Diplomacy of Fear: Canada and the Cold War 1941–1948* (Toronto: University of Toronto Press, 1988), 13; Lawrence Martin, *The Presidents and the Prime Ministers. Washington and Ottawa Face to Face: The Myth of Bilateral Bliss 1967–1982* (Toronto: Doubleday, 1982), 113–46; and James Eayrs, *In Defence of Canada: Appeasement and Rearmament* (Toronto: University of Toronto Press, 1965).

17. C.P. Stacey, *Canada and the Age of Conflict: A History of Canadian External Policies. Volume 2: 1921–1948. The Mackenzie King Era* (Toronto: University of Toronto Press, 1981), 275.

18. Robert Bothwell, *Canada and the United States: The Politics of Partnership* (New York: Twayne Publishers, 1992); and Richard A. Preston, *The Defence of the Undefended Border: Planning for War in North America 1867–1939* (Montreal: McGill-Queen's University Press, 1977).

19. Quoted in Dallek, *Franklin D. Roosevelt and American Foreign Policy*, 321.

FRANKLIN ROOSEVELT AND THE ORIGINS OF THE CANADIAN-AMERICAN SECURITY ALLIANCE, 1933–1945

Chapter 1

A Perfectly Logical and Sensible Thing: Canadian-American Security Relations Prior to 1937

On 4 March 1933, Franklin Delano Roosevelt, the Democratic Party's proud and victorious standard-bearer stood before the Capitol on an inclement day to be sworn in as the twenty-sixth president of the United States. Having campaigned for a "New Deal" designed to elevate a moribund and desperate United States from the grips of the greatest depression it had ever known, Roosevelt asserted his "firm belief that the only thing we have to fear is fear itself—nameless, unreasoning, unjustified terror which paralyzes needed efforts to convert retreat into advance." As the nation had asked for "action now," he promised great works to provide employment, programs to revive agriculture, banking reform, and national supervision of key industries and utilities. As to the question of foreign affairs, although the domestic emergency certainly had priority, he promised to restore world trade and dedicated "this Nation to the policy of the good neighbor—the neighbor who resolutely respects himself and, because he does so, respects the rights of others—the neighbor who respects his obligations and respects the sanctity of his agreements in and with a world of neighbors."[1]

Probably no nation on the planet was more interested in Roosevelt's "good neighbor" pledge than Canada, for as Hanford MacNider, the American minister to the Dominion during Herbert Hoover's administration, had pointed out, "[t]he shadow of the United States and everything that happens in it rests very heavily on Canada."[2] For Canadians, the United States was both the fabled "city on the hill," and a feared rival. Thousands of Canadians had migrated south in search of a better life, but many more who stayed in Canada had descended from refugees who had fled the American

Revolution after 1783. This sense of grievance, exacerbated by American invasions during the stalemated War of 1812, had created a strong and popular notion of the Canadian as "the first anti-American, the model anti-American, the archetypal anti-American, the ideal anti-American as he exists in the mind of God."[3] Canadian nationalists had no doubt which society was superior; Canada, unlike its empoisoned neighbor to the south,, had "no polygamous Mormondom; no Ku-Klux terrorism; no Oneida communism; no Illinois divorce system; no cruel Indian massacres."[4] Writing in 1930, Canadian university professor and commentator P.E. Corbett had remarked on "the co-existence of two apparently contradictory phenomena—a network of intimate friendships between Canadians and Americans, and a widespread distaste for Americans in general," a tendency "so ingrained in us that it passes without comment or justification."[5]

Could President Franklin Roosevelt alter this relationship for the better? Many Canadians hoped that would be the case. Although the *Toronto Globe and Mail* greeted Roosevelt's election cautiously—"[t]he victorious campaigner's speeches were more conspicuous for what they omitted than what they included"—four years of Herbert Hoover's administration and three years of economic chaos prompted it to say that as candidate Franklin Roosevelt "gave the impression that he did understand the really big issues surrounding the world depression, the next four years may tell a story different from the last."[6] Possessing fewer doubts, the *Montreal Herald* predicted that the United States, "fundamentally a member of the British family," would find "in this Dominion and in this Empire their truest friends, ready, willing and anxious to cooperate" in economic reconstruction and rehabilitation.[7]

Canadian-American relations certainly were not Roosevelt's major priority in 1933, and though State Department official J. Pierrepont Moffat noted in April 1933 that "the White House control over foreign affairs" rivaled only that wielded by "the great Theodore [Roosevelt],"[8] Franklin Roosevelt had inherited an administrative approach to Canadian affairs dominated by isolationism, a global preoccupation that transcended parochial Canadian-American concerns, and a proclivity to subordinate Canadian issues under the rubric of relations with Britain.[9] American isolation may be traced to George Washington's 1796 caution to have "as little political connection as possible" with foreign countries, but it was World War One that made isolationism, or "independent internationalism"as some have termed it,[10] the dominant American foreign policy creed. Appalled by that conflict's cost and the punitive peace that had followed the 1918 armistice, millions of Americans thus had embraced a dogma that preached the avoidance of all overseas military commitments, the freedom to make totally independent decisions regarding war and peace, and the taking of action only in the national interest.[11] And despite one American statesman's claim that Canada and Canadians were "bound to us by race and so many ties and community of interest,"[12] Canada was not excluded either from the effects of America's isolationist drift. Indeed, shocked by the 60,000 dead it had incurred on Europe's bloody battlefields, the Dominion too had lapsed into isolation after 1918. Although it hag gained a separate seat in the new League of Nations, Canada opposed the League's collective security provision, arguing that Canadians lived "in a fire-proof house, far from inflammable materials."[13] Liberal governments in the interwar period, led by Prime Minister King, spent much effort resisting attempts by Britain and sympathetic Canadians and other empire supporters to centralize imperial diplomatic and military decision-making.

Such introversion on both sides of the forty-ninth parallel made transcending the parochial difficult, particularly as Canada and the United States did not exchange diplomatic missions until 1927. President Calvin Coolidge had opposed a legation in Canada, telling reporters that there was "no real necessity" for it because American consular agents could easily handle trade relations. Not surprisingly then, when the legation finally was established, American diplomats had to be reassured that the State Department considered an Ottawa posting "a real job."[14] Hopes that Herbert Hoover's accession to power in March 1929 would reverse this neglect were dashed. American minister William Phillips advised President Hoover that if Canada was not recognized as "a separate country with all the patriotic vigor of a recently realized nationalism, I am afraid there is trouble ahead."[15] There was. Although King told Phillips that Canada should be "the medium for the cultivation of the closest possible relations between the United States and Great Britain," when Hoover suggested using King to present America's position on naval disarmament to Britain, an aide quickly dissuaded him from approaching the Canadian prime minister.[16] Relations soon bogged down over steep American tariffs on Canadian exports and the smuggling of vast quantities of Canadian liquor into a prohibitionist United States. Secretary of State Henry L. Stimson warned Hoover of the dire consequences to American exports if the tariff issue brought Canada's pro-imperial Conservatives back to power, and Phillips, frustrated by a lack of State Department support or guidance, resigned as minister and returned to Washington.[17]

Hoover's next steps little ameliorated the situation. Hanford MacNider took Phillips's spot; his job qualifications, aside from the obvious good fortune of having had a Canadian grandfather, were his strong Republican ties and a very public support for President Hoover. Although MacNider was liked in Ottawa, the fact that his was a political appointment at a time when Hoover's administration was touting the steps it had taken to professionalize the diplomatic corps did not go unnoticed north of the border.[18] A hastily arranged 1931 summit with King's Conservative successor, R.B. Bennett, proved a frustrating disappointment too. Eager to develop the St. Lawrence River's potential power supply, Hoover found Bennett most reluctant to undertake the expensive project for fear of alienating Quebec voters. Both men came away from that meeting quite unhappy: Hoover thought that Prime Minister Bennett had failed the test of a good neighbor, and Montreal's American consul general reported that he "had caught an intimation that Bennett would not be entirely displeased if the Democratic Party should come into power in the United States."[19]

But it was the decided American propensity for lumping Canadian affairs into its relations with Britain that most hindered ties with the Dominion. As Britain's ambassador to the United States had reported in 1929, Canada's development, "both internally and as a world force," had "confronted the United States for the first time in her history with a neighbour whom she can neither ignore nor overawe." Canada's treatment, he believed, would be an index of how the United States would interact with nations it could no longer remain isolated from, and would offer a point of contact "between the 'American thing' and that philosophy of life which is presented by the British Commonwealth of Nations."[20] Unfortunately, the United States did not know how it should treat Canada. Although Canada had become a self-governing Dominion in 1867, not until the British Parliament passed the Statute of Westminster in 1931 did Canada assume full control of its foreign affairs. And even though most Americans probably did not share President Ulysses S. Grant's tart opinion of Canada as "this semi-independent and irresponsible agency," many probably agreed with a 1924 State Department ruling that Canada existed as a person under international law, but "only in a limited sense."[21]

So, quite uncertain of Canada's international standing and noticeably unsure if their acceptance of Canada's right to have a legation in Washington constituted formal recognition of the Dominion's autonomous status,[22] Americans puzzled about relations with their neighbor to the north. For some the matter seemed simple enough: Canada was a British Dominion, and because Britain was America's traditional rival, so too then was Canada. In 1812 Andrew Jackson had sought "security against future aggressions, by the conquest of all the British dominions upon the continent of North America," and James Monroe, speaking seven years earlier, noted that "[w]hen the pear is ripe it will fall of itself."[23] Between these two extremes lay other, and perhaps not much less dangerous, options. Annexation, Secretary of State James Blaine wrote in 1892, seemed the ideal remedy. Continental unity with the United States would prevent Canada "from being turned into an outpost of European reaction antagonistic in spirit and institutions to the rest" and banish war from North America, whereas an independent Canada would leave open "an endless vista of dispute." The United States could either arrange a simple transfer of sovereignty; or by developing "the commercial autonomy of the continent," encourage Canada to "feel that to enjoy her full measure of prosperity she must be economically a community of this hemisphere, not an outlying dependency of a European power."[24]

Both alternatives had their supporters. In 1869 Senator Charles Sumner had suggested that Britain could atone for the damages inflicted upon Union shipping by British-built Confederate warships by handing over Canada to the United States, and the *Boston Post* proposed in 1926 that Britain trade Canada to America in order to repay outstanding vast World War One loans. Such talk accomplished little except to convince Canadians, as Prime Minister John A. Macdonald put it in 1890, that "every American statesman covets Canada."[25] Macdonald may have had a point. In 1879 President Rutherford B. Hayes had written that Manifest Destiny dictated that Canada and the United States one day "should come under one government" and therefore no "artificial stimulants" were required.[26] Thirty-two years later President Howard Taft proposed reciprocal tariff reductions that, if accepted, would have seriously impacted Canada's independent economic and political development. Though Taft may not have had annexation explicitly in mind, his stated goal of guaranteeing American access to plentiful and cheap Canadian resources (and perhaps the wider imperial market) by preventing Canada's evolution into an advanced industrial state, was ambitious enough to convince a great many Canadians that he did.[27] Initially accepted by a reigning Liberal government eager to develop the Canadian economy, Taft's program crumbled when pro-imperialist Conservatives won the bitterly contested 1911 Canadian election on a virulently anti-American and pro-British platform.

Some American officials thought Canada should be treated as an independent player. Charles Evans Hughes, Coolidge's secretary of state, thought Canada was "no longer a subsidiary corporation in a British holding company" but a "sister nation."[28]

William Phillips agreed, yet even though he was advising Washington to allow Canada to develop its own identity, years of experience had convinced him that the United States and Canada were "one economic unit." If the United States erected steep tariff barriers to Canadian trade, then Phillips had no doubt that there would be a Canadian reaction, and "[o]f course nothing in the world would suit the British Empire better than just some reaction."[29]

Bureaucratic strictures made policy reform difficult. Encouraged by Hoover to "develop an exploitative, neo-mercantilist philosophy which asserted that Canada should supply the United States with raw materials and provide a market for manufactured goods," the Department of Commerce pursued this ambitious goal so single-mindedly that the American legation in Ottawa warned that Canadians saw the United States as "a great octopus planning and longing to encompass Canada in its economic meshes."[30] The State Department was ill-equipped to fight its governmental rival. Its Canadian desk, manned by John (Jack) Hickerson from 1927 to 1941, was subsumed within the 15-man Division of Western European Affairs (48 personnel by 1941), and as Hickerson related much later, he had his hands mostly full fighting his isolationist and anti-British superiors. Policy formulation, in such a climate, definitely took a back seat.[31]

Given Secretary of State Cordell Hull's opinion that Canadian-American relations had reached a low ebb by 1933, Roosevelt's first dealings with Canada were low-key. He sounded out Bennett about organizing an international wheat conference and appointed his maternal cousin, Warren Robbins, to head the legation in Canada.[32] Obviously pleased with Bennett's cooperative attitude and assured by Phillips that Prime Minister Bennett, "a one man show," was "in a position to obtain approval of virtually any program which he should desire to sponsor," Roosevelt happily invited the Canadian leader to Washington in April to discuss mutual tariff reductions. They quickly reached an agreement in principle to negotiate a trade pact, prompting an ebullient Prime Minister Bennett to praise the president as a man of "wide vision, unselfish purpose, steady courage and sincerity, rare patience and determination."[33]

Roosevelt would need that patience. A determined and obstructive Congress opposed any steps to liberalize trade policy while so many millions of Americans remained jobless or underemployed, prompting a very discouraged Canadian minister, William Herridge, to warn State Department officials that if Canada could not get an American deal, it would "have to look elsewhere." Frustrated himself, Roosevelt told Stimson in May 1934 that he was considering visiting Ottawa, a trip the Republican statesman thought "would be a fine thing" from "the standpoint of world politics."[34] Roosevelt did not make that journey, but Canadian affairs acquired a fresh importance thanks to an American army air corps desire to send 10 bombers winging to Alaska across western Canada's vast expanses so as "[t]o further friendly diplomatic relations with Canada and to conduct a goodwill flight to Alaska."[35] In reality the matter was anything but simple, for a great many hopes accompanied those planes and their able crews. In the first instance, the interwar period had been most unkind to the American army. Though the 1920 National Defense Act had formally established a regular army of 280,000 troops, congressional reluctance to vote the necessary fiscal appropriations ensured that there were just 159,000 personnel in army uniforms by 1936. Matters could have been much worse because Roosevelt had intended to chop $144 million and 16,000 men from the army in 1934, a reduction stopped only when army chief of staff General Douglas MacArthur strode into the White House and confronted the president personally. Still, the military budget fell to its lowest outlay since before World War One.[36]

Though the army as a whole therefore badly needed the prestige a successful Alaskan mission would bring, air corps desperation was palpable. Army aviators, led first by Brigadier General William (Billy) Mitchell, had campaigned fruitlessly for years to establish a separate air force complete with an independent mission. For the air power disciples the stark military truth was self-evident and ominous: Given America's geographic isolation, no enemy fleet or army could successfully bridge the oceanic barriers as long as the United States possessed an adequate military capable of speedy mobilization. But if an adversary gained predominance in the air, then its aircraft "could reach our vital centers with comparatively little trouble, and cause inestimable damage," perhaps even win the war.[37] However, the air power prophets found honor difficult to obtain even within their own service. Army leaders attacked General Mitchell for "notoriously" overestimating air power's efficacy, labeled his many theories "unsound," and dismissed his numerous and lengthy reports as agencies "of propaganda for a unified Air Service and other pet lobbies."[38] Although Mitchell resigned his beloved commission in 1926 rather than face the consequences of his conviction for insubordination, other flyers carried on his work and their efforts paid off with a 1931 pronouncement that the air corps was responsible for defending the coasts. Unhappy naval aviators appealed that ruling in 1933, and the matter still was very much in doubt in 1934.[39]

The naval challenge might not have seemed so threatening had the air corps not been reeling from a major setback. Unhappy with air mail contracts awarded by Hoover's administration, Roosevelt had voided those controversial deals in February 1934 and given the job, temporarily at least, to the military. Using craft ill-equipped to fly in poor weather or at night, employing pilots lacking sufficient long-distance flight experience, and flying in the worst winter many could remember, the air corps performed miserably. By the time it was forced to relinquish the mail runs on 1 June 1934, the army had suffered 66 crashes, 12 fatalities, and had amassed considerable public, congressional, and presidential criticism.[40] Most importantly, this very poor performance, following as it did a number of well-publicized practice missions in which bombing efficiency had been unspectacular, left many Americans wondering if the army air corps could carry out long-distance wartime operations. A success, any success, was badly needed, and the Alaskan flight offered at least partial redemption for a tattered aerial reputation.

But the issue was even more complicated. Although the War Department had said publicly that furthering relations with Canada was the flight's main purpose, in truth the mission had been designed with some very practical military applications in mind. While in Alaska, the aviators would survey and photograph possible airfield sites and contribute to the formulation of defense plans for that isolated territory. But most importantly, the mission's secret instructions included a line about testing "the practicability of dispatching an air force to Alaska should necessity therefor [sic] arise."[41] With Japan's spectacular rise to power in east Asia and the Pacific, some War Department officers worried that Alaska might be particularly vulnerable to a surprise

Japanese assault. Although that view was anything but unanimously accepted,[42] there existed sufficient concern for the Alaskan flight to receive War Department backing. The rub was that the most expedient method of despatching aircraft to Alaska meant their flying over Canada. A series of military overflight agreements between Canada and the United States had existed since the 1920s (and the Canadian government had agreed on 2 June 1934 to extend those pacts for another year[43]), but those accords applied only to local flights conducted in eastern North America, not long-distance trips across half a continent. Although the air corps certainly desired to investigate the technical requirements of an Alaskan air route, its definition of practicability extended as well to testing Canada's willingness to cooperate militarily and diplomatically with the United States in a war against Japan.

This vague notion of Canada and the United States as natural military allies (at least against Japan) was a relatively new concept for most Americans. Senator William Henry Seward may have been the first American official to publicly suggest an alliance with Canada in 1853, but he had spoken then in the context only of what he saw as the converging economic development between the two North American nations.[44] For the American military, far more accustomed to viewing Canada either as a potential base for British aggression or as a target, the notion of Canada as a friend was only slowly taking root. Certainly World War One had played some role in encouraging that train of thought. Though the United States entered the conflict in 1917 as an "associated power" rather than as a full-fledged ally of Britain and France, American and Canadian forces had cooperated in the use of ports and transportation networks, training, censorship, intelligence gathering, and munitions production. And though that interaction had stopped somewhat abruptly after 1918, Canada's military had agreed in 1926 "to make specific reply to any requests for information which" the War Department might desire to make, albeit via Britain's military attaché in Washington.[45]

The air corps wanted more than just an exchange of information. As early as 1919, Billy Mitchell, having returned from World War One an aerial hero, had set out a triangular defensive system for the North American continent composed of a series of interconnected flyways anchored on Alaska, the Panama Canal, and Canada. Seeking to capture public support at home and in Canada for his complex scheme, in 1920 Mitchell had organized a four-plane flight from New York City to Alaska in the hope that the flight would establish a Canadian air route that would aid the despatch of air service units to Asia (if needed), and ensure that the airways to Europe and Asia would be controlled "by the two great English speaking races."[46]

Although Canada had permitted that mission, the extensive logistical effort needed to ensure the flight's success (including the placement of supplies at scattered air strips throughout the vast Canadian northwest) demonstrated that even though Mitchell's flyway notions were theoretically sound, in 1920 they remained technically impossible given range limitations and the rather primitive nature of contemporary aeroplane construction.[47] Not easily discouraged (Royal Air Force chief Lord Trenchard had said that if Mitchell could "break the habit of trying to convert his opponents by killing them, he'll go far"[48]), the general was re-energized by his participation in an Asian tour (which doubled as his honeymoon) in late 1923 and early 1924. Convinced that Japan could build "the greatest military machine the world ever saw, such as the armies of Genghis Kahn and Tamerlane," and that armed conflict between the white and yellow races was inevitable, Mitchell wanted 300 aircraft in Alaska poised for a "decisive" bombing offensive against congested Japanese cities made of "paper and wood and other flammable structures."[49] Worried that Japan might seek to preempt such an assault by attacking Alaska first, Mitchell thought that only a speedy despatch of forces to that territory would save the day, and geography dictated Canadian aid. Would Canada help? Mitchell was sure that it would be happy to do so. In the first case Canada's Conservative government, unwilling to be a "partner to an arrangement that could by any possibility be said to be directed against the United States or that might endanger the good relations between" the empire and America, had aided the demise of the Anglo-Japanese alliance in 1921–22.[50] Mitchell's brief visit to Canada in 1923 removed all doubts from the general's inquiring mind: "In their tastes, ideas, and manner of living," Mitchell wrote, Canadians were more American than British, and as a Japanese invasion of Alaska threatened Canada as much as the United States, "[u]nder these circumstances, a distinct understanding with Canada is a perfectly logical and sensible thing, one in accordance with all our traditions and our position in the Northern Hemisphere."[51]

Though Mitchell had long since put his uniform away by 1934, that year's Alaskan flight finally offered his beloved air corps a good chance to test his untried Canadian speculations. Canada's chief of the general staff (CGS), Major General A.G.L. McNaughton, had little sympathy for such aspirations. Although McNaughton had told a senior visiting British official that "any estrangement from the United States plays into" the hands of those in Canada "opposed to co-operation with the Empire in time of war,"[52] having noted American interest in Canadian airspace as early as 1923, McNaughton charged that the proposed 1934 flight constituted "nothing more than a military reconnaissance designed to open an air route from the United States to Alaska which would facilitate reinforcing that territory in the event of war between the United States and Japan." Should Canada acquiesce, it would set an unhappy precedent that "might make it very difficult to maintain our neutrality or to terminate the custom" in a crisis, and might encourage other nations (Japan) to request similar privileges.[53]

McNaughton's concerns could not be taken lightly. Fiercely intent on transforming Canada's moribund militia-based army into a professional force capable of decisively shaping Dominion security policy and playing a major role in any future European conflict, the cerebral general (trained as an engineer by McGill University), according to his bitter service rival Brigadier J. Sutherland Brown (a self-described conservative "Imperialist"), unfortunately possessed a"radical temperament" and was known as a "little Canadian" (an anti-imperialist). Most importantly, Brown thought that McNaughton "had made himself very strong with the Government, particularly with R.B. Bennett, not military, and therefore his recommendations will receive high considerations in high places."[54] So, following up on a 1920 warning by another CGS that with Germany's defeat "the centre of interest had shifted from the North Atlantic to the North Pacific,"[55] McNaughton, echoing C.F. Hamilton's 1921 warning that the United States easily could become "an uncommonly ugly neighbour" if Canada could not prevent the Japanese from using Canadian territory and waters to attack American targets, cautioned in 1933 that Canada could find itself "in an invidious and even dangerous position" if it could not adequately defend its neutrality, a position a specially appointed tri-service committee affirmed. Unless Canada could successfully fend off Japanese incursions, the United States probably would intervene militarily, and given the obvious power disparity, "it would doubtless commend itself to the Canadian Government to exercise great forbearance to the United States in this matter as long as it could convince Japan that it was not conniving at unneutral service." The Canadian military's solution was to suggest a modest West Coast defense buildup and a proper defensive scheme that would emphasize Canadian neutrality in the Pacific.[56]

If McNaughton had been the final arbiter in the matter, the American flight certainly would have not taken place, but the real decision-making power rested firmly with Canada's Under-Secretary of State for External Affairs (USSEA), O.D. Skelton. Recruited from a senior ivory tower post at Queen's University in the 1920s by Prime Minister King, the hardworking, incisive, and indispensable Skelton was "the ablest man in the public service of Canada" according to King, and even Bennett, who had firmly intended to fire Skelton after winning the 1930 election, found that he simply could not get along without him.[57] Though Canadian and British imperialists blamed Skelton for Canada's resistance to military and economic empire centralization prior to World War Two (less-restrained critics sniped about Skelton's Irish heritage), the USSEA was not so much anti-British as he was pro-Canadian. Britain had interests to pursue, and when its statesmen trumpeted about the need for imperial solidarity, Skelton "assumed that the rhetoric concealed a hard-headed attempt to exploit colonial loyalties for the benefit of Great Britain."[58] Also suspicious that General McNaughton was attempting to commit Canada piecemeal to Britain's side in any future bloody European conflict—"how many hypotheses make a commitment," the USSEA had pondered in 1926—Skelton declined to participate in joint defense planning with the Department of National Defence (DND) and had done much to prevent the creation of a Canadian equivalent of Britain's Committee of Imperial Defence (CID) until the 1930s.[59]

Such suspicion, however, did not extend to the United States and Americans. Described by an American diplomat "as a man who has always been a friend of the United States and an advocate of more confident relations with us," Skelton, doubting that the United States desired a political union, thought that Canada's security lay "in her own reasonableness, the decency of her neighbour, and the steady development of friendly intercourse, common standards of conduct, and common points of view."[60] Such reasonableness clearly characterized Skelton's response to the Alaskan overflight request. Arguing that allowing American warplanes to overfly British Columbia once would not "necessarily commit" Canada to a more permanent arrangement, Skelton reminded General McNaughton that America's position was quite unique "as it alone possesses territories on this continent between which a route through Canada is a natural one." But as a sop to the unhappy McNaughton, Skelton suggested that the American planes should fly via a central British Columbia route rather than the more sensitive, and commercially promising, Mackenzie Valley.[61]

Although a most puzzled State Department appealed this restriction on the grounds that American aircraft had already used the Mackenzie Valley route twice (DND had asked Skelton not to reveal the reasons behind its objections[62]), its Ottawa legation reported that Canadians feared that as American bombers would use Alaska to fly to Japanese or Russian objectives, "they may feel that it is in the interest of

Canadian neutrality not to facilitate any flights which might contribute to develop this route for this purpose." So when Skelton told First Secretary Pierre de la Boal that allowing the warplanes to use the Mackenzie Valley route was problematical, Boal made it quite clear that a Canadian refusal to allow the flight "was likely to be looked upon in both countries as a measure prompted by military considerations quite unusual in the existing relations between Canada and the United States and reminiscent of the inhibitions which exist in other parts of the world." This unsubtle threat had its desired effect. Skelton advised Bennett that if he wished to decline the American petition, "it would be preferable to refuse it on the ground that the route is not available rather than bringing in any military defence issues." Bennett agreed, and over McNaughton's renewed objections, he ruled that the United States could use the Mackenzie flyway if it so chose.[63]

This arrangement, however, very nearly blew apart just days later after the *Washington Herald* claimed that the Alaskan mission would test how well the route would function "if it were necessary in war time to concentrate power" in Alaska.[64] Livid, Skelton maintained that the news, regardless of its veracity, would make further military overflights impossible and would further upset the already "very suspicious" Japanese. Skelton did not advocate canceling the flight or the renewal of the overflight pact, but Robbins, reporting the hands of those in DND who were "inclined to view our military operations with some suspicion" had been strengthened, had "no doubt" that some Canadian officers were working "to render any incursions from the United States in time of war as difficult as possible."[65]

Robbins was quite correct. McNaughton's staff continued to beaver away at the neutrality scheme, and the general complained to the British War Office that "the gradual establishment of a practice of despatching aircraft to Alaska over Canadian territory might give rise to a rather awkward situation on some future occasion."[66] The flight itself, which left Washington, D.C., on 19 July and arrived safely in Alaska five long days later, was a technical success. The air corps had demonstrated that its newer B-10 bombers could handle long-distance operations, although Alaska, in the mission commander's opinion, would require a considerable infrastructure to make it a suitable military staging area. Colonel H.H. Arnold also praised the British Columbia route for its excellent weather and hoped that Canada's "[m]ilitary element have gained a very favorable impression of our Air Corps and its personnel." Edmonton's American consul felt certain that Arnold was correct. Although the local press had played up the mission's martial rationale, Canadian military personnel in that northern city had expressed great pleasure "over what they regard as a symbol of identity between the interests of Canada and the United States in the matter of Alaskan defense."[67]

Roosevelt had demonstrated little personal interest in the Alaskan overflight issue, but another situation drew his attention to Canada. By mid-1934 the task of replacing the 1922 Washington Naval Agreement, slated to expire in 1936, occupied military planners in a number of countries. Japan, which had accepted a level of naval inferiority relative to Britain and the United States (a ratio of 3:5:5) in 1922, no longer found that arrangement suitable, and Britain, already concerned by the growing power of Adolf Hitler's Germany, could ill afford a renewed Pacific arms race. So when the British suggested a modest shipbuilding program that might mollify Japan, Roosevelt argued instead for imposing a 20 percent reduction in naval tonnage on each signatory, a proposal that the Japanese, not surprisingly, declined to accept. Roosevelt therefore instructed his delegate at the London Naval Conference to impress the British, "in the most diplomatic way," with the fact "that if Great Britain is even suspected of preferring to play with Japan to playing with us, I shall be compelled, in the interest of American security, to approach public sentiment in Canada, Australia, New Zealand and South Africa in a definite way to make these dominions understand clearly that their future security is linked with us in the United States."[68] Norman Davis did as he was told, intimating to the British government that "Anglo-American cooperation is of more vital importance to the British Empire than to us and that in case of trouble with Japan, Canada as a practical matter would in fact become our hostage."[69]

The move worked. Britain disavowed any naval deal with Japan, but success could not hide the simple fact that Roosevelt's threat to detach the Dominions from the empire, albeit by political means only, was nothing less than "astonishing."[70] What had prompted it? From a British perspective the answer seemed crystal clear: Roosevelt was pursuing a long-standing American goal to uncouple Canada from the empire.[71] The threat also may have been a ploy designed to pressure Britain, a theory that has some considerable credence given that Roosevelt quickly dropped the proposal after Britain gave way. But to label the tactic only a ruse designed for the short term would be to deny some crucial evidence that the geopolitically-minded Roosevelt already was tentatively exploring the possibility of forming a hemispheric defense system. Having told Assistant Secretary of State Sumner Welles the previous June that as the world was "rapidly trending towards a continental policy," with Japan reigning supreme in Asia and the various European powers again instituting "a balance of power regime," Roosevelt had thought that "we here on this Continent must work out a continental understanding of identification of interests." Great Britain would "be left more or less out on a limb," holding on to a few scattered possessions here and there for an uncertain period of time.[72]

Before issuing his threat, Roosevelt had informed the British ambassador that Britain and its Dominions, "as they could not afford" to face a larger Japanese fleet, should adopt his opposition to naval parity. But even though he assured Lord Lothian that he wanted to aid Britain as much as possible against the revisionist dictatorships in Europe and Asia, Roosevelt said that any definite commitments were impossible because their validity would depend greatly "on the personal views of the incumbent of the White House, and no President could bind his successor." It is unclear whether Roosevelt had specifically mentioned Canada in any capacity at that meeting, but Lothian told a Canadian diplomat later that the Dominion could "play a leading part" in convincing the United States to reach an understanding with Britain.[73]

Lothian, though, had mentioned Canada very prominently when he met with William Phillips at the State Department on 11 October. Discussing the distrust of the United States manifested by Prime Minister Stanley Baldwin and Chancellor of the Exchequer Neville Chamberlain, Lothian feared that Britain might accept a Japanese peace guarantee to avoid a damaging arms race it might not be able to win. Moreover, W.L.M. King, expected to replace Bennett as prime minister when Canadian elections were held in late 1935, was now in London for meetings with the British government, and though King could be expected to urge Anglo-American cooperation,[74] Lothian deliberately may have left Phillips with the impression that Britain was recruiting

King's support in the event that Japan drove a wedge between the United States and Britain. If so, that impression was duly noted for when Stimson met with Roosevelt on 30 October, the president remembered that the former secretary previously had spoken of Canada as "the key log" in the Pacific jam.[75]

Perhaps Roosevelt might have carried through with his threat to detach the Dominions from the empire had the British government not backed down on the naval parity issue, though that might ascribe to the president a single-minded determination that he probably did not possess at that time. His governing style emphasized a capacity for innovation and a need for novelty and daring that was neither systematic nor consistent, and that "provided no clearly articulated break with the inherited faith." Britain's ambassador to the United States in World War Two had a more colorful and British analogy appropriate to his privileged British upbringing: The president's policy-making style, Lord Halifax said, was "rather like a disorderly line of beaters out shooting; they do put the rabbits out of the bracken, but they don't come out where you expect."[76]

However, the Canadian rabbit, much to Roosevelt's chagrin, soon popped out from another more familiar hole. Despite the Alaskan flight's technical success, when the army-navy Joint Board promulgated a new air doctrine later in 1934, the USN reassumed primary responsibility for coastal defense. But the major blow to the army air corps came in July 1934 even before Arnold's planes had winged their way north to Alaska. Charged with studying air corps operational capabilities after the air mail fiasco, the Baker Board concluded that air power, though an obviously important strategic element, was not a decisive weapon and therefore the United States need not fear aerial attack.[77] The report's one saving grace, at least from an aviator's point of view, was that its support for developing major airfields throughout the United States echoed army recommendations (the Drum Board report) made the previous October.[78] Few disputed that new bases were required; the argument instead centered around the number to be constructed, as well as their location and cost. Alaskan representative Anthony Dimond, who had come to the Congress in 1932 on a mission to expose the Japanese threat to Alaska, wanted a $16 million base built at Fairbanks, whereas J.J. McSwain, the powerful chair of the House of Representatives's Committee on Military Affairs, desired seven new bases, three each on the nation's Atlantic and Pacific coasts, with the seventh on the Gulf of Mexico, constructed at a projected cost of $150 million.[79]

Far more ambitious was bill H.R. 4130 presented by Florida representative Mark Wilcox on 17 January 1935. Asking for $190 million to finance the creation of 10 massive bases, each capable of handling a wing (132 aircraft), Wilcox's plan, according to army assistant chief of staff Brigadier General C.E. Kilbourne, had two major problems: It specified the number and location of the bases, something which only the secretary of war had the legal power to do; and it proposed specific sizes for said installations, a provision that general doubted "would meet with the approval of air tacticians" given their natural aversion to the over concentration of aircraft at any one aerodrome.[80] But when the Committee on Military Affairs began three days of mostly secret hearings on the air base issue in February, very much more was on the agenda. Billy Mitchell proved to be the star attraction. Aiming a salvo directly at his hidebound service enemies, the retired and ailing warhorse dramatically claimed that "[a]ir power can neutralize anything standing still or moving on the surface of the earth or the water, further declaring that because Alaska was "the most central place in the world for aircraft," he believed that "in the future he who holds Alaska will hold the world."[81]

Although Alaska proved to be a most popular subject over the course of the hearings, a proposed base somewhere in the Great Lakes region induced far more fascinating testimony. All but two of Wilcox's bases would be located along ocean frontiers; only the Great Lakes facility and a Rocky Mountains installation were exceptions, although the latter was designed to back up West Coast bases. Opening the hearings, Wilcox explained that he had chosen those sites so as to provide for the absolute protection for the nation's frontiers from enemy aircraft carriers operating 300 to 500 miles out to sea, or "from bases established in nearby territory" such as Newfoundland, eastern Canada, or the Caribbean islands. His bases would provide the capability to break up such assaults and prevent any hostile force from occupying those key regions.[82]

Kilbourne agreed that a Great Lakes air base was most desirable from a practical point of view, but he warned that the United States had to employ caution in putting new military stations near its northern border for fear it "would look as though we contemplated passing away from the century-old principle that our Canadian border needs no defense." Such discretion was sorely lacking in many of the officers who followed Kilbourne's testimony to the committee. Captain H.L. George warned that Britain had the capability to shuttle aircraft to bases in Labrador or Hudson Bay before concentrating them to strike vital points in the northeast United States,[83] but it was General F.M. Andrews and air corps officer Lieutenant Colonel J.D. Reardan who uttered the most-arresting comments. Head of the newly created General Headquarters (GHQ) Air Force, Andrews very much doubted that Canada willingly would join an anti-American coalition, but if it did, then the proposed bases in New England and the Great Lakes region would permit American aircraft to dominate Canada's industrial heartland and its most important urban areas. If that awful image of American planes raining bombs upon Canada and its major cities had not adequately chilled the assembled congressional audience, Reardan made certain that task was completed. Complaining that the previous testimony had not accounted for the hazard posed by hostile air forces operating on short lines of operation, Reardan, stressing that such a threat could only come from the north, coolly noted that the assumption of neutrality involved responsibilities as well as rights for any state. If Canada could not prevent hostile violations of its airspace, then he concluded that the United States "would have to do so, I imagine."[84]

These were not the ramblings of marginalized men, working in isolation on the fringes of a military planning process; moreover, nothing they had said on Capitol Hill had not been mentioned already within air corps planning circles. The 1933 Drum report, an air corps submission to the Baker Board, and a preliminary GHQ report all had as their foundation the basic assumption that if the United States faced a hostile Anglo-Japanese coalition, it would have to command the Great Lakes and undertake a ground advance into eastern Canada. Further, even the USN was pondering its options should an enemy attempt to launch planes from carriers hidden in Hudson Bay or use British Columbian bases to attack the American northwest.[85] Moreover, these concepts sprang naturally from Joint Army and Navy War Plan Red, the strategy for a conflict with Britain. Not surprisingly, given geographic fact and the Royal Navy's potency, Plan Red identified Canada as the one place where American military power could be brought to bear against a British foe with effect. Indeed, the plan's designers had concluded somewhat cynically that Canada (code-named Crimson) could best help the American cause by siding with Britain because as "CRIMSON neutrality would be of little military advantage to BLUE [the United States], since the duration of such neutrality would always be a matter of doubt, and might be employed to protect CRIMSON during the period when the Dominion was weakest."[86] Designing such military plans, however, did not necessarily mean that they would ever be used. Plan Red assumed that war would come when Britain reacted to American economic pressure and expansion into areas previously under British control, a questionable assumption at best because Britain officially had stopped seeing the United States as a possible enemy in 1904.[87] Such plans existed also to train officers for any situation no matter how unexpected or unlikely, and because the army, confronted by the USN's domination of war planning regarding Japan, concentrated on the one region where it seemed that its talents might prove useful.[88]

Indeed, the testimony on Capitol Hill might have not even been especially ill-advised except for one crucial fact: In late April 1935 the committee somehow managed to accidentally release the entire transcript, closed sessions and all, to the general public, thus giving ordinary Canadians and Americans unprecedented access to the military planning process. Reactions were sharp, especially in the United States. Newspapers spoke of the threat to the "century-old peace bond of two nations" and the "hypocrisy" of the president emphasizing a good neighbor policy while the military plotted against those neighbors, and Americans flooded the White House with earnest and angry letters demanding the sacking of Kilbourne and Andrews.[89] But the public response in Canada and Britain to the revelation was surprisingly low-key. Many Canadian and British dailies simply reported the story without editorial comment, perhaps as the American legation reported, because they were "inclined to treat the matter with a good deal of ridicule at the expense of the Congressional Committee and of our military authorities."[90]

But a very angry William Phillips informed the Canadian legation's Hume Wrong most decidedly on 29 April that the American officers' "provocative references to Canada" most definitely were not shared by the American government.[91] Phillips was far from being the only very upset American official. Pointedly remarking that testimony did "not represent either the policy of this administration or that of the commander-in-chief," Roosevelt publicly repudiated the McSwain hearings, a rebuke that drew praise from the American and Canadian press.[92] But while McSwain and Secretary of War George Dern apologized for the controversy (Dern reprimanded Kilbourne and Andrews), McSwain took the time to unwisely remind the president that the 1817 Rush-Bagot treaty concerning Great Lakes naval disarmament applied only to ships, not aircraft. Moreover, McSwain pointed out that the army still maintained forts near the Canadian frontier, and "these have never been in any way regarded as unfriendly gestures," for like French fortifications near Belgium, they were meant to guard against what might come "over and through" the neighbor.[93]

Although Boal reported that Skelton's initial response to the contents of the transcripts had been "amusement" rather than alarm, his concern that the USSEA was far more "disturbed" than he had let on proved to be on the mark. When the two men met on 2 May, Skelton revealed that he had no inherent problem with the creation of a Great Lakes air base; had the project been quietly undertaken, the USSEA said no Canadian "objection would have been forthcoming." Skelton's major concern, beyond the fact that the revised bill (H.R. 7022) unsuccessfully had tried to "camouflage" the base's exact location and purpose by describing it as an intermediate station, was the effect the committee revelations might have on Canada's neutrality should the United States and Japan go to war. He also revealed that the Alaskan overflight had bothered him far more than he had let on in 1934. Particularly upsetting had been the fact that the air corps had publicly announced that the mission was going ahead before it had obtained Canadian approval, a step seemingly calculated by the American military to force the Canadian government's hand. Concerned that such military flights should not "become a matter of course" now or in the immediate future, Skelton suggested that American planes might use an overwater route that avoided Canadian airspace. But when Boal protested that such a sudden switch would result in undue risks to the lives of American crews, Skelton counseled choosing a flight path that would minimize Canadian exposure both geographically and politically.[94]

McNaughton was far more bothered than Skelton. The Alaskan overflight, a May 1934 USN survey of the Aleutian Islands for possible base sites, and north Pacific maneuvers by the American and Japanese fleets had caught his attention even before the committee leak. So when Bennett decided in the spring of 1935 to again slash the already paltry Canadian military budget, McNaughton had counterattacked. Predicting a major conflict in Europe by 1939, his 5 April review of Canada's defense called for an expeditionary force and a home defense detachment, no small task when Canada had not one modern antiaircraft gun, possessed only enough artillery shells for 90 minutes of normal firing, and could muster just 25 obsolete warplanes. A draft letter meant to accompany the review put the matter even more bluntly. If Canada failed to safeguard its neutrality, the United States could occupy British Columbia, thus possibly "bringing to an end the political independence of this country."[95] Perhaps worried by the letter's blunt tone, McNaughton had not forwarded the missive to Bennett before the McSwain committee news broke, but such self-restraint did not last once the transcripts had emerged. Convinced more than ever that the United States would "not hesitate for one moment to occupy our country in order to deny potential bases to their enemy," and that the McSwain hearings presaged "the institution of an American protectorate over" Canada, McNaughton toughened up his defense review considerably, asked for additional money so that the Royal Canadian Air Force (RCAF) could station more warplanes on the West Coast, and sent his dire warning to Bennett. It had some effect. The government decided to add almost $3 million to the air force budget, not exactly what McNaughton had hoped for, but enough to form two maritime patrol squadrons and to buy four new torpedo bombers.[96]

That Canadian authorities had responded so reservedly and politely to the air corps indiscretion, Boal credited to Roosevelt's quick repudiation. But the matter was more complicated. Although McNaughton's response to the McSwain revelations had been most angry, his general staff, claiming that a study of the transcripts had revealed not "one syllable of hostility towards Canada" from the most "responsible servants" of the American government, concluded that "[n]o umbrage can properly be taken by Canada at these disclosures" for given Canada's military weakness, "not only are our gates wide open but we have not even the semblance of a fence and our neighbour is, in consequence, obliged to provide against our lack of provision."[97] Moreover, given their familiarity with Defence Scheme No. One (unfairly ridiculed by historians and scrapped by McNaughton in 1929), which envisaged a limited Canadian offensive into the United States in anticipation of substantial British aid if the United States ever attacked Canada, few Canadian officers could hardly plead strategic innocence.[98]

The Wilcox National Defense Act finally became law in August 1935, but though it authorized Dern to pick and prioritize base sites, the legislation's refusal to allocate funds for any projects meant that there would be no Great Lakes base under construction anytime soon.[99] Nor had the good news for Canadians ended. Only days after rebuking McSwain and the air corps, Roosevelt chose career diplomat Norman Armour to replace Robbins as the minister in Ottawa. The nomination was very well received. The *New York Times* said the selection assured Canada that the United States was sending one of its very best diplomats to Ottawa, and Wrong related Armour's reputation as "one of the crack men in the Foreign Service."[100]

Still, the Armour appointment was not nearly enough for Wrong. An often very harsh judge of Americans (in 1928 he had described the United States as "a barbarous country"[101]), in July 1935 Wrong had composed a lengthy draft analysis of American-Canadian relations. Although Wrong had hoped that Franklin Roosevelt's election to the presidency in 1932 would presage settlement of the more grievous economic injustices inflicted upon Canada by an insensitive United States, three years later the Canadian diplomat found it difficult "to find one positive action taken by the Roosevelt Administration which has been beneficial to Canada." As to international affairs, excepting only improving relations with Latin America, "this Administration has proved itself to be more strongly isolationist than its two predecessors." Admitting that President Roosevelt and most of his closest advisers "undoubtedly" possessed a spirit of good will towards Canada, Wrong thought that spirit "has been shown in words and not in deeds," and unless something useful was quickly accomplished, the good neighbor policy would be seen as nothing "more than a slick and hypocritical phase."[102]

But early indications hinted strongly that Wrong's hopes about an American transformation would be cruelly disappointed. After months of dueling with Congress in the wake of Italy's invasion of Ethiopia, Roosevelt approved the first Neutrality Act in August 1935. With its mandatory embargoes on arms sales to all belligerents, the controversial act appeared to penalize poorly armed victims, but "more sensitive to the public mood, more ready to translate it into action, more willing to be guided by it" than many politicians, Roosevelt chose to give way to congressional concerns, an action he later regretted.[103] Progress towards better Canadian-American relations also stalled as an economically depressed Canada lurched without much enthusiasm towards the polls in October 1935. Despite Bennett's protestations that Conservative party fortunes finally were on the rise, in Robbins's opinion "it is all over but the shouting." Disgusted by Bennett's lack of action on the St. Lawrence power project and a proposed reciprocity agreement with the United States, Robbins thought that perhaps King and the Canadian Liberal Party were "*a little bit*" more inclined "than the other party to play the game with us."[104] Armour would get the chance to see if Robbins was right for despite Bennett's desperate electoral deathbed appropriation of Roosevelt's New Deal principles (prompted and encouraged by William Herridge), when Canadians trudged to the polls, the Conservatives retained just 39 seats as King and his Liberals swept convincingly to victory and power with 171 seats.

Hope for a better relationship between Canada and the United States came almost immediately. Meeting with Skelton, Armour learned that the USSEA desired closer economic ties with the United States and the development of what he called a "North American mind." If that did not come to pass, then Skelton feared that Canada would be drawn inevitably and unhappily into a "world-wide British economic empire whose interests, as progressively developed from London, might soon diverge seriously from" American needs. Armour could not have agreed more. As Canada consistently ranked as the United States's best or second-best customer, it seemed vitally important to the new minister that the United States had to do something concrete to interest Canadians to further develop their trade with the United States, to support American policies in regard to Latin America (possibly as a member of the Pan-American Union), the Far East and elsewhere, and to feel "that in a thousand and one ways that they are bound to us in practical things even though sentimentally and politically they are part of the British Empire."[105] Armour happily discovered that King shared similar sentiments. Speaking very fondly of his many years spent in the United States, first as a graduate student at the University of Chicago and then at Boston's Harvard University, and later as a labor conciliator for the wealthy Rockefeller family, King thought that a speedy and satisfactory working out of Canadian-American trade problems might positively affect the European situation. Though not naturally inclined to undertake radical steps (King once had told a British diplomat "that his experience of political life had taught him that any success he had attained had been due far more to avoiding action rather than taking action"[106]), musing that he and Canada "could be of great use as a link" between Britain and the United States during the London Naval Conference and in settling the Ethiopian situation, for "we [Britain, America and Canada] must stand together on all these questions," King preferred "the American road" rather than a British one. Urged by Armour to write Roosevelt, King intimated instead that he intended to travel to Washington in November to meet with the president.[107]

An invitation to visit the White House quickly arrived, and with the logjam in the trade talks broken, King found himself in Washington on 8 November ready to meet Roosevelt for the first time, although the two men had corresponded since 1929. A lengthy discussion concerning the reciprocity treaty's remaining problems ensued, but shifting to other matters, Roosevelt said that whereas Canada and the United States understood each other far better than did America and Britain, Britain "had been much too slow in dealing with Japan, and with Germany." As to Germany's "troublesome" attitude, Roosevelt postulated that the imposition of an air and land blockade against Germany might change German behaviour for the better.[108] A week later a jubilant King, buoyed by the clearly delighted Canadian reaction to the trade pact, returned to Washington for the pact's formal signing ceremony. And while Herbert Hoover sourly observed that the "more abundant life" promised by Roosevelt with the signing of the trade agreement seemed to be reserved for Canadians, Hull told Stimson that the

United States had "got all the advantages in the concessions made."[109]

Writing to the president just over a week later, King effused that the treaty's "herald of *a better day*, and *a better way*" had been generally recognized in Europe. Even the cynical Wrong thought that Roosevelt was feeling his way to a new foreign policy, "the definition of which is of immense importance to Canada as a North American country, as part of the British Commonwealth, and as a member of the League of Nations."[110] But Wrong tasted bitter disappointment again when Congress began discussing new neutrality legislation in January 1936. Saying that the proposed measure "may well prove to be the most important legislative act of the New Deal in its effect on the rest of the world," Wrong hoped that its provisions—the banning of all military exports, loans and credits, or travel to belligerent states—might lead to American support for sanctions against aggressors, but the immediate effect would be the withdrawal of the United States from real participation "in any system of collective security." In addition, Wrong feared that the restrictions on extending American credit to other nations could have a serious impact on a belligerent Canada.[111]

Wrong's concerns were shared. Maintaining that his fellow Americans could not remain indifferent to aggression overseas, Norman Davis pleaded that the United States could not prevent war "as long as we embrace the fallacy that by a policy of neutrality and isolation we can escape war and the consequences of war." Roosevelt seemed to understand that contradiction. His notion of a German blockade, although it never materialized, reflected his growing apprehension that Germany deliberately was creating a war psychosis in anticipation of a war of aggression.[112] The fact that his German blockade proposal went nowhere might be blamed on Roosevelt's scattershot approach to foreign policy. But the problems he faced were more serious than that. Given a State Department (and public) view that "high though the price may be we will *not* be drawn into a future war in Europe" and Roosevelt's conclusion that Britain's clear "national selfishness" made "mutual helpfulness very difficult to accomplish,"[113] American diplomacy seemed to have few useful or practical roles to play.

But Roosevelt's State of the Union address on 3 January 1936 appeared to offer an approach that might combat the predatory revisionist powers and assure wary Americans that preserving their security did not demand military intervention in Europe's immoral and bloody power politics. Declaring that America would maintain its neutrality, and blaming autocratic Asian and European rulers for the chaos that threatened the peaceful 90 percent of the world's population, Roosevelt said, "A point has been reached where the peoples of the Americas must take cognizance of growing ill-will, of marked trends towards aggression, of increasing armaments, of shortening tempers—a situation which has in it many of the elements that lead to the tragedy of general war."[114] Before the month ended, Roosevelt had invited the leaders of the Latin American states to gather together soon with him to determine how to best maintain peace in the Americas, and even though that conference did not convene until the following December, the initiative thrust the perceived German and Italian threat to Latin America firmly "to the forefront of America's collective consciousness."[115]

Bringing Canada to the forefront of the American collective consciousness took a bit more doing. Writing to Sumner Welles in February, Armour thought that although Canada was not a member of the Pan-American Union and had not "shown a very definite desire to be included," Welles might persuade the King government to despatch an official observer to the upcoming conference.[116] Welles, who had pushed his friend Roosevelt for years to acknowledge that hemispheric matters "must be regarded as the keystone of our foreign policy" and that the Monroe Doctrine defended all of the Americas from assault, splashed cold water on Armour's notion. His view of American foreign policy, the basis of which "should always have been, and should now be more than ever for the future, the political and economic union of the American republics," excluded Canada on the grounds that the United States could not then logically deny entry to those European powers still maintaining colonies in the Western Hemisphere. Most importantly, Welles said Roosevelt feared that extreme American nationalists, and most especially the often vitriolic Hearst press, would immediately claim "that we were proposing an offensive and defensive alliance with the British Empire."[117]

Statements such as these have earned Welles an historical reputation "as a man completely unfitted for dealing with balanced power relationships,"[118] but such criticism did not apply to him alone. When Boal met Loring Christie in March 1936, Christie sounded much like Welles. Having returned to the Department of External Affairs (DEA) at Skelton's request in 1935 after a decade's absence from government service, Christie had established a reputation as a Canadian nationalist and an opponent of military commitments by penning a foreign policy analysis that had asked pointedly how Canadians could "expend energy across the Atlantic without weakening our resistance to events impinging from the south or from across the Pacific?"[119] Boal heard an answer to that complex question a year later. Canada, Christie averred, should keep clear of any European conflict, and when Boal asked for confirmation that the axiom that "if Britain went to war, Canada went to war" still held true, Christie declared that though that was technically correct, the legal notion of a "divided crown" (the king being seen as the ruler of Britain and each Dominion separately) might permit Canada to declare its neutrality if Britain went to war. Believing that King was inclined to accept that notion, Christie advised that much would depend on whether Britain's very survival "appeared to be menaced" in such a conflict. Although Christie clearly had given Boal much to consider, what had stuck out to the American diplomat was a "distinct impression" that Canadians looked to the United States to preserve the peace as long as American policy did not actively harm Britain.[120]

It appears hardly coincidental therefore that just weeks later, after stalling since January to meet Canadian Governor General Lord Tweedsmuir's request to visit Canada, Roosevelt announced his plans to go to Ottawa in June 1936. Observing that Canada was the only important Western Hemisphere country not to have been invited to the Pan-American conference, the *Manchester Guardian* concluded that Roosevelt would "seek Canadian participation in plans for the redefinition of the rights of neutrals in the event of war." Political gossip in Washington thought so too, but added the possibilities that the visit might have been designed to elicit a joint declaration of Canadian-American aloofness from the European crisis or to diminish publicity for the Republican national convention slated for early June.[121]

Domestic political considerations forced the president to delay his trip to Canada until 31 July. Exactly what Roosevelt intended was a mystery, but Skelton asserted that the idea that Canada should recognize "a certain community of interest with the other states in this hemisphere by participation in the Pan American Union and otherwise cannot be said to be a live subject here." Given developments elsewhere, however, Skelton was willing to approach the subject with "an open mind."[122] Roosevelt's trip to Quebec City instead of Ottawa—complete with "G. men literally armed to the teeth. They even had a machine gun!"[123]—was a smashing public relations success. Thousands of enthusiastic Canadians lined the route from where the presidential ship had docked up to the imposing Chateau Frontenac where Roosevelt delivered a speech in English and French. Recalling many fond summers spent at his family's isolated Campobello Island retreat off the southern coast of Canada's eastern province of New Brunswick, Roosevelt drew prolonged cheers from the assembled with his comment that Canadians and Americans never referred to each other as foreigners, only as Canadians and Americans. Such sentiment, moreover, had been made real by the undefended boundary that separated the two nations, a border that set an example "to the other Nations of the world."[124] Roosevelt's private discussion later with King assumed a far different tone. Mentioning that some unidentified senators recently had said they would favor intervening if Japan attacked British Columbia, Roosevelt added that a highway through Canada could prove to be an important means for reinforcing Alaska quickly in a crisis.[125]

That unsubtle message, followed by Roosevelt's public comments on 14 August at Chautauqua, New York, that those nations wishing the United States ill "know that we can and will defend ourselves and defend our neighborhood,"[126] had not been entirely unexpected given a Canadian army intelligence report "that the major military schemes and problems discussed at the [US army] War College were all based on the general idea of a Far Eastern country making an attack on the United States by way of Canada."[127] Still, although King worried that Roosevelt's good intentions regarding the achievement of world peace had been undermined by going "too far in his policies" and the influence of not having "the right men around him,"[128] he must have been surprised to hear Roosevelt, the man who had taken his military to task in 1935 for discussing American intervention in Canada, imply that that option was now feasible just one short year later.

But if Roosevelt had intended solely to spur the Canadians to think more seriously about hemispheric defense, he had convinced them instead that they had a potentially serious problem with the United States. The Canadian army's lengthy 5 September appreciation portrayed American and Japanese naval exercises, the rise of a "Big Navy" lobby in America, Alaskan overflights, and an Alaskan highway as "distinct portents of a trend of events." If the United States and Japan went to war, Canada would confront three choices: siding with America regardless of Britain's position; membership in an Anglo-American coalition; and neutrality. As the first seemed unlikely, the appreciation's author, Colonel H.D.G. Crerar, thought that only the coalition and neutrality need be worried be considered. And even though General McNaughton no longer haunted DND's modest halls (reading the political tea leaves well, the general had resigned his commission prior to the 1935 election to head up the National Research Council), his ideas about the American threat to Canada still had currency. If Japan invaded British Columbia or used Canadian waters to attack American targets, Crerar warned that "American public opinion will demand what would amount to the military occupation of British Columbia by U.S. forces." Crerar's prescription was extensive and expensive because existing Canadian forces were "incapable of ensuring anything approaching adequate supervision of the Western coast," let alone fighting a major war in the Pacific or Europe. The navy would need six destroyers (it had two) and four minesweepers, the air force 23 squadrons (almost 400 aircraft), and the army required coastal and antiaircraft guns, 64 West Coast observation posts, and six modern and highly mechanized divisions, two of which should be able to mobilize quickly in a crisis (Mobile Force). Total cost for the program over five years would be $200 million, with $65 million being required in the first year.[129]

Rightly described as "among the key documents in Canadian history" for its repudiation of isolationism and the claim that the end of hostilities in 1918 "was but an armistice,"[130] Crerar's appreciation received a mixed response in Canada's halls of power. To the Department of External Affairs, the document's emphasis on a military capable of fighting at home *and* overseas confirmed Christie's fears that military support for home defense masked a desire to create an expeditionary force.[131] The cabinet's objections were more practical: How could such a program be paid for, and would the electorate accept such a costly rearmament? King, revealing himself to be "a more committed proponent of military expansion than anyone had suspected,"[132] acted. Six days after Roosevelt's Chautauqua speech, and almost eight months after Minister of Defense Ian Mackenzie had first suggested the idea, King's government created the Canadian Defence Committee (CDC), chaired by King, to oversee defense policy.[133] Loosening the public purse strings, however, took a bit more hard work. Assuming that the government would "have the least trouble" with the public if it met the situation "boldly," King, who had told the cabinet on 5 August that coastal defense had to be a priority, had a plan. Emphasizing the need to adequately protect Canada's neutrality, the prime minister suggested putting forward formal neutrality legislation followed by "a defence program on [the] Atlantic & Pacific, being certain that British protection means less & less, U.S. protection danger of losing our independence." Even so, $200 million gave King pause enough to favor stretching the expenditure over 10 years. Mackenzie, understanding that the first year's allocation was the prime sticking point, cut the initial outlay to $36 million. And though this meant that there would be money enough only for proper defenses on one coast (and certainly not enough for an expeditionary force), the cabinet and the military agreed "[v]irtually without discussion" that the Pacific frontier would be strengthened.[134]

The Alaska highway issue was not so easily dealt with. Ironically, an Alaskan route had been raised first by British Columbia in 1929 as a means of encouraging economic development and American tourism. King's government had demonstrated very little interest in the project then, although President Hoover had been sufficiently intrigued to appoint a board, including three Canadians, to consider it. Its 1931 report favored construction for the economic benefits it would bring to the United States. But when the body's Canadian members suggested that the road would naturally facilitate Alaska's military development, although their American counterparts said the highway "would have no more military significance than any other road that might extend north beyond the British Columbia boundary," the Americans admitted that the route would have a "very definite value from an aviation standpoint in cases where Canada and the United States might be allies."[135]

The ongoing economic depression and the Canadian federal government's lack of support dictated that the expensive project remained only an idea for the time being. But by 1935 the highway scheme was again on the American agenda, and with congressional support, Dimond petitioned Roosevelt to initiate serious negotiations with Canada and to appropriate $2 million for a link between Alaska and the Yukon. Roosevelt and the Department of the Interior did express some interest, but given the Bureau of the Budget's firm opposition, on 26 August 1935 Roosevelt would approve only a joint resolution calling for talks with Canada.[136] But when Canada was formally approached the following February, Deputy Minister of the Interior J.M. Wardle, a former Canadian member of Hoover's commission, thought that Canada should talk with the Americans as long as it was understood that the Dominion had not committed itself to any expenditure. Also seeing an Alaskan highway in primarily economic and political terms and describing it as "a perfectly intelligible aspiration on the part of the Pacific coast people," Skelton worried that neither British Columbia nor Canada could justify the cost and that Canadians might resent money spent on a north-south road into the United States rather than purely Canadian east-west communications. As to apprehensions about the highway's military utility, the USSEA doubted in September 1935 that "unless Canada incurred a 'moral' obligation by allowing the United States to assume the whole or part of the cost of building the highway in Canadian territory," such concerns should not "be allowed to overcome such a project." He therefore favored more studies rather than a firm commitment.[137]

Not surprisingly, General McNaughton had seen Dimond's efforts as a clear indication that the United States wanted improved military communications to Alaska, and that American use of that route in a crisis "would confront us with a somewhat delicate situation." His successor as CGS, Major General E.C. Ashton, put matters more forcefully. Admitting that the highway could bring some substantial economic advantages to an economically depressed British Columbia, Ashton believed that the road's primary purpose lay in reinforcing Alaska quickly during a war with Japan. And even though the United States claimed to have no such intentions for the road, Ashton "regretfully" concluded that if America and Japan came to blows, that in the context of such "a great international struggle military necessity would tend to overcome political scruples." Canada, he therefore concluded, "would be more than foolish" if it subsequently created "what would then become a military asset of a very high order if possessed or utilized by our neighbours to the south."[138]

Roosevelt's August 1936 comments about the highway's military utility struck a Canadian nerve. Not only had the president broken with the standard American practice of denying the road's potential military role, he had indicated a strong personal interest in the project. Perchance shell-shocked by the unwelcome possibility that McNaughton had been right all along—that the United States wanted to ensure Canadian partiality in a Pacific conflict—External Affairs did not know what to do. When an American official asked Christie in October 1936 for Canada's official stand on the viability of the Alaska highway project, Christie said that the matter was still under consideration, but that the primary problem was not military but financial; therefore, in Christie's opinion, the objections of the Canadian general staff did not require any consideration. Whether Ely Palmer believed that explanation is unclear, but he did report to the State Department that Canada likely would reject an Alaskan highway project based on its probable inability to assume a proportionate share of the cost.[139] Roosevelt, however, was far from finished with Canada, as the events of 1937–1938 would indicate.

NOTES

1. Kenneth S. Davis, *FDR: The New Deal Years 1933–1937* (New York: Random House, 1979), 29–31.

2. Hanford MacNider to Harry R. Lewis, 8 February 1932, Herbert Hoover Presidential Library [HHL], West Branch, Hanford MacNider Papers, box 46, file Canada, Minister to, Correspondence 1932 January–June.

3. Frank Underhill quoted in J.L. Granatstein, *Yankee Go Home? Canadians and Anti-Americanism* (Toronto: HarperCollins, 1996), 8.

4. *Canadian Methodist Magazine*, XI (February 1880), 188.

5. P.E. Corbett, "Anti-Americanism," *Dalhousie Review*, 10 (October 1930), 295.

6. Editorial, *Toronto Globe and Mail*, 9 November 1932.

7. "Greetings From A Blood Brother," *Montreal Herald*, 6 March 1933.

8. Quoted in Frank Freidel, *Franklin D. Roosevelt: A Rendezvous with Destiny* (Boston: Little, Brown and Company, 1990), 108.

9. Robert Bothwell and John Kirton, "A Sweet Little Country," in Norman Hillmer, ed., *Partners Nevertheless: Canadian-American Relations in the Twentieth Century* (Toronto: Copp Clark Pitman, 1989), 46–47.

10. Joan Hoff Wilson, *American Business and Foreign Policy, 1920–1933* (Boston: Beacon Press, 1973), x.

11. Wayne S. Cole, *Roosevelt & the Isolationists, 1932–45* (Lincoln: University of Nebraska Press, 1983), 6–8; and Thomas G. Paterson, J. Garry Clifford, and Kenneth J. Hagen, *American Foreign Policy: A History/1900 to Present*. 3rd edition (Lexington: D.C. Heath, 1991), 305.

12. John W. Foster to Michael H. Herbert, 21 August 1892, in United States State Department, *Papers Relating to the Foreign Relations of the United States* (Washington, D.C.: Government Printing Office, 1893), 301–4.

13. Senator Raoul Dandurand speech, 2 October 1924, in Walter A. Riddell, ed., *Documents on Canadian Foreign Policy 1917–1939* (Toronto: Oxford University Press, 1962), 464.

14. Quoted in Peter Charles Kasurak, "The United States Legation at Ottawa, 1927–1941: An Institutional Study," doctoral dissertation, Duke University, Durham, 1976, 17–18; and William R. Castle to Ferdinand L. Mayer, 21 February 1929, HHL, William R. Castle Papers, box 2, file Canada 1929–1932.

15. William Phillips to Castle, 23 February 1929, HHL, Castle Papers, box 2, file Canada 1929–1932; and William Phillips, *Ventures in Diplomacy* (Boston: Beacon Press, 1953), 149.

16. "Memorandum of conversation between the Prime Minister and Minister Phillips on February 26, 1929, at Ottawa," HHL, Herbert Hoover Presidential Papers, Subject File [PPS], box 276, file St. Lawrence River 1929; and Castle diary, 21 March 1929, HHL. Castle was the aide who had advised Hoover to drop the idea of using Prime Minister King to explain the American naval position to the British.

17. Stimson diary, "Re: Talk with Senator Borah," 22 June 1929, YU; and Castle diary, 6 November 1929, HHL.

18. Richard N. Kottman, "Hoover and Canada Diplomatic Appointments," *Canadian Historical Review*, 51 (September 1970), 296. Although Canada's chargé d'affaires in Washington thought that MacNider lacked "mental subtlety," he likely would appreciate Canada's viewpoint and possessed "sufficient independence of mind and position to encourage him to urge on his own Government the Canadian aspect of affairs"; Hume Wrong to the Secretary of State for External Affairs [SSEA], no. 1673, 23 August 1930, National Archives of Canada [NAC], Ottawa, R.B. Bennett Papers, reel M–1026.

19. Castle diary, 31 January 1931, HHL; Richard N. Kottman, "The Hoover-Bennett Meeting of 1931: Mismanaged Summitry," *Annals of Iowa*, 42 (Winter 1974), 213; and Wesley Frost to MacNider, 13 June 1931, HHL, MacNider Papers, box 46, file Canada, Minister to, Correspondence 1931 January–June.

20. Sir Esme Howard to A. Anderson, "Annual Report of the United States for the Year 1928," 9 August 1929, in D.K. Adams, ed., *British Documents on Foreign Affairs: Reports and Papers from the Foreign Office Confidential Print. Part II. Series C, North America, 1919–1939. Volume 20. Annual Reports 1928–1932* (Bethesda: University Publications of America, 1995), 39.

21. John W. Holmes, *Life with Uncle: The Canadian-American Relationship* (Toronto: University of Toronto Press, 1981), 44; and Peter Kasurak, "American Foreign Policy Officials and Canada, 1927–1941: A Look through Bureaucratic Glasses," *International Journal*, 32 (Summer 1977), 544.

22. Jack Hickerson to Mr. Barnes, 15 January 1931, National Archives and Records Administration [NARA], Washington, D.C., Department of State Records, RG59, Decimal File 1930–39, 711.42/69.

23. Quoted in James Chase and Caleb Carr, *America Invulnerable: The Quest for Absolute Security from 1812 to Star Wars* (New York: Summit Books, 1988), 13; and Michael H. Hunt, *Ideology and U.S. Foreign Policy* (New Haven: Yale University Press, 1987), 32.

24. James Morton Callahan, *American Foreign Policy in Canadian Relations* (New York: Macmillan, 1937), 412.

25. Frederick Merk, *Manifest Destiny and Mission in American History: A Reinterpretation* (New York: Vintage Books, 1966), 230–31; "Trade War Debt for Canada," *Boston Post*, reprinted in the *Calgary Herald*, 21 July 1926; and Granatstein, *Yankee Go Home?*, 46–47.

26. Quoted in Martin, *The Presidents and the Prime Ministers*, 37.

27. Robert Hannigan, "Reciprocity 1911: Continentalism and American Weltpolitik," *Diplomatic History*, 4 (Winter 1980), 2–3.

28. Quoted in Kasurak, "American Foreign Policy Officials and Canada," 548.

29. Phillips to Secretary of State, 14 December 1928, NARA, Department of State Post Records, Ottawa, RG84, Entry 2195A, file 631; and Phillips to Hickerson, 13 July 1928, Ibid.

30. Kasurak, "The United States Legation at Ottawa," i–ii; and Mayer to Castle, 26 September 1928, NARA, RG84, Entry 2195A, file 631.

31. Bothwell and Kirton, "A Sweet Little Country," 47.

32. Cordell Hull, *The Memoirs of Cordell Hull. Volume II* (New York: Macmillan, 1948), 1479; Henry Morgenthau to Franklin Roosevelt, 21 January 1933, Franklin Delano Roosevelt Presidential Library [FDRL], Hyde Park, President's Secretary's File [PSF], file Departmental File Treasury: Morgenthau, Henry Jr.: 1933–36. Castle thought that Robbins's selection for the ministership was "wicked" for his "sole qualification for the job is that he is a cousin of F.D.R."; Castle diary, 17 April 1933, HHL.

33. Phillips to Marvin H. McIntyre, 26 April 1933, FDRL, Roosevelt PSF, file Diplomatic Correspondence Canada: 1933–35; and Martin, *The Presidents and the Prime Ministers*, 109.

34. Hickerson memorandum, 7 August 1934, NARA, RG59, Decimal File 1930–39, 611.4231/883; and Stimson diary, 17 May 1934, YU.

35. Secretary of War George Dern to Cordell Hull, June 1934, NARA, RG59, Decimal File 1930–39, 811.2342/421.

36. Keith D. McFarland, *Harry H. Woodring: A Political Biography of FDR's Controversial Secretary of War* (Lawrence: The University Press of Kansas, 1975), 84 and 120; and Dallek, *Franklin D. Roosevelt and American Foreign Policy*, 36.

37. William Mitchell to Director of Air Service, 9 January 1920, Library of Congress Manuscript Division [LC], Washington, D.C, William Mitchell Papers, box 8, file General Correspondence 1920.

38. Brigadier General Harry A. Smith, "Report of Brigadier General William Mitchell, on trip to Pacific Ocean," 18 November 1925, NARA, War Plans Division [WPD], RG165, file WPD 2050.

39. John F. Shiner, "The Air Corps, the Navy, and Coast Defense, 1919–1941," *Military Affairs*, 45 (October 1981), 113–20; and John F. Shiner, *Foulois and the U.S. Army Air Corps 1931–1935* (Washington, D.C.: Office of Air Force History, 1983), 220–21.

40. John F. Shiner, "General Benjamin Foulois and the 1934 Air Mail Disaster," *Aerospace Historian*, 25 (December 1978), 221–30.

41. Adjutant General to the Chief of the Air Corps, "Alaskan Flight," NARA, Army Air Forces Central Decimal Files 1917–38, RG18, Entry 166, box 706, file 373.

42. Alaskan defense prior to World War Two is discussed in Galen Roger Perras, "Stepping Stones on a Road to Nowhere? The United States, Canada, and the Aleutian Islands Campaign, 1942–1943," doctoral dissertation, University of Waterloo, 1995.

43. Under-Secretary of State for External Affairs [USSEA] O.D. Skelton to the United States Minister for Canada, 2 June 1934, no. 54, NARA, RG59, Decimal File 1930–39, 811.2342/422,

44. Reginald Stuart, *United States Expansionism and British North America, 1775–1871* (Chapel Hill: The University of North Carolina Press, 1988), 217.

45. Lieutenant Colonel G.T. Perkins, "Canadian Trip," June 1926, NARA, Military Intelligence Division [MID] Correspondence 1917–41, RG165, file 2694–36. World War One cooperation is explored in Greg C. Kennedy, "Strategy and Supply in the North Atlantic Triangle, 1914–1918," in B.J.C. McKercher and Lawrence Aronsen, eds., *The North Atlantic Triangle in a Changing World: Anglo-American-Canadian Relations, 1902–1956* (Toronto: University of Toronto Press, 1996), 48–80; and R.D. Cuff and J.L. Granatstein, *Canadian-American Relations in Wartime: From the Great War to the Cold War* (Toronto: Hakkert, 1975).

46. Major General T. Monoher to the Chief of Staff, "Authorization for the Alaska Flying Expedition," 8 April 1920, LC, Mitchell Papers, box 8, file General Correspondence Apr.–Dec. 1920; Mitchell to General Charlton, 18 October 1919, Ibid., box 7, file General Correspondence October–December 1919; and H.H. Arnold, *Global Mission* (New York: Harper & Brothers, 1949), 97–98.

47. Nancy Fogelson, *Arctic Exploration & International Relations 1900–1932* (Fairbanks: University of Alaska Press, 1992), 81.

48. Eugene M. Emme, "The American Dimension," in Alfred F. Hurley and Robert C. Ehrhrat, eds., *Air Power and Warfare: The Proceedings of the 8th Military History Symposium United States Air Force Academy 18–20 October 1978* (Washington, D.C.: Government Printing Office, 1979), 64.

49. Mitchell, "Strategical Aspect of the Pacific," 1924, LC, Mitchell Papers, box 46, file Pacific Problem Strategical Aspect; and "Report of Inspection of Air Service Activities by B.G. William Mitchell," 1924, United States Air Force Academy Library Special Collection [USAFA], Colorado Springs, William Mitchell Papers.

50. Loring C. Christie, "The Anglo-Japanese Alliance," 1 June 1921, reprinted in *External Affairs*, 18 (September 1966), 402–13. Canada's role in ending the alliance is discussed in Robert S. Bothwell, "Loring C. Christie and the Failure of Bureaucratic Imperialism," doctoral dissertation, Harvard University, 1972; and A.R.M. Lower, "Loring Christie and the Genesis of the Washington Conference of 1921–1922," *Canadian Historical Review*, 47 (March 1966), 38–48.

51. "Report of Inspection of Brig. General Wm. Mitchell, Assistant Chief of Air Service during Winter—1923," USAFA, Mitchell Papers; and "Col. William Mitchell's Opening Statement before the President's Board of Aeronautic Inquiry on Conditions Governing our National Defense and the Place of Air Power beside Sea Power and Land Power," 1925, LC, Mitchell Papers, box 20, file Statements from Gen. Mitchell's Desk 1925.

52. "Impressions of Canadian Defence Policy—December, 1934, by Sir Maurice Hankey," 1 January 1935, Public Record Office [PRO], Kew, Maurice Hankey Official Papers, CAB 63/8; and Hankey to Prime Minister Stanley Baldwin, 3 January 1935, Ibid.

53. McNaughton to Major General J.H. MacBrien, 13 March 1923, NAC, A.G.L McNaughton Papers, box 109, file Otter Committee 1919–1920; Deputy Minister of National Defence L.R. LaFleche to Skelton, 9 June 1934, NAC, Department of External Affairs [DEA] Records, RG25, vol. 1684, file 53–AB; and McNaughton memorandum, 15 June 1934, Ibid.

54. Brigadier General J. Sutherland Brown to Colonel W.W. Foster, 31 December 1932, Queen's University Archives [QUA], Kingston, J. Sutherland Brown Papers, box 1, file 11; and Brown to Grote Sterling, 6 January 1932, Ibid., box 3, file 43. The best account of McNaughton's attempt to transform the army is Stephen J. Harris, *Canadian Brass: The Making of a Professional Army 1860–1939* (Toronto: University of Toronto Press, 1988).

55. MacBrien to the Secretary of the Militia Department, 30 April 1920, NAC, Department of National Defence [DND] Records, RG24, vol. 2324, file HQS 66.

56. McNaughton to Bennett, "Sino-Japanese Dispute. Possible Canadian Commitments in Respect to the Maintenance of Neutrality," 24 February 1933, in Alex I. Inglis, ed., *Documents on Canadian External Relations: Volume 5. 1931–1935 [DCER]* (Ottawa: Department of External Affairs, 1973), 336–39; and Sub-Committee of the Joint Service Committee, "The Maintenance of Canadian Neutrality in event of war between Japan and the U.S.A.," 10 March 1933, NAC, RG24, vol. 2692, file HQS 5199–A. Defense Scheme Number 2, the neutrality plan, was ready by 1938; Department of National Defence, Directorate of History and Heritage [DHH], Ottawa, Kardex Files, "Defence Scheme No. 2. Plan for the Maintenance of CANADIAN NEUTRALITY In the Event of War between the United States and Japan," 11 April 1938, file 322.016 (D12). C.F. Hamilton, a former militia officer and civil servant, thought that while Canadian interests would be best served by an American triumph over Japan (though he did not want too resounding an American victory), if Japan invaded Alaska or used Canadian waters and territory to attack American targets, Hamilton thought that the United States likely could become "an uncommonly ugly neighbour" and would occupy British Columbia; C.F. Hamilton memorandum, March 1921, NAC, C.F. Hamilton Papers, vol. 3, file 12.

57. Diary entry, 7 August 1930, William Lyon Mackenzie King Papers, Diaries, NAC; and John Hilliker, *Canada's Department of External Affairs. Volume I: The Early Years, 1909–1946* (Montreal: McGill-Queen's University Press, 1990), 137. King believed that O.D. Skelton's judgment deserted him when Skelton had strong personal feelings about an issue, something King put down to the USSEA's "extreme radical sympathies" and perhaps an Irish "inferiority complex"; King diary, 26 December 1936, NAC.

58. H. Blair Neatby, *William Lyon Mackenzie King. Volume Three, 1932–1939: The Prism of Unity* (Toronto: University of Toronto Press, 1976), 134–35.

59. Norman Hillmer, "Defence and Ideology: The Anglo-Canadian Military 'Alliance' in the 1930s," in B.D. Hunt and R.G. Haycock, eds., *Canada's Defence: Perspectives on Policy in the Twentieth Century* (Toronto: Copp Clark Pitman, 1993), 87; and Stephen Harris, "The Canadian General Staff and the Higher Organization of Defence, 1919–1939," in Hunt and Haycock, *Canada's Defence*, 77.

60. Pierre de la Boal to Hickerson, 23 June 1934, NARA, RG59, Decimal File 1930–39, 811.2342/460; and Norman Hillmer, "The Anglo-Canadian Neurosis: The Case of O.D. Skelton," in Peter Lyon, ed., *Britain and Canada: Survey of a Changing Relationship* (London: Frank Cass, 1976), 76.

61. Skelton to LaFleche, 12 and 13 June 1934, NAC, RG25, vol. 1684, file 53–AB; and Skelton to Robbins, no. 59, 14 June 1934, NARA, RG59, Decimal File 1930–39, 811.2342/425.

62. LaFleche to Skelton, 13 June 1934, NAC, RG25, vol. 1684, file 53–AB.

63. Robbins to Hull, no. 648, "Discussion in Canadian Senate of Canada's Neutrality," 18 June 1934, NARA, RG59, Decimal File 1930–39, 811.2342/431; Boal to Hull, no. 644, "Projected good will flight from the United States to Alaska," 15 June 1934, Ibid., 811.2342/426; Skelton to Bennett, 15 June 1934, "United States' Request re Flight to Alaska," NAC, RG25, vol. 1684, file 53–AB; and Bennett to Robbins, no. 62, 18 June 1934, Ibid.

64. Frank Waldrop, "Army to make mass flight to Alaska," *Washington Herald*, 21 June 1934.

65. Robbins to Hull, no. 659, "Projected Washington–Alaska Flight," 22 June 1934, NARA, RG59, Decimal File 1930–39, 811.2342/431.

66. McNaughton to General A.A. Montgomery-Massingberg, 31 July 1934, NAC, Ian Mackenzie Papers, vol. 30, file X–28.

67. Colonel H.H. Arnold, "Report on the Alaskan Flight," October 1936, NARA, RG18, Entry 166, box 705, file 373; and Harold M. Collins, "Visit of United States Army Bombing Squadron," 28 July 1934, Ibid.

68. Roosevelt to Norman H. Davis, 9 November 1934, in Edgar B. Nixon, ed., *Franklin D. Roosevelt and Foreign Affairs. Volume II: March 1934–August 1935* (Cambridge: Belknap Press of Harvard University Press, 1969), 263.

69. Davis to Roosevelt, 27 November 1934, Ibid., 291.

70. James MacGregor Burns, *Roosevelt: The Lion and the Fox* (New York: Harcourt, Brace and Company, 1956), 250.

71. D.C. Watt, *Succeeding John Bull: America in Britain's Place 1900–1975* (Cambridge: Cambridge University Press, 1984), 78.

72. Sumner Welles memorandum, 14 June 1934, FDRL, Sumner Welles Papers, box 149, file Roosevelt 1934.

73. Wrong to Herridge, 11 October 1934, plus "Memorandum of views expressed by Lord Lothian in a conversation on October 9th, 1934," NAC, RG25, vol. 2961, file 57.

74. Phillips, "Memorandum of conversation with Philip Kerr (Lord Lothian)," 11 October 1934, NARA, RG59, Decimal File 1930–39, 711.41/280.

75. Stimson, "Memorandum of visit to President Roosevelt on October 30, 1934," 31 October 1934, YU, Stimson Papers, vol. 27.

76. Richard Hofstadter, *The American Political Tradition and the Men Who Made It* (New York: Vintage Books, 1989 edition), xxxv–xxxvi; and Halifax quoted in J. Garry Clifford, "Both Ends of the Telescope: New Perspectives on FDR and American Entry into World War II," *Diplomatic History*, 13 (Spring 1989), 220.

77. Robert W. Krauskopf, "The Army and the Strategic Bomber, 1930–1939," *Military Affairs*, 22 (Summer 1958), 88; and Shiner, *Foulois and the U.S. Army Air Corps*, 215.

78. "Report of Special Committee, General Council, on Employment of Army Air Corps under Certain Strategic Plans," [Drum Report], 11 October 1933, NARA, WPD General Correspondence 1920–1942, RG165, Entry 281, file WPD 888.

79. Anthony J. Dimond speech, 5 March 1934, *Congressional Record*, vol. 78, 3754–55; and J.J. McSwain to Roosevelt, 28 May 1934, FDRL, Roosevelt Official Files [OF], file OF25u. Dimond saw himself as a modern Cato, "the ancient Roman who was so much alarmed about the danger to his country for the strength and power of Carthage that he never ended a speech without saying, 'Carthage must be destroyed'"; and Mary Childers Mangusso, "Anthony J. Dimond: A Political Biography," doctoral dissertation, Texas Tech University, 1978, 315.

80. H.R. 4130, 17 January 1935, *Congressional Record*, vol. 78, 1331–33; and Brigadier General C.E. Kilbourne to Wilcox, 28 January 1935, NARA, RG165, Entry 281, file WPD 3798–5.

81. Mitchell testimony, 13 February 1935, *Hearings before the Committee on Military Affairs House of Representatives Seventy-Fourth Congress, First Session, on H.R. 6621 and H.R. 4130, February 11–13, 1935* (Washington, D.C.: Government Printing Office, 1935), 113–21.

82. Wilcox testimony, 11 February 1935, Ibid., 7–8.

83. Kilbourne and George testimony, 11 February 1935, Ibid., 16–17 and 51–52.

84. Andrews and Reardan testimony, 11–12 February 1935, Ibid., 60–61 and 72.

85. Drum report, 11 October 1934, NARA, RG165, Entry 281, file WPD 888; WPD, "Suggestions for the Secret Annex," 5 July 1934, Ibid., file WPD 3828; Reardan and Captain C. W. Connell, "Preliminary Report of the Board of Officers on Airdrome Requirements of the GHQ Air Force," 5 November 1934, Ibid., file WPD 3809; Rear Admiral E.J. King to Clark Howell, 13 December 1934, LC, Ernest J. King Papers, box 5, file Correspondence 1936–38 H; and Commander H.H. Frost, "Blue Strategy against a Coalition of Great Powers," May 1932, Naval Historical Center [NHC], Washington, D.C., Strategic Plans Division [SPD] Series III, box 39, file Blue [United States] Strategy.

86. "Joint Estimate of the Situation Blue-Red," 8 May 1935, NARA, Records of the Joint Board 1903–1947, RG225, JB 325, reel 10.

87. Ibid. With the CID's 1904 ruling that the United States "need not be taken into consideration" in defense planning, when the Anglo-Japanese alliance was renewed in 1912, Britain insisted that it not be obligated to go to war with the United States on Japan's behalf; Hankey, "The origins and present position of the decision to make no defensive preparations against America as a possible enemy," May 1929, PRO, Hankey Papers, CAB63/40.

88. Preston, *The Defence of the Undefended Border*, xi. Although Army War College Commandant Major General W.D. Connor admitted that conflicts could arise from "the most unexpected situations," he was "no alarmist about war with" Britain. Even if his service invaded Canada, no easy task given the army's "skeleton" strength, Connor expected "a public clamor against it," though he could not "conceive of the President agreeing to any such move"; Connor to Assistant Commandant, 10 March 1928, United States Army Military History Institute [MHI], Carlisle Barracks, Army War College Curriculum Records, file 111–12.

89. "Air Bill Provides Secret Base near Canada to Protect Lakes," *Washington Post*, 29 April 1935; and "The Good Neighbor?" *Washington Post*, 2 May 1935. Letters demanding the firings are found in FDRL, Roosevelt OF, file OF25.

90. Boal to Hull, no. 1241, 2 May 1935, NARA, RG59, Decimal File 1930–39, file 811.248/77; "U.S. Air Base near Canadian Border Is Aim," *Ottawa Morning Journal*, 29 April 1935; "Army Men Get Sharp Warning from Roosevelt," *Ottawa Citizen*, 30 April 1935;

"Seizing British Islands," *Manchester Guardian*, 29 April 1935; and "U.S. Air Base Plan near Border," *London Daily Telegraph*, 30 April 1935.

91. Wrong to SSEA, no. 515, 29 April 1935, NAC, RG25, vol. 1746, file 408. Wrong said Phillips had been "more angry than he had ever seen him before"; Skelton memorandum, 29 April 1935, Ibid.

92. Roosevelt to McSwain, 29 April 1935, Duke University Archives [DUA], Durham, John Jackson McSwain Papers, box 11, file Correspondence 1935: April 22–Aug.; "Earned Rebuke," *Baltimore Sun*, 1 May 1935: "A Well Merited Rebuke," *New York Herald Tribune*, 2 May 1935; and "U.S. President Repudiates Boundary Air Base Plan," *Ottawa Journal*, 30 April 1935.

93. Dern to Roosevelt, 30 April 1935, NAC, RG25, vol. 1746, file 408; White House memorandum on McSwain, May 1935, FDRL, Roosevelt OF, file OF48b; and McSwain to Roosevelt, 1 May 1935, DUA, McSwain Papers, box 11, file Correspondence 1935: April 22–Aug.

94. Boal to Phillips, 30 April 1935, NARA, RG59, Decimal File 1930–39, 811.248/80–1/2; Boal to Hull, no. 1246 plus enclosure no. 1, 2 May 1935, Ibid., 811.248/82; and House of Representatives Report No. 755, "Army Air Corps Stations and Frontier Air Defense Bases," and H.R. 7022, 24 April 1935, copies in NAC, RG25, vol. 1746, file 408.

95. McNaughton, "The Defence of Canada (A Review of the Present Position)," 5 April 1935, NAC, RG25, vol. 1747, file 469; and McNaughton to Bennett, April 1935, DHH, file 014.014.

96. McNaughton, "Canada and the United States Security against Air Attack," 29 April 1935, NAC, RG25, vol. 744, file 162; McNaughton, "The Defence of Canada (A Review of the Present Position)," 28 May 1935, DHH, Kardex file 74/256; and Roger Sarty, *The Maritime Defence of Canada* (Toronto: The Canadian Institute of Strategic Studies, 1996), 79–109.

97. Boal to Hickerson, 2 May 1935, NARA, RG59, Decimal File 1930–39, 811.248/80–1/2; Canadian army general staff, "Note, from a Canadian aspect, on a Report of the hearings before the Committee on Military Affairs, House of Representatives, on H.R. 7022," 4 May 1935, DHH, Kardex file 74/256.

98. Claiming that Defence Scheme Number One mistakenly had regarded "friends as enemies," James Eayrs thought that it had resulted from "a creeping paralysis of the imagination when it comes to assessing the influence of a changing political and technological environment upon the fortunes of this country." Brigadier J. Sutherland Brown, concluding that an Anglo-American war was not unthinkable and that America intended to squeeze Canada whenever possible, thought his plan reasonable because "[w]hen a great nation makes such demands from another nation, we not only want to fear God and honour the King, but to keep our powder dry." The Canadian army, deeming Brown's hopes "chimerical," opted for a more cautious defensive strategy; James Eayrs, *In Defence of Canada: From the Great War to the Great Depression* (Toronto: University of Toronto Press, 1964), 71–73; Brown to the Chief of Staff, 11 November 1927, NAC, RG24, vol. 2925, file HQS 3496; Brown memorandum, 29 December 1923, QUA, Brown Papers, box 8, file 163; Colonel H.H. Matthew to Chief of Staff, 26 January 1929, NAC, RG24, vol. 2925, file HQS 3496; and Harris, *Canadian Brass*, 170–71. A copy of the plan can be found in NAC, RG24, vol. 2926. Brown's career is sympathetically discussed in Charles Taylor, *Six Journeys: A Canadian Pattern* (Toronto: Anansi, 1977), 3–38.

99. John Haile Cloe and Michael F. Monoghan, *Top Cover for America: The Air Force in Alaska 1920–1983* (Missoula: Pictorial Histories, 1984), 21.

100. "Our Minister to Canada," *New York Times*, 22 May 1935; and Wrong to Skelton, 4 May 1935, NAC, RG25, vol. 1726, file 26–u.

101. Quoted in J.L. Granatstein, "Hume Wrong's Road to the Functional Principle," in Keith Neilson and Roy A. Prete, eds., *Coalition Warfare: An Uneasy Accord* (Waterloo: Wilfrid Laurier Press, 1983), 63.

102. Wrong, "What Has the Good Neighbour Policy Accomplished in the Case of Canada?" 6 July 1935, NAC, Hume Wrong Papers, vol. 1, file 2.

103. Dexter Perkins, *The New Age of Franklin Roosevelt 1932–45* (Chicago: The University of Chicago Press, 1957), 9 and 96–97.

104. Robbins to Roosevelt, 18 December 1934, FDRL, Roosevelt PSF, file Diplomatic Correspondence Canada: 1933–35.

105. Armour to Phillips, 22 October 1935, Ibid.

106. F.L.C. Floud to Sir Harry Batterbee, 24 May 1938, PRO, Dominions Office Records [DO], DO35/586, file G88/55.

107. Armour memorandum, 25 October 1935, FDRL, PSF, file Diplomatic Correspondence Canada: 1933–35; and King diary, 24 and 25 October 1935, NAC.

108. King diary, 8 November 1935, NAC. Roosevelt had sought to meet King in 1929, but concerned that the meeting might worsen ongoing tariff disputes, King gracefully declined; Roosevelt to King, 17 June 1929, NAC, W.L.M. King Papers, Correspondence, reel C2313, 142151; and King to Roosevelt, 3 July 1929, Ibid., 142153–58.

109. Quoted in Neatby, *The Prism of Unity*, 146; and Hull to Stimson, 27 November 1935, LC, Cordell Hull Papers, box 37, file Nov. 1–28 1934.

110. King to Roosevelt, 25 November 1935, NAC, King Correspondence, reel C2313, 181549–50; and Wrong to SSEA, no. 1293, 14 December 1936, Ibid., reel C3685, 183253–54.

111. Wrong to SSEA, no. 6, 7 January 1935, NAC, King Correspondence, reel C3695, 197514–23.

112. Davis to Hull, 3 February 1936, LC, Hull Papers, box 37, file Jan. 7–Mar. 29, 1936; and Roosevelt Press Conference No. 142, 7 September 1934, in *Complete Press Conferences of Franklin D. Roosevelt, Volume 3* (New York: Da Capo Press, 1972), 58–61.

113. J. Pierrepont Moffat to Mayer, 22 January 1934, HHL, Ferdinand Mayer Papers, box 1, file Disarmament Conference (Geneva) 1934 Jan–April; and Roosevelt to Robert W. Bingham, 11 July 1935, FDRL, Roosevelt PSF, file Great Britain: Bingham, Robert W.

114. Dallek, *Franklin D. Roosevelt and American Foreign Policy*, 117.

115. David Haglund, *Latin America and the Transformation of U.S. Strategic Thought, 1936–1940* (Albuquerque: University of New Mexico Press, 1984), 3.

116. Armour to Welles, 18 February 1935, FDRL, Welles Papers, box 25, folder 7.

117. Irwin F. Gellman, *Secret Affairs: Franklin D. Roosevelt, Cordell Hull, and Sumner Welles* (Baltimore: The Johns Hopkins University Press, 1995), 68; and Welles to Armour, 24 February 1935, FDRL, Welles Papers, box 25, file 7.

118. Watt, *Succeeding John Bull*, 75.

119. Quoted in J.L. Granatstein, *The Ottawa Men: The Civil Service Mandarins, 1935–1957* (Toronto: Oxford University Press, 1982), 71–73. Christie's nationalism and isolationism came across so strongly that some questioned his mental stability; Stacey, *Canada and the Age of Conflict, Volume 2*, 83.

120. Boal memorandum, 18 March 1936, FDRL, Welles Papers, box 25, file 7.

121. "President Roosevelt's Possible Visit to Canada," *Manchester Guardian*, 21 April 1936; and Wrong to SSEA, no. 458, 30 April 1936, NAC, King Correspondence, reel C3695, 197847–51. Tweedsmuir (John Buchan) had asked Roosevelt on 9 January to become the first American leader to visit Ottawa. Roosevelt responded affirmatively on 16 April; Armour to Roosevelt, 9 January 1936, NARA, RG59, Decimal File 1930–39, 811.001 Roosevelt Visit/148–1/4; and Roosevelt to King, 16 April 1936, in Elliot Roosevelt, ed., *F.D.R.: His Personal Letters 1928–1945 Volume I* (New York: Duell, Sloan and Pearce, 1950), 578–79.

122. Skelton to Vincent Massey, no. 100, 14 May 1936, University of Toronto Archives [UTA], Toronto, Vincent Massey Papers, vol. 406, file 4.

123. Tweedsmuir to W. Carruthers, 4 August 1936, QUA, John Buchan Papers, box 7, file Correspondence July–August 1936.

124. "Address on the Occasion of a Visit to Quebec, Canada by President Roosevelt, July 31, 1936," copy in NAC, William Lyon Mackenzie King Papers, Memoranda and Notes, reel C4279, C141959–64.

125. King diary, 31 July 1936, NAC.

126. Quoted in Dziuban, *Military Relations between the United States and Canada*, 3.

127. "Militia and Air Force Confidential Intelligence Summary Volume XIV. Serial No. 3/36," 30 June 1936, DHH, Kardex file 112.3M1023 (D23).

128. King diary, 30 September 1936, NAC.

129. Joint Staff Committee (JSC), "An Appreciation of the Defence Problems Confronting Canada with Recommendations for the Development of the Armed Forces," 5 September 1936, DHH, Kardex file 74/256.

130. Eayrs, *Appeasement and Rearmament*, 138.

131. Christie, "Notes on the Defence of Canada," 20 February 1936, NAC, RG25, vol. 721, file 47; and Christie, "Memorandum on Defence Policy," 1 September 1936, NAC, Loring Christie Papers, vol. 27, file 9.

132. Roger Sarty, "Mr. King and the Armed Forces," in Norman Hillmer, Robert Bothwell, Roger Sarty, and Claude Beauregard, eds., *A Country of Limitations: Canada and the World in 1939* (Ottawa: Canadian Committee for the History of the Second World War, 1996), 217. The traditional account is found in Eayrs, *Appeasement and Rearmament*; and C.P. Stacey, *Arms, Men and Governments: The War Policies of Canada 1939–1945* (Ottawa: Department of National Defence, 1970).

133. Ian Mackenzie to King, 7 January 1936, NAC, King Correspondence, reel C3695, 189607; and Privy Council Order 2097, 20 August 1936, Ibid., 189615.

134. King diary, 3 February 1937, 5 August and 9–10 September 1936, NAC; Sarty, *The Maritime Defence of Canada*, 99; Mackenzie to King, plus JSC to the cabinet, "An Appreciation of the Defence Problems Confronting Canada with Recommendations for Development of the Armed Forces," 16 November 1936, NAC, King Papers, Correspondence, vol. 221, file Mackenzie-1936; and C.P. Stacey, *Six Years of War: The Army in Canada, Britain and the Pacific* (Ottawa: Department of National Defence, 1955), 11–13.

135. J.M. Wardle to J.B. Harkin, 13 January 1932, NAC, Bennett Papers, reel M–1336, 414746; Alaska Road Commission Report, "The Proposed Pacific Yukon Highway," 1 April 1931, HHL, Hoover Papers, PPS, box 172, file Highways; and Robin Fisher, "T.D. Pattullo and the British Columbia to Alaska Highway," in Kenneth Coates, ed., *The Alaska Highway: Papers of the 40th Anniversary Symposium* (Vancouver: University of British Columbia Press, 1985), 10.

136. Roosevelt to Marvin McIntrye, 3 May 1935, FDRL, Roosevelt OF, file OF1566; Mr. Kannee to McIntyre, 27 April 1935, Ibid.; and H.R. 160, 3 January 1935, Senate Report 114, "Highway from the United States to Alaska through British Columbia," 15 February 1935, and S. 1374, 26 August 1935, copies in NAC, RG25, vol. 1739, file 221 pt. 1.

137. Wardle to Skelton, 10 March 1936; NAC, RG25, vol. 1739, file 221 pt. 1; and Skelton to Major General E.C. Ashton, 6 September 1936, in Inglis, ed., *DCER: Volume 5*, 265–66.

138. McNaughton to Montgomery-Massingberd, 31 January 1935, NAC, RG24, reel C4975, file HQS 3367; general staff, "U.S.A.–Alaska Highway, via British Columbia & Yukon," 24 August 1935, NAC, RG25, vol. 1739, file 221 pt. 1; and Ashton to Skelton, 14 September 1935, in Inglis, *DCER: Volume 5*, 267.

139. Ely Palmer memorandum of interview with Christie, 19 October 1936, NARA, RG84, Series 2195A, file 815.4 Alaska Highway.

Chapter 2

The United States Will Not Stand Idly By: Defending Canada, 1937–1939

On 4 January 1937, Adolf A. Berle and Sumner Welles, having recently attended the Pan-American conference in Argentina, consumed numerous hours on their slow passenger liner voyage home discussing what the United States could or should do if Europe slid into another continental conflagration. Berle, a Columbia University law professor, feared that allowing belligerents to purchase American arms would lead to "the kind of situation which led to our participation in the World War of 1914," but felt that prohibiting all but normal trade would not work either as banned nations likely would obtain American military goods via a third party. As to refusing to trade only with one party in the conflict—"politically impracticable" because that meant the United States would be taking sides—Berle thought it "slightly more dangerous than flat and equal prohibition."[1] Confronted with such unhappy alternatives, Berle and Welles concluded that the best hope lay in preventing war rather than trying to keep the United States unentangled if Europe tore itself apart again. Informal discussions might determine the minimum concessions required "to detach Germany from the project of a Russian war and her Japanese alliance," and liberate that nation from its economic difficulties. And if that went well, the United States might then convene an international congress to address Europe's broader economic and political problems. But after reflecting that public opinion might not support American intervention and using the 1921–22 Washington naval talks as their guide, they sought to convince European leaders to discuss disarmament, a subject most Americans likely would gladly champion. Roosevelt, they agreed, "would be receptive to the idea."[2]

Receptive Roosevelt was, but as Britain's ambassador had already told Hull, faced with German, Japanese, and Italian bellicosity, Britain had discerned it had little alternative but to "arm heavily" and await the explosion.[3] But though the conference initiative failed to get off the ground, importantly it represented a more interventionist approach by Roosevelt's administration. Exactly why this shift occurred in 1937 remains a matter of debate. Sumner Welles has argued that Roosevelt entered office in 1933 with a complete foreign policy agenda designed to improve hemispheric relations and solve European and Pacific problems. And whereas historian Arthur M. Schlesinger, Jr., has contended that Franklin Roosevelt demonstrated considerable foreign policy consistency at least in principles,[4] others have argued that Roosevelt drifted without "any clearly defined strategy," that he crusaded publicly for collective security but was a private appeaser,[5] or that having suffered some painful domestic policy defeats, Roosevelt had entered his second term determined to experiment with foreign affairs, "especially when this sector began to show some dangerous trends."[6]

If Roosevelt had determined to experiment, former British Prime Minister Ramsay Macdonald hoped that something good would come of that effort for "[i]f the international influence of the United States were to be written [now] every paragraph would indict that country." More sanguine than Macdonald, as 1936 came to an end, Permanent Under-Secretary of State Robert Vansittart advised that care should be taken in accommodating the dictators lest Britain "alienate Franklin Roosevelt the Second—who may be a person very different from Franklin Roosevelt the First."[7] Vansittart's guarded optimism stemmed from the fact that the American naval attaché in London had approached the Admiralty in March about exchanging intelligence data, and Roosevelt himself had told British officials in March 1936 and January 1937 that he favored such cooperation.[8]

But British policy makers, preoccupied with European troubles and their own bitter internal squabble over the need for rearmament in the face of German power, believed that a brash United States, burdened by a fragmented political system, could not deliver the political "goods." Moreover, they perceived Roosevelt to be an intellectual meddler seeking to usurp Britain's global leadership role.[9] Attempting to alter this British perception and taking a not inconsiderable political risk, Roosevelt told reporters in April 1937 that if he had senatorial support, he would offer Britain and France an offensive and defensive alliance. But when Roosevelt tried to arrange a meeting with Prime Minister Neville Chamberlain in June, Chamberlain, fearful that a visit to the United States might arouse undue expectations among the British public and might convince Germany and Italy that the democracies sought to encircle them, declined the chance to meet with the president.[10]

Prime Minister King, however, was quite eager to undertake the trek to the American capital when so requested in February 1937. Convinced that any new war would be far more "destructive of human life and civilization" than the last global conflict, King hoped that Roosevelt would exploit his recent re-election to call a world conference to address the threat posed by communism and fascism. Thus, when Roosevelt's invitation came to his desk, King felt that the journey south was a "duty, and may offer a chance of being of some real service in the world situation."[11] King's arrival in Washington on 5 March sparked two days of often intense and wide-ranging conversations with Roosevelt. Claiming no intention to seek a third presidential term, Roosevelt mentioned demilitarizing all Pacific islands "other than those which were in territorial waters," and defended the discernible lack of presidential discretionary power in the third neutrality act as necessary given that he could not guarantee a successor "might be of a different frame of mind or have a different attitude." As the first day wound down though, Roosevelt raised a now familiar topic. Although uncertain about the project's long-term viability, he thought that a $30 million Alaskan highway "would be of a great military advantage, in the event of trouble with Japan." Unable to justify such an expenditure, although British Columbia might construct the road at some future point if it so desired, King made it clear that even though some Canadians thought that the American Monroe Doctrine would provide well for their nation's defense, "no self-respecting Government could countenance any such view." Roosevelt's response was "significant." Saying that Canada need not worry about securing its Atlantic coast, the president divulged that "[w]hat we would like would be for Canada to have a few patrol boats on the Pacific Coast, and to see that her coast fortifications around Vancouver were of a character to be effective there."[12]

King was most pleased that Roosevelt had discussed Canada's West Coast defenses in such "a nice way and without in any way suggesting how Canada should handle her own affairs."[13] External Affairs was relieved as well for both Christie and Skelton, employing language that McNaughton might have used, had warned King before his departure for Washington that reliance on the United States for protection risked Canada becoming an outright American protectorate. Skelton in particular had emphasized that Canada should count on neither American nor British aid, adding that although it could not "escape being affected by developments elsewhere," the Dominion was "still the most secure, the least exposed of all countries," an opinion shared by the American army's Military Intelligence Division (MID).[14]

Still, Roosevelt's reference to the Alaska highway's military utility compelled Canadians to rethink the implications of closer ties to the United States. For King the problem seemed easily solved. Although he sought British support for Roosevelt's planned peace symposium while visiting London in May 1937 (where he had advised Chamberlain "to try to make friends with America"), he rejected the notion, raised by his minister in Washington, that Canada and the United States shared a common North American point of view. That sort of thinking "was all right up to a certain point," King had told Herbert Marler, but it "should never be permitted to run counter to the advantages" that Canada gained from its membership in the British commonwealth. King desired only to be a bridge linking the two great Anglo-Saxon powers together while Canada continued its modest rearmament program, a role the State Department was content to let Canada have as it wanted the Dominion free of the American bloc ostensibly so that it could act as an interpreter between the United States and Britain.[15]

The risk of such a role, as Skelton bitterly remarked to a visiting American, was that a bridge was meant "to be walked on," and as 1937 unfolded with little or no progress internationally, American policy-makers became increasingly frustrated. In July Japanese soldiers engineered a military clash with China, sparking a massive conflict that threatened Western interests throughout the region. So when Canada was slow to endorse Hull's July eight-point peace plan, Assistant Secretary of State for Western European Affairs J. Pierrepont Moffat had Norman Armour browbeat a reluctant Skelton into signing King's name to the American initiative.[16] The frustration extended right to the top. Roosevelt told Hull on 4 August that he desired an Alaskan highway to be "completed as soon as possible." Also wanting to acquire a small piece of Canadian land in order to improve communications between southeastern Alaska and that territory's vast northern bulk, Roosevelt, no doubt recalling cousin Theodore Roosevelt's victory in the Alaska boundary dispute at the turn of the century, thought Canada might build the highway if the Alaskan town of Skagway was designated a free port for Canadian goods. Unfortunately, Roosevelt's mood improved very little when Hull reluctantly reported to the president that he had found "little inclination" within Canada's government to "even to discuss the matter." Promising that immediate consideration was being given to ways to "enlist the active interest and cooperation" of Canada, Hull promised to report back immediately to President Roosevelt when those plans had advanced.[17]

Roosevelt disliked waiting, and thanks to Armour's initiative, the president found himself with an opportunity to relay his interest in the Alaskan highway in a most satisfactory public fashion. Noting Roosevelt's intent to pay a short visit to Seattle in September while returning from a trip to Alaska, Armour thought that a British Columbia stopover by the president could demonstrate solidarity "between our own northwest and the stretch of territory separating Alaska from the continental United States." Though Hull thought the proposal certainly had some merit, Moffat, noting Tweedsmuir's caution that the trip, given current high anti-Japanese feelings on Canada's West Coast, might be misinterpreted especially as British Columbians shared Roosevelt's "great interest" in the highway, doubted that few Americans were so keen. Only the Department of the Interior and congressmen from Alaska and Washington State had been pushing the project, and the State Department had not received "any intimation that either the Army or the Navy has the slightest interest in this matter."[18]

Roosevelt, however, liked Armour's idea and chose to stop in the provincial capital of Victoria for a few brief hours on 30 September. Met by enthusiastic crowds and an equally boisterous Premier T.D. Pattullo in the most British of Canadian cities, Roosevelt departed for Seattle leaving behind an invitation for Pattullo to visit Hyde Park and considerable journalistic praise for his charm and bonhomie.[19] What the president failed to obtain was any Canadian promise, firm or tentative, to build an Alaskan road. Roosevelt's offer for formal negotiations, transmitted to King on 14 September, bogged down once more over finances and politics. Canada, Skelton told Armour, would consider the matter, but the development of east-west communications had first priority. But feeling that Roosevelt might not accept that ruling and desirous of keeping the matter on an "economic plane," Christie suggested undertaking a joint Canadian-American study of the project's feasibility. However, if Washington insisted on paying for even part of the planned Canadian section, Christie reluctantly acknowledged that the Canadian military's objections "presumably would have to be considered."[20]

Christie was right. Quite unhappy with Ottawa's stalling, his West Coast trip had led President Roosevelt to summarily conclude that Canada's defenses in British Columbia were "not only inadequate, but almost non-existent." Though reminded by Armour that Canada recently had undertaken to begin a rearmament program designed to correct those obvious deficiencies over the next few years, Roosevelt felt that the current situation required "a coordinated plan of defense for that important section of territory lying between northern Washington and the 'panhandle' of Alaska" and an exchange of military information between the Canadian and American militaries. Recalling that Britain and the United States had worked out a similar deal for the north Pacific prior to the American entry into World War One (when Roosevelt had been the assistant secretary of the navy), the president thought that the USN's chief of naval operations [CNO], Admiral William D. Leahy, might quietly send an officer in civilian clothes to Ottawa to explore the matter. Taken aback and certain that Prime Minister King should be sounded out first before any American officers headed north, Armour managed to convince Roosevelt to let him "handle the matter as I thought best."[21] Handling the matter meant a quickly arranged meeting with Under-Secretary of State Sumner Welles later that same day. Although Armour favored having King or Ian Mackenzie visit Washington rather than sending an officer to Ottawa, Welles wanted first to ascertain Roosevelt's "more considered views on the advisability of approaching the Canadians at this time."[22] Welles had very good reasons for caution as just the suggestion of even an informal defensive pact with Canada had potentially stunning implications. Not only would it mark a major departure from the American practice of avoiding prior foreign military commitments, but because of Canada's status as a British Dominion, such an accord would leave the Roosevelt administration vulnerable to accusations from its domestic political enemies that it was seeking to broker a wider-reaching alliance with Britain, an alliance that could involve the United States in another European conflict.

Indeed, much more than just talks with Canada was underfoot. Roosevelt's major foreign policy initiative in late 1937 had been his (in)famous "Quarantine Speech" on 5 October. Strongly urged by Hull, the lecture's condemnation of "terror and international lawlessness," its claim that the United States could not escape danger from overseas, and its use of the medical analogy of a quarantine to isolate aggressors struck a nerve at home and abroad. Initial American public reaction was favorable but waned quickly when Roosevelt said he had been thinking only of a general treaty guaranteeing "lasting peace," not a program of political and military sanctions.[23] And though historians debate about exactly what Roosevelt had hoped to accomplish, Dorothy Borg's interpretation that the speech's many ambiguities reflected Roosevelt's groping for a new policy after the outbreak of the Sino-Japanese war and his need to hide behind a "glittering" figure of speech seems most satisfactory.[24]

Glittering metaphors seemed quite useless, though, when Japanese aircraft sank the USS *Panay* without warning or provocation on China's Yangtze River on 12 December 1937. Although Japan apologized for the "accidental" assault, Roosevelt, convinced that "wild, runaway, half-insane men" had deliberately perpetrated the incident,[25] looked again to Britain for cooperation. In fact, inspired by the Quarantine Speech, which Chamberlain had regarded as evidence that President Roosevelt finally had recognized "the need for the education of public opinion," Ambassador Sir Ronald Lindsay, with Chamberlain's approval, had approached Welles on 27 November about initiating Anglo-American naval staff conversations. Though that initial offer had been politely declined, on 16 December, while the American cabinet discussed and then rejected a possible Anglo-American naval blockade of Japan, Roosevelt told Lindsay that he now would welcome such talks. USN War Plans Division director Captain Royal E. Ingersoll arrived in London two weeks later with vague instructions to determine what might be jointly done with Britain to restrain Japan.[26]

So, whereas the proposal for talks with Canada had preceded the taking up of Britain's offer, the two issues became intertwined thanks to an internal battle over the direction of American foreign policy. Having accepted in late 1937 an offer to take up the post of assistant under-secretary of state, Berle found himself, with Welles and Moffat, a "realist" confronting Wilsonian "idealists" like Cordell Hull, Norman Davis, interior secretary Harold Ickes, and treasury secretary Henry Morgenthau. Having long resisted enticements to join the Roosevelt administration because everything it touched had devolved "into a mess of trouble," Berle, obviously not suffering from a shortage of self-confidence, thought that he should handle the nation's foreign affairs rather than leaving "it to some second-rate intriguer picked from the political basket who will get us in a British alliance and a European Asiatic war."[27]

The realists, who had adopted a form of "Europhobic-hemispherism," had viewed Captain Ingersoll's mission with very little sympathy. Welles complained that the British were pressing for cooperation but "had not felt it necessary to inform us of what they are proposing," and Berle thought the current situation was reminiscent of the Anglo-French machinations that had intended to drag the United States into World War One in 1916. Equally critical, Moffat ridiculed Norman Davis's "premise that the existence of British Empire is essential for the national security of the United States and that while we should not follow Great Britain nevertheless we should not allow the Empire to be endangered." So when Davis, incensed by the strong Canadian opposition to applying sanctions against the dictatorships, groused that the Dominion desired to benefit from its geography, its imperial ties, and its friendship with the United States "without assuming any responsibilities," Moffat's immediate response was to utter a heart-felt "three cheers for Canada."[28]

It is hardly surprising then that the realists evinced little enthusiasm for any sort of security agreement with Canada given their belief that the idealists were seeking to tie the American diplomatic wagon to a British horse. Just two days after receiving the British staff talk proposal, Welles, explaining his desire not to trouble a "miserable" Roosevelt just before the president departed Washington for a warm southern cruise, thought that "it would be better to let the [Canadian] matter rest" until Roosevelt's return. Perhaps fearing that Welles seek to use the presidential vacation as an excuse never to broach the topic with Roosevelt, Armour offered a suggestion put forward originally by Colonel Crerar. Having recently met with army chief of staff General Malin Craig while on a personal trip to Washington to visit a British friend (although that half-hour discussion consciously had avoided military topics, Craig had told Crerar that should he write personally to him "if at any time some matter arose in which he could be of assistance"), Colonel Crerar firmly believed that having a few Canadian officers covertly visit Washington would be far less conspicuous than having American officers arriving in Ottawa. If the United States desired "cover," then Crerar suggested mounting formal ceremonies like a warship launching where no one would regard the presence of any foreign officers as extraordinary, or inviting the Canadians officers to lecture at American service colleges.[29]

Keeping his word, Welles contacted the president on 20 December about the possibility of talks with Canada. Still very interested in the subject, Roosevelt favored having the Dominion send an army officer and sailor to the United States for "off the record" discussions with their relevant American service counterparts, and having

Prime Minister King come to Washington too for additional consultations.[30] But fearful that his presence in the American capital might endanger ongoing negotiations for an Anglo-American trade agreement, King hoped to delay making any such trip until at least the early spring. And though King would not make any binding decisions, he thought Ashton and Commodore Percy Nelles might be able to visit Washington.[31] Seeing "very great advantages" flowing from military and diplomatic exchanges with the United States, Skelton thought there "was much to be said for getting our defence programme on a realistic North American basis." But the suspicious under-secretary, quite predictably, had serious doubts about the desirability of having such important discussions taking place between "technical defence officials" from both countries without the benefit of diplomatic guidance. Furthermore, having seen a series of recent Canadian newspaper stories asserting that the United States had asked Canada already to improve its West Coast defenses, Skelton naturally worried that continued leaks might seriously complicate matters, an opinion Armour shared.[32]

One doubts that Skelton, or anyone else working at External Affairs, thought any talks with the United States would lead inevitably to a formal defensive alliance. When Escott Reid, the national secretary of Canadian Institute of International Affairs [CIIA] (and a future DEA staffer), had discussed the notion of a Canadian-American alliance in early 1937, External Affairs officer (and native British Columbian) Hugh Keenleyside, accusing Reid of excessive rationality, had pointed out that governments and their peoples could not be expected to be "intelligent enough" to logically see the necessities of their positions. Practical politics seemed to rule out any "serious and well-thought-out defensive agreement between Canada and the United States" because such an agreement could operate well only when it was "based on effective technical co-operation."[33]

But Roosevelt's proposed talks seemed to offer a chance for such effective cooperation, except that the Canadian military's support for those discussions was long on domestic politics and short on cooperation. Although DND had sent two officers to Washington in April 1937 to carry out a study of American industrial mobilization planning,[34] Crerar's hope was that any enhanced security cooperation with the United States would "knock the feet from under" any and all subversive Canadian elements who opposed any and all military initiatives on the grounds that such steps probably resulted from British pressure. Ashton put matters even more bluntly. Criticizing "the frequent difficulties experienced by this Department [DND] in the pursuit of its approved objectives through obstruction or, at least, lack of sympathetic action, elsewhere," General Ashton attacked the "ultra-isolationist" view that Canada need not fight at Britain's side. Not only would such a dishonest policy be "tantamount to an act of secession from the Commonwealth," a defenseless Dominion naturally would be a matter of some serious concern to the United States. If the American discussions proceeded as planned, Ashton wanted definite assurances from the United States government that it "would safeguard Canada's situation and would not force her into a serious situation."[35]

Ashton got his opportunity to get those assurances when King agreed to send him and Commodore Nelles to Washington for just two days of talks at the Canadian legation beginning on 19 January.[36] Although Roosevelt's delegation (Generals Craig and S.D. Embick and Admiral Leahy[37]) followed a direct presidential order to keep no written records of the discussions, fortunately for historians the Canadians had far different instructions. Asked immediately by General Craig what subjects he wished to explore, Ashton responded somewhat uneasily that he and Nelles had come to Washington without any real indication as to what topics the talks would cover and with authorization from his government only "to give and receive information, but to make no commitments," binding or not. Admitting that he too had received "very limited instructions" from his political superiors, but fully prepared to talk "soldier to soldier," Craig broke the ice by outlining American arrangements for the defense of Puget Sound and the Juan de Fuca Straits. Invited to reciprocate, Ashton provided "in general terms" details concerning Canadian forces and West Coast plans.[38] But then Craig stunned the Canadians. Offering to extend the American army's area of defensive operations to cover the British Columbia's lengthy coastline, he requested information on Canadian West Coast landing fields capable of supporting American bombers. Willing to outline basing capabilities but not at all eager to address the potentially stunning strategic implications of Craig's proposal, Ashton, playing up imperial ties to Britain, explained that Canada faced three different Pacific scenarios: the possibility of an Anglo-Japanese conflict in which the United States opted to remain neutral; British imperial neutrality in a fight between the United States and Japan; and joining an Anglo-American coalition directed against the Japanese. But although Craig maintained that only the third option bore consideration, the evasive tactic seemed to bear fruit as Craig returned to the topics of landing fields and coastal defenses.[39]

Ashton's relief likely increased exponentially after Leahy took the lead the next day's discussions. Far less interested in or concerned by British Columbia's peculiar strategic circumstances, the American admiral's main preoccupation was his service's battle plan to destroy Japan's fleet in the western Pacific. Compared to that monumental task (Plan Orange), Leahy thought Canada's strategic situation was "very minor." The Japanese might raid North America, possibly even with aircraft carriers, but such raids would not presage any invasion of British Columbia or the American West Coast. Moreover, though fairly certain that Japanese naval units would try to use Canadian territorial waters to attack American targets, Leahy believed that such forces could be hunted down and disposed of with "no trouble." Having thus dismissed the Japanese threat to Canada, the Americans concluded the meetings by asserting that the United States currently could offer no formal defense commitments, an assertion the Canadians felt no need to dispute.[40]

Ashton and Nelles probably did not know that the contradictory comments made about British Columbia reflected an ongoing dispute between the American services about Plan Orange's soundness.[41] What they could be certain of was that Craig had not abandoned many of the notions about Canada that had emerged during the McSwain hearings. Therefore, Ashton's staff speedily completed Defence Scheme No. Two (the neutrality scheme) and advised King's government that extensive military contacts with the Americans could prove embarrassing if the empire opted for neutrality in a war between Japan and the United States, a risk that hardly seemed commensurate with the quite minor and subservient role Canada might possibly play in any such conflict at America's side. Maintaining that the formulation of Canada's Pacific strategy could not be seen in isolation from events elsewhere, the general staff advised telling the United States government that Canada would or could offer "no military commitments in advance of an actual crisis developing."[42] Such caution, however, did not extend to Canada's actual defense equipment needs. Requiring new fighter aircraft and antiaircraft guns but doubtful that Britain could provide the items, DND received permission to send a small team to the United States in March to examine suitable models. Given the fact of "the singular geographical relationship of Canada and the United States," Craig waived existing security considerations that would have prohibited the foreign officers from inspecting American armaments.[43]

Curiously, the reaction within Canada civilian circles to Craig's proposal was practically mute. Even the normally overly sensitive King seemed to take the matter in stride. Although the prime minister pushed the cabinet to buy two British destroyers primarily for West Coast duty, not until mid-March did his voluminous diary record any thoughts about West Coast security. Having read over a number of general staff submissions regarding Canadian neutrality, King noted that he now "felt more strongly than ever how inadequate are Canada's defence forces, and how necessary for us to do something to preserve this country to future generations against nations that place all their reliance upon force."[44] O.D. Skelton and Loring Christie too likely had other matters on their minds. As the men most likely fitting General Ashton's pejorative ultra-isolationist definition, they were worried not about American intentions in the Pacific, but what Canada's military was attempting to do across the Atlantic in Europe. Although Crerar told an American diplomat in March that Canada would limit its overseas role if Britain went at war (Crerar said Canada could do little else because the tempo of modern warfare would not allow for time to prepare and then despatch a large Canadian expeditionary force), by July Canada's military chiefs, perhaps reassured that the United States would guard Canada's West Coast from any and all Japanese incursions, thought that the Dominion's Atlantic defenses "should receive prior consideration" because the German menace from the Atlantic "is now fully equal to, if not considerably greater than, that which exists on the Pacific."[45] Convinced that heeding this military advice would lead inevitably to an expeditionary force being despatched to fight in a future European conflict, Christie demanded the government concentrate on building up the air force and navy while stripping the army "to the bone, excepting those [units] designed for coast defence."[46]

The Canadian legation deliberations apparently had little impact south of the border either. Craig's service did not follow up his idea to extend its operational zone to include British Columbia. In fact, when Army War College officers presented their Canadian theater study on 28 January, nowhere did it mention even the possibility that the Dominion might become an American ally. Instead, the report's section dealing with Canada's ability to wage war emphasized that even a limited American offensive "would greatly cripple the economic life of Canada."[47] If one accepts the commonly held precept (at least within Canadian circles) that Canadian-American relations often have fallen victim to an American global preoccupation, the fact that the Canadian legation discussions unfortunately had become inextricably linked with the Ingersoll mission to Britain probably dampened any American enthusiasm for the Canadian initiative. Ten days of talks in London had ended on 13 January with only a set of very vague Anglo-American plans to concentrate American ships at Hawaii if Japan made trouble, a nebulous proposal to blockade Japan at some unspecified future point, and the need for continued Anglo-American liaison pending further policy developments.

But whereas Ingersoll's mission had been a necessary beginning, leaks in Washington compelled President Roosevelt to order Leahy to say that Captain Ingersoll had gone to London to discuss only shipping tonnage rules under the 1936 London naval treaty, not Anglo-American naval cooperation.[48]

Enthusiasm for an Alaska highway had not diminished though, thanks in part to T.D. Pattullo. Enthused by his autumn 1937 visit with the president at the latter's Hyde Park estate, British Columbia's premier urged Roosevelt and King the following March to get construction underway as soon as possible. Inclined to view Pattullo as a "shockingly egotistical" man "ready to become a demagogue of the worst type if he did not get his way," and knowing that British Columbia could not afford to go ahead with the project without substantial federal financial aid, King told Pattullo that if he wanted any such road built, then he should authorize a private contractor to construct it. However, if the project went ahead, "the Dominion was not prepared to make any commitments of a military nature with respect to the route."[49] Pattullo found a slightly more receptive audience in Washington. Meeting with Dimond and Harold Ickes, who had favored such a highway "for some time," Pattullo discussed having the United States loan British Columbia $15 million to finance the road. Although Ickes and his officials offered moral rather than financial support,[50] King thought Pattullo "had acted like a child" for suggesting that American government money might fund Canadian public works; if the United States formally suggested such a thing to him, King made it quite clear that he would respond negatively.[51] Skelton's response proved far less restrained. Describing Pattullo's misguided initiative as "a high water mark (or a low water mark) in provincial diplomacy," the under-secretary said that its acceptance would amount "to regarding Canada or British Columbia as a subdivision of the United States" for the Americans certainly would not "spend money abroad without a very definite *quid pro quo*," and that understanding would involve the highway's use in a war with Japan whether or not Canada joined such a conflict.[52]

Although Congress was preparing to pass Warren G. Magnusson's bill (H.R. 8177) calling for an Alaskan international highway commission to negotiate with Canada, Herbert Marler thought that the bill had been designed primarily to boost Magnusson's political prestige and fortunes in his home state of Washington. And though the State Department fully supported the measure, one American official told Marler that the legislation only restated what had been approved three years earlier. Unfortunately, Pattullo foiled King's hopes that the matter might fall by the wayside by visiting Roosevelt again on 24 May. According to the British Columbia premier, Roosevelt had indicated both his willingness to spend $20 million to see the project through to fruition, and a desire to discuss the matter personally with King.[53] So when Roosevelt signed H.R. 8177 into law at May's end, King reluctantly instructed Skelton to form a committee composed of representatives from the DND, the DEA, and the Departments of Justice and Natural Resources to study the matter "from all its angles" in anticipation of a "conference with the President, if and when the subject is raised by him." Its report, ready in August, advised that an Alaskan highway "would not be justified" for strategic or economic reasons. Instead, the committee proposed that Canada build a road to the Canadian town of Prince Rupert on the Pacific coast, "a blatant piece of bribery aimed at buying off proponents of the highway."[54]

Yet when Roosevelt and King next met in August, the highway was not on the agenda although security matters definitely dominated the proceedings. Roosevelt likely would have preferred another subject for he had entered 1938 intent on allowing Sumner Welles the chance to mount his long-awaited world peace conference. But when Roosevelt had presented the idea to Neville Chamberlain on 11 January, the British leader declined to act upon the notion. While Chamberlain had thought that the *Panay* incident had been "a Heaven sent opportunity and you can bet your bottom dollar I am making the most of it," he also thought that it was "always best and safest to count on *nothing* from the Americans except words but at this moment they are nearer to 'doing something' than I have ever known them and I can't altogether repress hopes." Those hopes had soon ebbed when Chamberlain realized that the United States intended to make no firm security commitments even after the *Panay* bombing, and concerned that the gathering would encourage the dictatorships to seek even more concessions, the British prime minister asked the president to delay the conference until ongoing British talks with Germany and Italy had played out.[55] Misinterpreting "Chamberlain's horror and fear of European war as cloaking a psychological affinity for the totalitarian powers,"[56] President Roosevelt opted for the realists' hemispheric approach. Encouraged by growing public support for increased defense expenditures, Roosevelt had told Congress on 28 January that more money was required so that the nation's armed forces could "keep any potential enemy many hundreds of miles away from our continental limits." In April he "heartily" approved the creation of a Standing Liaison Committee to handle, among other tasks, building military cooperation with the Latin American republics.[57]

Canada's place in that American-led hemispheric defense system was not so easily established. Although most Americans likely knew little about their large neighbor to the north or its complex strategic needs (and probably cared even less), some prominent Americans indeed believed that the United States and Canada shared a common North American strategic destiny. In April the *New York Sunday News* announced its support for reaching a mutual defense treaty with Canada, whereas a Foreign Policy Association report, noting that Canada's increasingly heterogenous population might mean a severing of the Dominion's ties to Britain, emphasized "the essentially North American quality of Canada's foreign policy."[58] Moreover, the American legation reported that King had begun to accentuate Canada's need for an independent stance towards Europe's many problems, a fact that was "of especial importance since Canada is obviously not militarily strong enough to go its own way and act with complete disregard of other nations in an international crisis." The inference, John Farr Simmons concluded, was that "there is and will continue to be a more definite leaning towards the United States both economically and in the field of international affairs than has been the case in the past."[59]

Roosevelt apparently took this intelligence to heart, for when he arrived in Kingston, Ontario, on 18 August to dedicate a new bridge spanning the St. Lawrence River, his dramatic speech delivered on the campus of Queen's University electrified Canadians. Speaking just as the crisis over Germany's demand for Czechoslovakia's Sudetenland had begun, Roosevelt made it clear that the Americas no longer could say that "the eddies of controversy beyond the seas could bring no interest or no harm." And though he publicly acknowledged Canada's membership in the British empire, the president boldly declared that "the people of the United States will not stand idly by if domination of Canadian soil is threatened by any other empire."[60] Although Simmons exaggerated somewhat when he declared that many Canadians regarded the speech already "as one of the most important events in the Dominion's history,"[61] Canadian public reaction to the address was nearly entirely positive. Terming the short the speech the "Roosevelt Doctrine," many Dominion newspapers heartily welcomed what they saw as the natural extension of the American Monroe Doctrine northwards and challenged Canadians to demonstrate that they deserved their American friends. Some in the press even went so far as to conclude that the speech marked Roosevelt's determination to stand with the British and French against the totalitarian states.[62] Strangely, the only reservations came from West Coast newspapers. The *Vancouver Daily Province* pointed out that President Roosevelt had not guaranteed that Canada's coastal areas would be secured against bombardment or that the safety of its seaborne trade would be assured. On the other hand, the *Vancouver Sun* fretted that although Roosevelt had made history by offering the Dominion military protection, Canadians did "not wish to lean, as a nation, on the United States or any other power."[63]

Though King thought that Roosevelt's speech had been "most significant," two days later, after reworking a Skelton draft, the prime minister delivered his own address in which he strongly emphasized that his government had "been putting our own means of defence in order" to make the Dominion of Canada "as immune from attack or possible invasion as we can reasonably expect to make it, and that should the occasion ever arise, enemy forces should not be able to pursue their way, either by land, sea or air to the United States across Canadian territory."[64] But the public reaction in the United States to the talk of improved Canadian-American security ties was strangely muted. Though the *New York Times* did acknowledge the many grateful Canadian responses to the president's security pledge, it paid far more attention to Roosevelt's comments about the need for a St. Lawrence power treaty.[65] Moreover, it seems that none of Roosevelt's aides thought the matter noteworthy enough to have recorded any comments about it. William Castle, Hoover's former assistant secretary of state, had noted the address, and his opinion was scathing. Complaining that the "extremely unwise" speech had "struck me between the eyes," Castle thought that not only had Roosevelt unwisely extended the purview of the Monroe Doctrine, he had virtually guaranteed American involvement in any future Canadian or British wars. And when President Roosevelt had claimed that he had not broadened the Monroe Doctrine's mandate because Canada had always fallen under its protection, Castle caustically noted that not "even the infallible speech of a self appointed divinity cannot make it mean such a thing."[66]

Whether Roosevelt really intended to spark a debate about Canada's place in an American-led hemispheric defense system is, well, debatable. He did tell Lord Tweedsmuir later that he had hoped the speech would have "some small effect in Berlin." Indeed, Roosevelt seemed to play down the speech's importance by claiming that what he had said "was so obvious that I cannot understand why some American President did not say it half a century ago."[67] But though his Kingston comments failed to much impress Adolf Hitler's dark regime,[68] they were at least consistent with the president's developing views about Canadian security, and Roosevelt had laid out the basis of a strategy that would guide American foreign policy towards Canada through and beyond the very dark days that lay less than two years hence. Simmons laid bare some of these implications in a 30 January 1939 despatch. Noting Canada's declared intent to spend $60 million on the military over the next fiscal year "as against about $35 million expended during the past two fiscal years," if one added funds intended to cover pre-existing contracts and the possibility of supplementary estimates being voted by Parliament, Simmons calculated that the total defense expenditure could reach $100 million, "the largest peace time armament outlay in the history of the Dominion." And whereas Canada could reasonably expect to face only some minor air and naval raids given the Royal Navy's overwhelming north Atlantic superiority, Simmons reported that most coastal defense guns were obsolete, and just four "reasonably efficient" antiaircraft guns and only 180 aircraft existed in all of Canada. Should an enemy attempt to raid Canada, possibly using planes hidden in disguised merchant ships or very long-range bombers, Canadian army Colonel Maurice Pope had told Simmons that a panicky public would demand protection for every eastern Canadian town, thus reducing forces at vulnerable points or the ability to send units "overseas where they would be of real military value." But if Canada could not defend itself and if British aid was not forthcoming, the United States might then find itself called upon to live up to Roosevelt's Kingston pledge; thus, Simmons warned, "the question of Canada's capacity to repel enemy attacks would appear to be a matter of immediate concern to the United States."[69]

Simmons had put his finger exactly upon the problem. Although Roosevelt's stated intent had been to warn Hitler against taking aggressive action, most Canadians thought instead that Roosevelt had guaranteed that the United States would always gallop to the Dominion's rescue in a military crisis. And although King cautioned his cabinet in September 1938 that should Britain be "worsted in a world struggle, the only future left for Canada would be absorption by the U.S., if we were to be saved from an enemy aggressor,"[70] the Canadian military welcomed Roosevelt's pledge. Confident that a guarantee of American protection had solved Canada's home defense problem because "under existing strategic conditions there is no risk of an armed invasion in strength," the army concluded that mobilizing even part of Mobile Force for home defense would serve no military need except to "re-assure public opinion."[71] Therefore when its chief planner submitted a new mobilization scheme in mid-January 1939, Colonel Kenneth Stuart, logically pointing out that a seven-division militia and two-division Mobile Force far exceeded any Canadian home defense requirements, cleverly noted that as Roosevelt was preparing the United States "to intervene against the dictators," Canada could do no less. Stuart therefore recommended forming four divisions, two for home defense duties, the others for service overseas.[72]

Although Mackenzie marked his copy of this important document with large question marks wherever Stuart had mentioned an expeditionary force, in what one historian has termed a "both curious and important" sequel,[73] Stuart's memorandum, with only the most blatant references to overseas service expunged, formed the basis of Mackenzie's defense estimates presented to Canada's Parliament on 26 April 1939. Personally vetted by King, Mackenzie's statement noted five vital home defense tasks for the army and two others with far more ominous overtones: The need for a reserve force to meet "unexpected" contingencies; and the development of a capability to field a "substantial force" capable of being ready within six months "for active service."[74] Why had King agreed to such "a daunting and open-ended commitment" to form a

Canadian expeditionary force if a major war erupted overseas? Certainly he had hoped that by allowing Mackenzie to reveal the military's price for rearmament, King's defense program would look quite modest especially to his recalcitrant and isolationist Quebec backbenchers.[75] But most importantly, having thought that war had been imminent the previous September over Czechoslovakia, King had made the choice that Christie had most feared. Believing that Britain's very survival would be at stake in a conflict with Germany, the prime minister felt "it was a self-evident national duty, if Britain entered the war, that Canada should co-operate lending every assistance possible; in no way asserting neutrality, but carefully defining in what ways and how far she would participate." That self-evident duty might not necessarily mean an expeditionary force for a European war—hence Mackenzie's quite deliberate emphasis on the army's home defense responsibilities. If war came, King hoped that Canada could provide materials and munitions rather than cannon fodder.[76]

But Simmons's caution about Canadians expecting help begged the question as to whether the United States could provide assistance. There was little doubt among most informed Americans that the United States simply could not tolerate any foreign power making military inroads in Canada, but intentions and capabilities are quite different things, and the American army showed little capability to counter any serious threats to Canadian or American interests. Seventeenth in the world in size (behind even Portugal), with just over 184,000 regulars and approximately the same number of national guardsmen scattered throughout four partially-formed divisions and just five brigades "in various stages of completion" (as opposed to more than 90 German divisions and 50 Japanese divisions in China alone), the army had only 329 light tanks and 1,800 planes, and most of its other weapons and its doctrine dated back to World War One.[77] Moreover, its guiding strategic defense policy, as of November 1938, though making no mention of the need to safeguard Canada, outlined some formidable tasks: The army had a duty "to maintain an immediately available force, adequate to defend the continental United States, Panama, and Hawaii (in conjunction with the Navy), during the period our vast resources in personnel, material, and industry are mobilized for war."[78]

This unhappy strategic situation began to change somewhat for the better after the Munich agreement was reached in late 1938. Although Roosevelt rejoiced with King "that the outbreak of war" had been averted and said that he was "not one bit upset over" Munich's final result,[79] in fact his administration had found the Czech crisis most unsettling. Berle, who had ridiculed British entreaties to the Czechs "to be reasonable" with the caustic comment "that when you want to make the lion lie down with the lamb, there is not much point in beating the lamb," blamed Britain for encouraging the Czechs to resist Germany's demands and then refusing to grant any "unequivocal assurances" about coming to Czechoslovakia's aid if threats led to shooting.[80] Idealists, recognizing that the United States had not assisted the Czechs either, likely agreed with Assistant Secretary of State George Messersmith's assertion that the Sudetenland would not be Germany's last territorial demand.[81] What all could agree on was that Germany was becoming a real problem, and Roosevelt, claiming that his caution during the crisis had emanated from his belief that Britain and France needed time to overcome the great military superiority wielded by the dictatorships,[82] found himself with few levers to use against Hitler. Trade between Germany and the

United States was insubstantial and bureaucratic ties practically nonexistent, leaving Roosevelt no real alternative other than the display of "a credible threat of force."[83]

Just what Roosevelt thought a credible threat of force might be came when he met with his senior aides and service officers on 14 November. Having already approved $300 million in new defense spending with the option of seeking $500 million, the president said that the "United States must be prepared to resist attack on the Western Hemisphere from the North Pole to the South Pole, including all of North America and South America." Doubtful that even a well-equipped 400,000-man army would deter Hitler, Roosevelt asserted that if the United States had possessed 5,000 warplanes the previous autumn, "Hitler would have not dared to take the stand he did." Estimating that Germany had nearly 10,000 aircraft now and could produce 12,000 more annually, whereas Britain and France had less than 3,000 planes and a yearly productive capacity of just 8,400, Roosevelt wanted at least 10,000 American-made warplanes delivered over the next two years plus the industrial ability to churn out annually another 10,000.[84] Pleased that the president had dropped an earlier idea to produce 50,000 aircraft (Morgenthau thought Roosevelt was becoming "more and more practical"[85]), the notion of building planes without thought for a balanced force, infrastructure needs, or personnel, not to mention ground combat units, compelled Craig and his deputy chief of staff, Brigadier General George C. Marshall, to oppose the presidential initiative. Facing army demands that it needed 58,000 new regulars and 36,000 additional guardsmen to adequately protect overseas possessions and to form a 29,000-man expeditionary force required to secure new bases, and vigorously complaining that he could not "influence Hitler with barracks, runways and schools for mechanics," Roosevelt was persuaded to accept a compromise in mid-December: Of the newly-voted $500 million for defense, $180 million would build 3,000 planes, and the rest of the money would go towards the provision of non-air armaments and "non-plane air items."[86]

Canada too had not been forgotten. Asked by a journalist on 15 November whether national defense now meant continental defense, Roosevelt replied that the United States had to rethink hemispheric orientation—"in other words from Canada to Tierra del Fuego"—but that the burden "does not rest solely on our shoulders."[87] Indeed, Roosevelt thought Canada might produce some of the airplanes that would deter Germany. That idea had originated with William Bullitt. Returning to the United States in October from the American embassy in Paris, Ambassador Bullitt believed that France and Britain would have successfully resisted German pressure over Czechoslovakia had their respective air forces been perceived as a better match for the Luftwaffe. Looking for ways to provide those nations with aircraft from secure plants without violating the American neutrality laws, Bullitt hit upon the unique notion of having France establish aircraft plants in a number of Canadian border communities, plants that would employ American workers and use American raw materials.[88]

Though Roosevelt found this notion appealing enough to suggest Britain's involvement, Morgenthau was unmoved by Bullitt's scheme. Agreeing that the idea could provide France with a safe supply of planes in wartime, the treasury secretary doubted that given the distances involved, security would override the need for speedy delivery of aircraft in a crisis. Further, because Canada was a British Dominion, France risked having its aviation industry falling under British control if relations with

Britain deteriorated, not to mention what might happen if Canada opted for neutrality in a European war. Moreover, large Canadian aviation plants might draw workers and resources away from domestic American efforts, and could further damage American interests if Britain, seeking to avoid defeat or destruction, sided with Germany or Japan. Chamberlain also displayed little enthusiasm for the idea, noting only that the plan should be put aside for future use.[89]

Prime Minister King, made aware of Roosevelt's air power proposal by Lord Tweedsmuir, found the president's "amazing" 15 November comments disquieting. Having already told Skelton in October that he did "not like to be dependent on the U.S. [for a] change of leaders there might lead to a vassalage as far as our Dominion was concerned,"[90] and fearful imperialist jingoes might interpret Roosevelt's remarks "as an effort to isolate North America," King did not want to seem unappreciative of the president's "generous attitude." Deciding it was best to say nothing and to "treat the matter simply as an application of what had been said at Queen's University by the President," that discretion served King well when he arrived in Washington on 17 November to sign a new trade agreement. Pleased that the United States and Britain also had agreed to their own bilateral trade pact, King found Roosevelt far more eager to continue discussions about aviation matters. Firmly believing that Germany sought a South American foothold and that Japan likely would soon make trouble too in the Pacific, Roosevelt hoped that his air program would "astound" friend and foe alike. Predicting that 100,000 airplanes would roll off production lines within two years, the president said that half of the models could be allocated to Britain, and that 5,000 other planes could be Canada-bound. Impressed by the "comprehensive and detailed way in which the president presented his proposed programme," King promised that Canadian industry would do nothing that might hinder the American effort.[91]

Canadian cooperation proved forthcoming on another matter. After months of stalling, King's government finally decided in December 1938 to respond to the formation of the American Alaska highway commission by setting up its own national commission. Enthusiasm for the new body, however, was sorely lacking in Ottawa. External Affairs, denying that the proposed body committed Canada "to any action in regard to the construction of the highway" and claiming that no "suitable official" could be spared, declined to appoint a representative. Moreover, wanting to avoid anything that might "publicly emphasize the defence angle," the DEA opposed any official military representation on the panel. Although the cabinet appointed a militia officer (a civil engineer by trade), King's selection of Charles Stewart to head the panel may have indicated a lack of real interest because Stewart was so seriously ill he could not fully participate in the commission's work for another six months.[92]

Events conspired, however, to push the Alaska highway into the background. In March 1939 Germany occupied the remaining rump of Czechoslovakia, took back Memel from Lithuania, and began eyeing former German lands held by Poland since the latter's creation after World War One's end. Shocked by the Munich settlement's collapse, on 31 March a shaken Chamberlain announced Britain's guarantee to support Poland should Hitler's Germany initiate "any action which clearly threatened Polish independence."[93] Appeasement clearly had ended, and the search for allies to contain Germany now began in earnest. At France's urging, Britain agreed to approach the Soviet Union for help, but having little faith either in Soviet military capabilities or

Joseph Stalin's political trustworthiness, the British cast their gaze across the pond to a certain former colony.

Would the United States help? The consensus among senior British officials, even before the sad events of March 1939, was that it would. Although Tweedsmuir described American public opinion on international questions as "a very delicate plant" that "may suddenly develop curious growths," he believed that American and British opinions concerning the European dictatorships now were "extraordinarily close." Lord Lothian, soon to become Britain's ambassador in Washington, agreed. Visiting the United States and Canada in early 1939 while the British government still debated whether his appointment should go ahead, Lothian said that the Americans finally had begun to realize that they would be able to obtain "no halfway house for the United States between abandoning the Monroe Doctrine, retreating to the North American continent and leaving the oceans to the control of the Fascist powers and to establish on unchallengeable foundations in conjunction with Great Britain and the Dominions a joint democratic control of the sea." Even Chamberlain, so notoriously suspicious of the Yankee cousins, thought that after its initially disappointing critical response to Munich, the United States seemed to be developing an appreciation for "the line the British Government has taken."[94]

But the crash of a test plane in California on 23 January threatened British hopes. The discovery that one of the doomed craft's two pilots was a French air force officer prompted the initiation of a Senate investigation to see whether military secrets had been disclosed to a foreign government in violation of American law. Though Roosevelt vigorously defended France's right to seek aircraft from private American manufacturers, that explanation failed to calm accusations that he was seeking a tacit alliance with France and Britain. The problem worsened when Roosevelt met with some senators on 31 January. Saying that "he was very much concerned over the future of the world," the president made it clear that American security depended upon the continued independence of Europe's democracies and neutral states, and that if Britain and France succumbed to a totalitarian assault, Africa and then Latin America would fall next in, leading to "the gradual encirclement of the United States by the removal of the first lines of defense." Not only did France's acquisition of American warplanes bolster that first defense line, but in Roosevelt's considered opinion, letting some 40 or 50 independent countries purchase American arms "on the barrelhead" was "the best foreign policy" the United States could follow because it could "mean the saving of our civilization."[95]

Roosevelt had hoped that his comments to the senators would remain strictly confidential, but newspaper headlines the next day quoted an unidentified senator as saying that the president had openly described the Rhine River as America's defensive frontier, thus strongly implying that the United States would physically defend France against a German invasion. Facing widespread condemnation and Hoover's charge that Roosevelt was involved "in the most momentous change in American policies of peace and war since we entered the Great War," the president angrily counterattacked. Calling the Rhine frontier statement a "deliberate lie," Roosevelt emphasized his opposition to "any entangling alliances" and his support for arms reductions and world trade, but repeated that the survival of 40 to 50 states was "of tremendous importance to the safety of the United States."[96]

Roosevelt's furious defense may have helped. Although polls taken prior to the Munich settlement consistently had found 95 percent of the American public firmly opposed to participation in a European war, by February 1939 17 percent were willing to consider giving military support to France and Britain, a figure that would rise to 46 percent by the following August.[97] Still, with less than one in five Americans favoring any aid to the Allies, Roosevelt faced some tough sledding especially because many of his aides adamantly opposed helping Britain. Although some Americans obviously regarded the United States as the Anglo-Saxon family's younger son ready to shoulder the role of an aging British "father," Moffat "mentally repudiate[d]" even the implied suggestion "that we have the slightest responsibility towards the British Commonwealth." If British and American interests, "selfishly considered," agreed, then Moffat had no objection to working with Britain against the dictatorships, but he opposed making common cause simply "because of sentimental considerations, racial considerations, cultural considerations, et cetera."[98] General Embick agreed. Having long argued that America should concentrate on hemispheric defense and that the Philippines should be abandoned in order to improve relations with Japan, Embick believed that Germany would easily overrun Poland and the Balkans, but that western front fighting would be "largely restricted" to indecisive aerial and submarine warfare between Germany and the Allies. Disheartened by arguments favoring American intervention that showed "less historical sense than the average European peasant," Embick thought the stage was being set for Americans to be duped again as had occurred in 1917.[99]

Yet when the British Foreign Office invited the United States on 19 March to resume naval discussions, Roosevelt showed no sign that the advice from Moffat and Embick was guiding his actions. He assented to the British invitation just two days later with the proviso that Britain send an officer to Washington disguised as a third military attaché assigned to the British embassy. The ensuing talks, delayed until June by Admiralty disinterest, presaged the division of responsibilities that would last until December 1941. In the event of war in Europe, most of the USN would remain in the Pacific to deter Japan, though some vessels would patrol the western Atlantic. Leahy also suggested basing some ships at Singapore, but only if the Royal Navy did so as well. And although Commander T.C. Hampton of the Royal Navy told his British superiors that American war plans were tentative and that the USN surprisingly had formulated no detailed schemes for cooperation with Britain, he happily had found both Roosevelt and Leahy to be "extremely pro-British."[100]

American plans for hemispheric defense, however, were more than just tentative. Although John Keegan has claimed that "[f]or all the awful warning that the Civil War and World War I uttered about the consequences of unpreparedness, Washington allowed Pearl Harbor to come round without having made any better provision for harnessing the energies of government to strategy,"[101] the Joint Board had formulated strategies to meet a number of contingencies. Acting without explicit instructions, the Joint Board, noting with some considerable alarm "the increased power of the Fascist nations of Europe, the demonstrated expansionist ambitions of Japan, and the probable secret undertaking between Japan, Germany and Italy in regard to national expansion," had directed its Joint Planning Committee (JPC) in November 1938 to study options in the event of a "violation of the Monroe Doctrine by one or more of the Fascist powers, and a simultaneous attempt to expand Japanese influence in the Philippines."[102]

The JPC's initial January 1939 findings proved a most interesting read. Foreshadowing the strategy that would guide the United States in World War Two, the committee argued that Germany and Italy could be deterred from attacking South America only if the USN had not committed the bulk of its strength to the Pacific. Thus, American national interests demanded undertaking a European offensive while remaining on the strategic defensive against Japan. The final report, issued on 21 April 1939, was more clear. Declaring Germany to be the main threat—followed by Italy and then Japan—the JPC thought that the Fascist powers, using subversion and revolution, would seek bases in Latin America and possibly the Iberian Peninsula and North Africa. Concerned that such bases would endanger the vital Panama Canal, the JPC again accepted the possibility of initial Pacific defeats so that the Atlantic frontier could be made secure. It also sought more military missions in South America; the enhancement of defenses in Hawaii, Panama, Alaska, Puerto Rico, and the Pacific possessions; increases in the navy and marine corps, and the speedy formation of a three-division army expeditionary force.[103] Very pleased with the report which it described as "a monument to the Joint Planning Committee," the Joint Board ordered the two services to use the JPC conclusions to design plans to address strategic alternatives ranging from hemispheric defense to offensive operations in the Pacific and European waters.[104] This process produced five "Rainbow" plans over the next year, all of which had at their core a commitment to hemispheric defense. Rainbow 1, which dealt only with the defense of the Western Hemisphere, was ready first and received Roosevelt's oral sanction on 14 October 1939.[105]

Roosevelt had anticipated Rainbow 1. Having participated in a two-week Caribbean naval exercise in February, Roosevelt came away from that pleasant voyage convinced that American security demanded additional bases in the western Atlantic. Meeting with Leahy and Welles on 23 March, Roosevelt asked the admiral to study prospective sites.[106] Leahy took little time to complete his task as his service, concerned that "trends in aviation have increased the importance of acquiring certain neighboring foreign concessions," had been considering such basing options since 1933, while the army in 1936 had judged Bermuda and the West Indies to be "of military value to the United States." On 24 March, Leahy produced for the president a list that included Trinidad; Bermuda; St. Lucia; St. John's, Newfoundland; Halifax, Nova Scotia; and some small British and Australian island possessions in the Pacific.[107]

Identifying possible bases was one thing; getting access to them was quite another matter indeed. However, the visit to North America of King George and Queen Elizabeth in May 1939 offered the Americans a chance to make the case at a most senior level. Entertaining the British royal couple and Prime Minister King at his Hyde Park home on 10 June, the president revealed his intention to prevent any hostile warships from operating in the western Atlantic. However, the very difficult task of "keeping the waters of the Atlantic free of German ships of war" would be rendered much easier if American warships, "without violating any neutral rights," could refuel in Halifax.[108] But the president saved most of the vital details for two chats with Ambassador Lindsay in late June and early July. Lindsay heard Roosevelt explain that an efficient wartime patrol encompassing the entire western side of the Atlantic, (including Canada, Newfoundland, and all British, French, and Dutch possessions in the Western Hemisphere) required foreign bases. Some of those facilities would be in Brazil, but the USN also needed sites on the British colonies of St. Lucia, Trinidad, Bermuda, and at Halifax. Roosevelt also made certain that Lindsay understood that reaching an agreement before any hostilities began was imperative so that Americans would accept their ships using foreign bases in wartime. Britain's answer came before mid-July; the United States was free to utilize any British bases the Atlantic patrol might require.[109]

Such permission, however, did not apply to Halifax. Having heard Roosevelt present his case to King George at Hyde Park, Prime Minister King was quite aware of the president's intent but was reluctant to commit himself or Canada to the naval scheme. Although Conservative Member of Parliament (MP) Howard Green had come out publicly in April in favor of "a clear-cut, honest alliance" between Canada and the United States, King had told his Liberal caucus in March that looking "to the U.S. to save us" would incur a price "much greater than we would have to pay to any other for assistance."[110] Whether Canada would allow American vessels to use Halifax, the prime minister told a visiting British official on 19 July, depended "on developments." If USN ships wished "to engage in or risk war by coming into our ports for fuel," King said that was "their doing & business." Canadians, however, would "not object to getting all the help we could."[111]

Always eager to see things for himself, in early August Roosevelt undertook a cruise of eastern Canadian waters aboard a USN cruiser. Stopping in Halifax on 15 August, the president demonstrated considerable interest in the port's facilities, the local defenses, and the development of Canadian antisubmarine tactics. Concerned that German submarines might be able to hide along the rugged and isolated Labrador coast, Roosevelt also discussed the possibility that Japan might try to use islands off British Columbia as advanced bases.[112] But Halifax was not included in the American rush to acquire base leasing rights on Trinidad, Bermuda, and St. Lucia after the German-Soviet nonaggression pact became known on 24 August. Instead, the United States received formal permission from Canada to use Halifax as an advanced naval air service base if needed, and if such American use did not interfere with Canadian activities.[113]

Fears of a new conflict were realized when Germany, falsely claiming that Polish troops had crossed the frontier and had murdered some German civilians, invaded Poland on 1 September. Two days later, after their ultimatum demanding Germany's withdrawal from Poland went unheeded, France and Britain honored their Polish guarantees and declared war on Germany. King had no doubt that Canada would choose to side with Britain in the war, but concerned about national unity and intent on demonstrating the Dominion's foreign policy powers, he wanted the nation to enter the conflict undivided and on its own accord. On 1 September the cabinet agreed that as soon as Britain "became engaged in the war," it would seek Parliament's "authority for effective cooperation by Canada at the side of Great Britain."[114] Nine days later, that authority was forthcoming (only two votes were cast against the declaration), and Canada formally opened hostilities against Germany for the second time in the century.

The United States remained neutral. During peace's final days Roosevelt had appealed to Adolf Hitler to choose negotiation over fighting, but knowing that such entreaties had almost no chance of success (though Harry Hopkins had hoped that the "grand" letter to Hitler would prevent Britain and France from opting for a "fatal" Munich-like settlement, Berle thought that the presidential appeal, though necessary, had "all that quality of naiveté which is the prerogative alone of the United States"[115]), the president had hoped to establish who was responsible for initiating the conflict. Roosevelt ordered his cabinet on 1 September to prepare only to meet war problems rather than waging war itself "because we were not going to get into this war." Two days later, he told the nation that although he could not "ask that every American remain neutral in thought," his government would make every effort to prevent a "black-out of peace in the United States."[116]

Though Prime Minister King listened to Roosevelt's broadcast "feeling an almost profound disgust" that the United States was keeping out of the "great issue" and "professing to do so in the name of peace when everything on which peace is based is threatened,"[117] Roosevelt and his administration were seeking to ensure that American neutrality would favor the Allied cause. Indeed, having unhappily estimated that the Fascist powers had "at least an even chance" of winning the war, the president had decided the previous May to seek the repeal of the neutrality act's arms embargo. Chosen to work with the Congress on the issue, Berle had approached the task with mixed emotions. Though he thought that central European territorial adjustments were "apparently necessary," he feared he was witnessing the rise of an "intolerably strong German-Italian empire" intent on achieving Britain's destruction within two or three years. And though the United States had no real interest in defending Britain's empire, Berle was certain that his nation "had a solid interest in having the British, and not the Germans, dominant in the Atlantic" because a victorious Germany would then launch "imperialist schemes in South and Central America," and that course of action would compel the United States to become militarist itself to ensure its survival.[118]

Despite Berle's best efforts, Congress took until November to rescind the various arms embargo prohibitions it had enacted, and as Europe plummeted into madness, Roosevelt's administration dithered about what could be done to safeguard American neutrality and aid the Allied cause. In the first case, Roosevelt had decided by 26 August to have the USN patrol a mid-Atlantic line from Canada to Guiana, a sort of "Pax Americana" that would seek to exclude all hostile belligerent warships. Though the Pan-American Union adopted the notion of a neutrality zone 300 to 1,000 miles out to sea from the American frontier with Canada down to the southern tip of South America, none of the belligerents accepted the proposal, and the USN found itself unable to enforce the prohibition.[119]

Far more confusing to American policy makers was Canada's status as the Dominion took until 10 September to formally side with Britain and France against Germany. Berle, Moffat, and Hickerson, still following the notion that Canada was a country only in a strictly limited sense, believed that Britain's declaration of war on 3 September "automatically" had brought Canada and the other British Dominions into the conflict; therefore there seemed to be no choice but to include Canada in the State Department's formal announcement of American neutrality on 5 September.[120] But the American consul general in Vancouver had quite a different idea, theorizing that

Canada's refusal to make clear its status was a designed imperial ploy to allow the Dominion to import American supplies needed for Britain's war effort. Although the consul demonstrated a particularly poor understanding of both Canada's constitutional position after the passage of the 1931 Statute of Westminster and Prime Minister King's outlook, Canada did hope to use its last days of peace to acquire badly needed American weapons, in particular 65 warplanes. Unfortunately, as Assistant Secretary of War Louis Johnson made clear to both the Canadians and Roosevelt, though some aircraft might be diverted from current American production lines to Canada, most of the models had yet to be manufactured and thus could not be delivered any time soon. Sympathetic to Canadian needs and rejecting Berle's claim that refusing to recognize Canada's belligerent status would spark British accusations that the United States was seeking to break up the empire, Roosevelt telephoned King on 5 September to ask if Canada considered itself to be at war. When King said that that decision had not been taken yet by Parliament, the president deleted Canada from the official neutrality proclamation.[121]

The president's decision to omit Canada sparked a small row within the State Department. Although New York City Mayor F.H. LaGuardia lobbied hard for the Roosevelt administration to convince Canada to defer its war vote so that the United States could send vital supplies to the Dominion until the very last moment—"[w]hat happened to such shipments after that would not be our concern" LaGuardia added—Moffat thought that would leave the administration open to charges that it was subverting the neutrality act's arms embargo section. To the relief of all, Canada's formal entry into the conflict on 10 September stopped the anxious debate. Roosevelt promptly signed the neutrality proclamation naming Canada as a belligerent, and in Berle's opinion, thus the mighty British empire was "reunited."[122] Yet as Escott Reid discovered, ways could be found around some of the embargo's provisions. Meeting with the Army and Navy Munitions Board's secretary on 9 September, Reid found that officer quite eager to outline those items, including key artillery pieces and optical instruments, not on the embargoed list. Moreover, noted isolationist Senator Arthur Vandenberg assured the legation on 29 September that the repeal of the neutrality act's arms embargo rule "was practically certain."[123]

Similar assurances were also forthcoming from the president. Asked on 12 September by a journalist whether his 1938 pledge to defend Canada still held true, Roosevelt replied that it did, although he quickly added that the pledge should not be interpreted in any way as an extension of the Monroe Doctrine beyond its original limits.[124] But Roosevelt was even more forthcoming in a private interview on 25 September with the new, and controversial, Canadian minister, Loring Christie. Revealing that he had made his August cruise to eastern Canada and Labrador "to see the lie of the land for himself" and to gauge the region's potential for hiding unfriendly submarines, the president suggested using USN ships to escort British vessels sailing from American ports into Canadian waters and outlined his plan for the western Atlantic neutrality zone.[125]

The arms embargo rule was scrapped in early November, but not without a bitter fight in which Canada unhappily found itself a star attraction thanks to Colonel Charles Lindbergh. Having moved to Europe in the mid-1930s after the murder of his infant son, the famed and impressionable aviator had formed two important opinions during his European tenure: First, that German air power far surpassed that of all other European states; and that a disastrous war between the Fascist nations on one side and Britain and France on the other would open the gates wide to Soviet expansion in western Europe.[126] Having returned to the United States in 1939, Lindbergh cautioned against undertaking any act that might endanger American neutrality, and as a radio address on 13 October demonstrated, the very fact that the United States bordered a belligerent Canada concerned him greatly. Asking what right Canadians had "to draw this hemisphere into a European war simply because they prefer the Crown of England to American independence," Lindbergh said "sooner or later" Americans "must demand the freedom of this continent from the dictates of European power." Although most critics assailed Lindbergh as naive, inept, and even stupid, some Americans, like General Hugh Johnson, the former head of the National Recovery Administration during Roosevelt's first term, argued that Lindbergh had exposed the contradiction in Roosevelt's pledge to both defend Canada and preserve American neutrality. Admitting that the United States had to defend the Western Hemisphere against assault, Johnson wished to pose an interesting question: "Suppose, as has now happened, one of our most powerful good neighbors attacks a country of the Eastern Hemisphere—what do we do when the counter-attack comes?"[127]

Public opinion supplied the answer to that query. Although many Americans continued to oppose military aid to the European democracies even after Congress repealed the neutrality legislation, by January 1940 polls showed that 74.2 percent of Americans favored defending Canada, 1.1 percent higher than a similar poll taken the previous January.[128] Loring Christie had a less prosaic explanation for the issue's quick demise: Colonel Lindbergh, "like some others in the public eye, may be a case for a psychiatrist."[129] Happy to see that the revised neutrality law now allowed Canada to purchase American arms to Canada "without hindrance" as long as the items were paid for within 90 days, King's government settled down to what it hoped would be a better and more easily manageable relationship with the United States. When Canada's finance minister visited Morgenthau in late December, although Colonel J.L. Ralston believed that this conflict would be "a long grinding economic struggle without the glamour and music which attended the world war," he "had no problems to bring up." Ralston had sought the meeting so that he could meet Morgenthau.[130] Such a luxury would be sorely lacking in 1940.

NOTES

1. Adolf A. Berle memorandum, 4 January 1937, FDRL, Welles Papers, box 39, file 5.

2. Ibid., plus second Berle memorandum, 4 January 1937, Ibid.

3. "Memorandum of Conversation between Secretary Hull and the British Ambassador, Sir Ronald Lindsay," LC, Hull Papers, box 58, file Great Britain 1936–38.

4. Sumner Welles, *The Time for Decision* (New York: Harper & Brothers, 1944), 50; and Arthur M. Schlesinger, Jr., "Franklin D. Roosevelt's Internationalism," in Cornelis A. van Minnen and John F. Sears, eds., *FDR and His Contemporaries: Foreign Perceptions of an American President* (New York: St. Martin's Press, 1992), 9.

5. Frederick W. Marks III, *Wind over Sand: The Diplomacy of Franklin Roosevelt* (Athens: The University of Georgia Press, 1988), 267, 277.

6. Mark M. Lowenthal, "Roosevelt and the Coming of the War: The Search for United States Policy 1937–42," in Walter Laqueur, ed., *The Second World War: Essays in Military and Political History* (London: Sage Publications, 1982), 51.

7. Ramsay Macdonald to Tweedsmuir, 7 December 1936, QUA, Buchan Papers, box 8, file Correspondence December 1936; Robert Vansittart memorandum, 16 December 1936, PRO, Foreign Office Records, FO371, 19787/A9996/9996/51.

8. Richard A. Harrison, "Testing the Water: A Secret Probe towards Anglo-American Military Co-operation in 1936," *The International History Review*, 7 (May 1985), 217.

9. Ibid., 219; and William R. Rock, *Chamberlain and Roosevelt: British Foreign Policy and the United States, 1937–1940* (Columbus: Ohio University Press, 1988), 12–13.

10. William E. Kinsella, Jr., *Leadership in Isolation: FDR and the Origins of the Second World War* (Cambridge: Schenkman Publishing, 1978), 88; and David Reynolds, *The Creation of the Anglo-American Alliance 1937–41: A Study in Competitive Co-operation* (Chapel Hill: The University of North Carolina Press, 1982), 17.

11. King diary, 3 and 12 November 1936, and 24 February 1937, NAC; and Armour memorandum, 12 November 1936, NARA, RG59, Decimal File 1930–39, 842.00/500–1/2.

12. King diary, 5 March 1937, NAC.

13. Armour memorandum of interview with King, 22 March 1937, NARA, RG84, Entry 2195A, file 800.

14. Christie, "Re Monroe Doctrine," 16 February 1937, in John A. Munro, ed., *Documents on Canadian External Relations: Volume 6. 1936–1939* (Ottawa: Department of External Affairs, 1972), 177; Skelton memorandum, February 1937, NAC, O.D. Skelton Papers, vol. 27, file 9; and MID report, "Canada: Political Estimate," 1 June 1937, NARA, RG59, Decimal File 1930–39, 842.00/504.

15. King diary, 1 December 1936 and 10 May 1937, NAC; and Armour memorandum, 5 March 1937, NARA, RG84, Entry 2195A, file 800.1.

16. Helen Moorhead to Raymond L. Buell, 22 March 1937, LC, Raymond L. Buell Papers, box 10, file Moorhead, Helen Howard; and J. Pierrepont Moffat diary, 12 August 1937, Houghton Library, Harvard University [HL], Cambridge, J. Pierrepont Moffat Papers, MS Am 1407, vol. 39. Sixty nations, including Germany and Japan, endorsed Hull's plan for the peaceful resolution of all conflicts; Dallek, *Franklin Roosevelt and American Foreign Policy*, 145.

17. Roosevelt to Hull, 4 August 1937, FDRL, Roosevelt PSF, file Hull, Cordell: 1933–37; and Hull to Roosevelt, August 1937, Ibid.

18. Armour to Moffat, 2 September 1937, NARA, RG84, Entry 2195A, file 800.1 1937 Chief Executive; Hull to McIntrye, 13 September 1937, FDRL, Roosevelt OF, file OF200–ss; Armour to Moffat, 10 September 1937, HL, Moffat Papers, MS Am 1407, vol. 12; and Moffat to Armour, 14 September 1937, NARA, RG84, Entry 2195A, file 800.1 1937 Chief Executive. Among the congressmen favoring the Alaska highway was Anthony Dimond of Alaska and Warren G. Magnusson of Washington State. Magnusson's tireless advocacy for an Alaskan highway is explored in Timothy J. McMannon, "Warren G. Magnusson and the Alaska Highway," paper presented to the symposium, "'On Brotherly Terms': Canadian-American Relations West of the Rockies," University of Washington, Seattle, 11–14 September 1996.

19. "President Roosevelt's Visit," *Victoria Daily Colonist*, 30 September 1937.

20. Armour to SSEA, no. 564, 14 September 1937, NAC, RG25, vol. 1739, file 221 pt.1; Skelton to Christie, 16 September 1937, Ibid.; and Christie memorandum, 12 November 1937, Ibid.

21. Armour memorandum, 9 November 1937, NARA, RG84, Entry 2195A, file 800 1937 Political Affairs Defense and Foreign Policy. As Canada currently had "few military resources and little munition production capacity," the American army thought that Canadian combat effectiveness "would be seriously hampered" unless it could obtain heavy weapons of all types "from allies or neutrals"; MID, "Supplement British Empire (Dominions Except

Newfoundland) Combat Estimate Canada," 1 September 1937, NARA, RG59, Decimal File 1930–39, 842.20 MID Reports/4.

22. Ibid.

23. Roosevelt "Quarantine" address, 5 October 1937, in Daniel J. Boorstin, ed., *An American Primer* (Chicago: The University of Chicago Press, 1966), 847–52; and John E. Wiltz, *From Isolation to War, 1931–1941* (New York: Thomas Y. Crowell, 1968), 63.

24. Dorothy Borg, "Notes on Roosevelt's 'Quarantine Speech,'" *Political Science Quarterly,* 72 (September 1957), 405–7. Richard Hofstadter and Charles Beard thought that the speech revealed Roosevelt's swing away from isolation, and James MacGregor Burns saw it as a "trial balloon" to test the public's mood. When that mood proved unheroic, the president "pulled in his horns further"; Hofstadter, *The American Political Tradition,* 446–47; Charles A. Beard, *American Foreign Policy in the Making, 1932–1940* (New Haven: Yale University Press, 1946), 190–91; and Burns, *The Lion and the Fox,* 318–19. Tweedsmuir claimed that the speech "was the culmination of a long conspiracy between" him and Roosevelt; Tweedsmuir to Gilbert Murray, 8 October 1937, QUA, Buchan Papers, box 9, file Correspondence October 1937.

25. Quoted in Dallek, *Franklin D. Roosevelt and American Foreign Policy,* 154.

26. Neville Chamberlain to Tweedsmuir, 19 November 1937, QUA, Buchan Papers, box 9, file Correspondence November 1937; and Mark M. Lowenthal, *Leadership and Indecision: American War Planning and Policy Process 1937–1942* (New York: Garland Publishing, 1988), 20–25.

27. Berle diary, 29 November 1938, FDRL, box 210, Diary 1937.

28. John Lamberton Harper, *American Visions of Europe: Franklin D. Roosevelt, George F. Kennan, and Dean G. Acheson* (Cambridge: Cambridge University Press, 1994), 60; Berle diary, 2 December 1937, FDRL, box 210, Diary 1937; and Moffat diary, 10 and 13 November, 1937, HL, MS Am 1407, vol. 39.

29. Welles to Armour, 29 November 1937, FDRL, Welles Papers, box 161, file Canada; and Armour to Welles, 10 December 1937, Ibid. Crerar's chat with Craig is described in Crerar to Ashton, 30 October 1937, NAC, H.D.G. Crerar Papers, vol. 10, file 958C.009.

30. Welles to Roosevelt, 20 December 1937, FDRL, Roosevelt PSF, file State: 1937; Roosevelt to Welles, 22 December 1937, Ibid.; and Roosevelt to King, 21 December 1937, NAC, King Correspondence, reel C3729, 207146.

31. King to Roosevelt, 30 December 1937, NAC, King Correspondence, reel C3729, 207148–49; and Armour to Welles, 8 January 1938, NARA, RG59, Decimal File 1930–39, 842.20/68 1/2.

32. Skelton, "Conversations on West Coast Defence," 10 January 1938, NAC, RG25, vol. 2959, file B–80. The articles intimated that although the American military was pressing Canada to do more to defend itself, the real threat to Canada was not serious; see M.H. Halton, "Defence Co-operation between Britain, U.S. Suggested in London," *Toronto Daily Star,* 6 January 1938; William Strange, "Three Experts See Invasion Just a Bogey," *Toronto Daily Star,* 6 January 1938; and "Guard for Alaska," *Toronto Globe and Mail,* 6 January 1938. Armour found the publication of these pieces "an extraordinary coincidence," perhaps explained by the American announcement of a billion-dollar defense program; Armour to Welles, 6 January 1938, FDRL, Welles Papers, box 44, file 13.

33. Hugh L. Keenleyside to Escott Reid, 14 May 1937, NAC, Escott Reid Papers, vol. 34, file Keenleyside, Hugh L.

34. The applicable correspondence is found in NARA, RG59, Decimal File 1930–39, 811.22742/27 to 811.22742/34.

35. Crerar to Colonel W.W.T. Torr, 13 January 1938, DHH, Kardex file 000.8 (D3); Ashton to Mackenzie, "Observations on Canada's Defence Policy," 14 October 1937, DHH, Kardex file 112.3M2009 (D27); Ashton to Mackenzie, "The Defence of Canada: A Survey of

Militia Requirements," 10 January 1938, DHH, Kardex file 114.1 (D11); and Ashton to Crerar, 29 November 1937, NAC, RG24, vol. 2448, file HQC 631–52–1.

36. Welles to Roosevelt, 14 January 1938, NARA, RG59, Decimal File 1930–39, 842.20/68 1/2.

37. In his diary, Leahy mentioned only that he, Embick, and Craig had met with Ashton and Nelles at the Canadian legation on 19 January for "an interesting talk"; William Leahy diary entry, 19 January 1938, LC, William Leahy Papers, container 2, reel 2.

38. Ashton to Mackenzie, "Conversations held in Washington, D.C., on the 19th and 20th January, 1938," 26 January 1938, DHH, Kardex file 112.3M2009 (D22).

39. Ibid.

40. Percy W. Nelles to Mackenzie, "Conversations held in Washington, D.C. on the 19th and 20th January, 1938," (late) January 1938, NAC, King Memoranda and Notes, vol. 157, file F1411.

41. For some very critical analyses of the USN's various incarnations of Plan Orange, please see Louis Morton, "Inter-Service Co-operation and Political-Military Collaboration," in Harry L. Coles, ed., *Total War and Cold War: Problems in Civilian Control of the Military* (Columbus: Ohio State University Press, 1962), 131–60; Edward S. Miller, *War Plan Orange: The U.S. Strategy to Defeat Japan, 1897–1945* (Annapolis: Naval Institute Press, 1991); and Brian McAllister Linn, *Guardians of Empire: The U.S. Army and the Pacific, 1902–1940* (Chapel Hill: University of North Carolina Press, 1997).

42. JSC to Mackenzie, 14 April 1938, DHH, Kardex file 181.006 (D276).

43. LaFleche to Skelton, 7 February 1938, NAC, RG25, vol. 1856, file 72–J pt. 1; Welles to Craig, 15 March 1938, FDRL, Welles Papers, box 161, file Canada; and Craig to Welles, 18 March 1938, Ibid.

44. King diary, 11 January and 12 March 1938, NAC.

45. David Key memorandum of interview with Crerar, 14 March 1939, NARA, RG59, Decimal File 1930–39, 842.20/79; and JSC, "A Review of Canada's Position with Respect to Defence, July 1938," 22 July 1938, NAC, Mackenzie Papers, vol. 30, file X–50.

46. Christie to Skelton, "Canadian Defence Policy," 24 June 1938, NAC, Skelton Papers, vol. 27, file 8.

47. Sub-Committee No. 2, "A Survey of Canada from the Theater Point of View," 28 January 1938, NARA, RG165, MID "Regional File" 1922–44, Entry 77, file 1000–Canada.

48. Lowenthal, *Leadership and Indecision*, 27–32; and Herbert Marler to SSEA, no. 158, 9 February 1938, NAC, King Correspondence, reel C3736, 216622–29.

49. T.D. Pattullo to Roosevelt, 4 March 1938, FDRL, Roosevelt OF, file OF1566; unsigned memorandum to King, "Alaska Highway," 5 April 1938, NAC, RG25, vol. 1739, file 221 pt. 1; King diary, 24 April and 1 August 18 1934, NAC; and King to E.A. Pickering, 7 April 1938, Ibid.

50. Harold Ickes diary, 21 April 1936, in *The Secret Diary of Harold L. Ickes. Volume II: The Inside Struggle 1936–1939* (New York: Simon and Schuster, 1954), 376; Pattullo to King, 23 April 1938, NAC, RG25, vol. 1739, file 221 pt. 1; and Skelton to King, "Alaska Highway," 28 April 1938, Ibid.

51. King diary, 26 April 1938, NAC; and King to Pattullo, 28 April 1938, NAC, King Correspondence, reel C3737, 218442–43.

52. Skelton to King, 23 April 1938, NAC, RG25, vol. 1739, file 221 pt. 1; and Skelton to King, "British Columbia–Yukon–Alaska Highway," 25 April 1938, Ibid.

53. Marler to SSEA, no. 603, 6 May 1938, NAC, King Correspondence, reel C3736, 216854–55; Pattullo to King, 28 May 1938, NAC, RG25, vol. 744, file 164; and Skelton to King, "Re: Interviews with Premier Pattullo," 31 May 1938, NAC, RG25, vol. 1739, file 221 pt. 1.

54. King to Skelton, 1 June 1938, NAC, RG25, vol. 744, file 164; interdepartmental committee, "Report to Council on the Proposal to Construct a Highway through British Columbia and the Yukon Territory to Alaska," August 1938, British Columbia Archives and Records Service [BCARS], Victoria, T.D. Pattullo Papers, vol. 72, file 1; and Fisher, "T.D. Pattullo and the British Columbia to Alaska Highway," 17.

55. John Charmley, *Chamberlain and the Lost Peace* (London: Hodder & Stoughton, 1989), 38; and Dallek, *Franklin D. Roosevelt and American Foreign Policy*, 155–56.

56. Donald Cameron Watt, *How War Came: The Immediate Origins of the Second World War, 1938–1939* (New York: Pantheon Books, 1989), 125.

57. Roosevelt to Congress, 28 January 1938, in Department of State, *Peace and War. United States Foreign Policy, 1931–1941* (Washington, D.C.: Government Printing Office, 1943), 405; and Dallek, *Franklin D. Roosevelt and American Foreign Policy*, 176. A 1937 poll found that 69 percent of Americans wanted a larger army, 74 percent a bigger navy, and 80 percent an enlarged air force; Ralph B. Levering, *The Public and American Foreign Policy, 1918–1978* (New York: William Morrow and Company, 1978), 74.

58. "U.S.-Canadian Defense," *New York Sunday News*, 17 April 1938; and James Frederick Green, "Canada in World Affairs," *Foreign Policy Reports*, 14 (1 July 1938), 88, 96.

59. John Farr Simmons to Hull, no. 2410, 21 July 1938, NARA, RG59, Decimal File 1930–39, 842.22741/2.

60. Roosevelt speech, "Reciprocity in Defense," 18 August 1938, copy in NAC, Skelton Papers, vol. 5, file 5–6.

61. Simmons to Hull, no. 81, 19 August 1938, NARA, RG59, Decimal File 1930–39, 711.00/1029.

62. "The New 'Roosevelt Doctrine,'" *Montreal Daily Star*, 19 August 1938; "The Good Neighbor," *Ottawa Citizen*, 19 August 1938; "A New Bond of Security," *Toronto Globe and Mail*, 19 August 1938, and "Monroe to Roosevelt," *Winnipeg Free Press*, 20 August 1938. The articles claiming that Roosevelt was seeking common cause with the European democracies include, "King and Roosevelt—Bridge Builders," 19 August 1938, *Montreal Daily Star*, and "The 'Roosevelt Doctrine' and the 'Monroe Doctrine,'" *Ottawa Journal*, 20 August 1938.

63. "A Friendly Gesture—No More," *Vancouver Daily Province*, 24 August 1924; and "Roosevelt Makes History," *Vancouver Sun*, 19 August 1938.

64. King diary, 18 and 20 August 1938, NAC; and King speech, "Reciprocity in Defence," NAC, Skelton Papers, vol. 5, file 5–6.

65. John MacCormac, "President Aids King's Policies," *New York Times*, 19 August 1938.

66. Castle diary, 18 and 25 August 1938, HHL; The Monroe Doctrine debate is discussed in C.G. Fenwick, "Canada and the Monroe Doctrine," *The American Journal of International Law*, 32 (October 1938), 782–85.

67. Roosevelt to Tweedsmuir, 31 August 1938, QUA, Buchan Papers, box 10, file Correspondence July–August 1938.

68. Dallek, *Franklin D. Roosevelt and American Foreign Policy*, 163. Canada's minister to France said that German newspapers described the speech either as an election address or a step towards preparing the American people for foreign intervention. An Italian newspaper, *La Tribuna*, sarcastically noted that Canada needed protection from invading polar bears; Philippe Roy to SSEA, no. 285, 19 August 1938, NAC, RG25, vol. 1873, file 359.

69. Simmons to Hull, no. 2896, 30 January 1939, NARA, RG59, Decimal File 1930–39, 842.20/98. The scope of Canadian service demands can be seen in "Synopsis of Presentations Made to the Defence Committee of Council, November 14, 1938," QUA, Charles

Gavan Power Papers, box 67, file D–2000; Sarty, "Mr. King and the Armed Forces," 222–29; and King diary, 14 November 1938, NAC.

70. King diary, 27 September 1938, NAC.

71. General staff, "Memorandum on Preparation for War (General Staff Branch)," 10 February 1939, NAC, RG24, vol. 2647, file HQS 3498 pt. 12.

72. Kenneth Stuart, "The Problems and Requirements of Canadian Defence," 16 January 1939, NAC, Mackenzie Papers, vol. 34, file B–30.

73. Sarty, "Mr. King and the Armed Forces," 230.

74. Mackenzie statement, *Debates*, House of Commons, 29 April 1939.

75. Sarty, "Mr. King and the Armed Forces," 231.

76. King diary, 13 September 1938, NAC; King's frustrated hopes for conducting a limited war is explored in J.L. Granatstein, *Canada's War: The Politics of the Mackenzie King Government, 1939–1945* (Toronto: Oxford University Press, 1975).

77. Brigadier General George C. Marshall, "Reinforcements for Overseas Possessions and Need for Expeditionary Forces," 7 February 1939, George C. Marshall Library [GCML], Lexington, George C. Marshall Papers, box 75, file 75/17; and John T. Nelsen II, *General George C. Marshall: Strategic Leadership and the Challenges of Reconstituting the Army, 1939–41* (Carlisle Barracks: Strategic Studies Institute, United States Army War College, February 1993), 1.

78. Marshall to Brigadier General Leigh R. Gignilliat, 4 November 1938, in Larry I. Bland, ed., *The Papers of George Catlett Marshall. Volume 1: "The Soldierly Spirit," December 1880–June 1939* (Baltimore: The Johns Hopkins University Press, 1981), 642–43.

79. Roosevelt to King, 11 October 1938, FDRL, Roosevelt PSF, file Diplomatic Correspondence Canada: 1938–39; and quoted in Arnold A. Offner, *The Origins of the Second World War: American Foreign Policy and World Politics, 1917–1941* (New York: Holt, Rinehart, and Winston, 1975), 127. Frederick Marks has said that Roosevelt regretted only his failure to assume a more prominent role in the Munich settlement; Marks, *Wind over Sand*, 145.

80. Berle diary, 29 August 1938, FDRL, box 210, Diary July–December 1938; and Ibid., 26 May 1938, box 210, Diary January–June 1938.

81. Offner, *The Origins of the Second World War*, 126.

82. Josephus Daniels record of conversation with Roosevelt, 16 January 1939, LC, Josephus Daniels Papers, box 7.

83. Manfred Jonas, *The United States and Germany: A Diplomatic History* (Ithaca: Cornell University Press, 1984), 229.

84. Major General H.H. Arnold notes taken at the White House, 14 November 1938, FDRL, Roosevelt OF, file OF25t; and Dallek, *Franklin D. Roosevelt and American Foreign Policy*, 173.

85. Henry Morgenthau diary, 13 November 1938, FDRL, Henry Morgenthau Jr. Papers, Presidential Diaries, fiche 5.

86. Craig, "Army Two-Year Augmentation Program," December 1938, NARA, RG165, Entry 281, file WPD 3674–10; and Dallek, *Franklin D. Roosevelt and American Foreign Policy*, 173.

87. Roosevelt press conference, 15 November 1938, in Samuel I. Rosenman, ed., *The Public Papers and Addresses of Franklin D. Roosevelt. Volume 6: The Continuing Struggle for Liberalism* (New York: Macmillan, 1941), 598–600.

88. Rock, *Chamberlain and Roosevelt*, 129–30.

89. Morgenthau, "Proposal that the French Government Establish in Canada Airplane Plants Capable of Constructing Several Thousand Planes a Year," October 1938, FDRL, Roosevelt PSF, file Treasury: Morgenthau, Henry Jr.; and Lowenthal, *Leadership and*

Indecision, 89–90.

90. King diary, 24 October 1938, NAC.

91. King diary, 15 and 17 November 1938, NAC.

92. Privy Council Order 3252, 22 December 1938, NAC, RG25, vol. 1739, file 221 pt. 2; Keenleyside, "Alaska Highway," 15 December 1938, Ibid.; and Fisher, "T.D. Pattullo and the British Columbia to Alaska Highway," 19.

93. Charmley, *Chamberlain and the Lost Peace*, 174.

94. Tweedsmuir to Sir Alexander Hardinge, 14 January 1939, QUA, Buchan Papers, box 10, file Correspondence January 1939; Lord Lothian to King, 9 March 1939, NAC, King Correspondence, reel C3745, 229407–11; and Chamberlain to Tweedsmuir, 7 February 1939, QUA, Buchan Papers, box 10, file Correspondence February 1939.

95. Transcript, "Conference with the Senate Military Affairs Committee, Executive Offices of the White House, January 31, 1939, 12.45 P.M.," FDRL, Roosevelt President's Personal Files, file 1–P.

96. Reid to DEA, no. 227, 17 February 1939, NAC, Reid Papers, vol. 30, file Washington Despatches 1939–1941; and Roosevelt press conferences, 3 and 17 February 1939, in *Complete Press Conferences of Franklin D. Roosevelt, Volume 12* (New York: Da Capo Press, 1972), 112–18, and 173–74.

97. Philip E. Jacob, "Influences of World Events on U.S. 'Neutrality' Opinion," *Public Opinion Quarterly*, 4 (March 1940), 58–60.

98. Moffat diary, 16 February 1939, HL, MS Am 1407, vol. 42.

99. General S.D. Embick to Marshall, 12 April 1939, GCML, Marshall Papers, box 67, file 67/36. Calling the Philippines a "military liability of constantly increasing gravity," Embick had proposed withdrawing from that possession as early as 1933. Also warning that carrying out Plan Orange "would be literally an act of madness," he wanted to avoid provoking Japan by pulling American forces back to a line from Alaska through Hawaii to the Panama Canal; Mark A. Stoler, "From Continentalism to Globalism: General Stanley D. Embick, the Joint Strategic Survey Committee, and the Military View of American National Policy during the Second World War," *Diplomatic History*, 6 (Summer 1982), 305; and Embick, "Military Aspects of the Situation that Would Result from Retention by the United States of a Military (Including Naval) Commitment to the Philippines," 2 December 1935, NARA, RG225, JB305, Serial 573, JPC Development File, item 3.

100. Lowenthal, *Leadership and Indecision*, 122–23; and Reynolds, *The Creation of the Anglo-American Alliance*, 61–62.

101. John Keegan, "A Generation of Victors," *New York Times Book Review*, 16 August 1987, 10.

102. Joint Board minutes, 9 November 1938, NARA, RG225, JB301.

103. Mark Skinner Watson, *Chief of Staff: Prewar Plans and Preparations* (Washington, D.C.: Department of the Army, 1950), 98–99; and JPC, "Study of Joint Action in Event of Violation of Monroe Doctrine by Fascist Powers," 21 April 1939, NARA, RG225, JB325, Serial 634.

104. Joint Board minutes, 6 May 1939, NARA, RG225, JB301.

105. Ray S. Cline, *Washington Command Post: The Operations Division*, 2nd edition (Washington, D.C.: Center of Military History, 1985), 56. Rainbow 2 dealt with a defensive effort in the Pacific with allies, Rainbow 3 dealt with a Pacific war without allies, Rainbow 4 envisioned taking the offensive in South America or the eastern Atlantic, and Rainbow 5 called for operations in Africa and Europe to defeat Germany and Italy.

106. David Beatty, "The 'Canadian Corollary' to the Monroe Doctrine and the Ogdensburg Agreement of 1940," *The McNaughton Papers*, 5 (1994), 32.

107. W.A. Moffet to CNO, 1 March 1933, NARA, General Records of the Navy Department, Office of the Secretary, RG80, box 218, file A–16; Brigadier General W. Kruger to Chief of Staff, "Acquisition of Colonial Territory," 18 December 1936, NARA, RG165, Entry 281, file WPD 3977; and Leahy to Welles, 24 March 1939, RG59, Decimal File 1930–39, 811.34500/3–1/4.

108. King diary, 10 June 1939, NAC.

109. Lindsay to FO, 30 June 1939, PRO, FO371, vol. 23901, file W10081/9805/49; Lindsay to FO, 8 July 1939, Ibid., vol. 23902, file W10354/9805/49; and Beatty, "The 'Canadian Corollary,'" 32–33.

110. Bruce Hutchison, "Alliance with the U.S.?" *Vancouver Sun*, 11 April 1939; and King diary, 23 March 1939, NAC.

111. King diary, 19 July 1939, NAC.

112. Commander H.E. Reid to Naval Secretary, DND, 16 August 1939, NAC, RG25, vol. 829, file 4; and Lieutenant Commander H.N. Lay, "Conversation between the President of the United States in U.S.S. Tuscaloosa and Officers of the Guard, Lieut. Commander H.N. Lay, R.C.N., Halifax, 15th August, 1939," Ibid.

113. Canadian Legation to DEA, no. 78, 29 August 1939, NAC, RG25, vol. 2453, file Secret 1939; and Skelton, "United States Halifax Proposal," 31 August 1939, Ibid., vol. 829, file 4.

114. Neatby, *The Prism of Unity*, 317–28; and King diary, 1 September 1939, NAC.

115. Harry Hopkins to Roosevelt, 31 August 1939, FDRL, Harry Hopkins Papers, box 96, file Roosevelt, Franklin D. (unsigned correspondence 1933–1940); and Berle diary, 24 August 1939, FDRL, box 210, Diary July–August 1939.

116. Dallek, *Franklin D. Roosevelt and American Foreign Policy*, 197–99.

117. King diary, 3 September 1939, NAC.

118. Berle diary, 26 May and 28 June 1939, FDRL, box 210, Diary April–June 1939.

119. Berle diary, 26 August 1938, in Beatrice Bishop Berle and Travis Beal Jacobs, eds., *Navigating the Rapids 1918–1971: From the Papers of Adolf A. Berle* (New York: Harcourt Brace Jovanovich, 1973), 245; and Dallek, *Franklin D. Roosevelt and American Foreign Policy*, 207–08.

120. Moffat diary, 2–3 September 1939, HL, MS Am 1407, vol. 43.

121. Paul R. Josselyn to Hull, no. 71, 1 September 1939, NARA, RG84, Foreign Service Posts Canada, Vancouver, Series 2238, file 800; Louis Johnson to Roosevelt, 25 August 1939, FDRL, Roosevelt PSF, file War: Johnson, Louis: 1937–40; Moffat diary, 5 September 1939, HL, MS Am 1407, vol. 43; Berle diary, 6 September 1939, FDRL, box 211, file Diary September–October 1939; and King diary, 5 September 1939, NAC.

122. F.H. LaGuardia to Hull, 5 September 1939, FDRL, Berle Papers, box 40, file LaGuardia, Fiorello; and Berle diary, 6 and 11 September 1939, Ibid., box 211, Diary September–October 1939.

123. Reid memorandum, 11 September 1939, NAC, Reid Papers, vol. 5, file 2; and Canadian legation memorandum, 29 September 1939, NAC, King Memoranda and Notes, reel H1560, C285557–58.

124. Felix Belai, Jr., "Pledge to Defend Canada Stands, Says President as It Enters War," *New York Times*, 13 September 1939.

125. Christie to Skelton, 27 September 1939, NAC, RG25, vol. 2459, file C-10. Both King and Skelton had agreed that Christie's extensive American contacts (he had been a lawyer in New York City prior to World War One), his obvious capacity, and a friendship with Lothian made him the best man for the job. Moreover, although Christie was fully committed to Canada's role in the conflict, his opposition to military commitments to Britain prior to 1939 was seen as an advantage in that he could be expected to counter the pro-imperialist Lothian. On the other hand, pro-imperialist Canadians found Christie's appointment "unfortunate," and Vincent

Massey, Canada's notably Anglophile high commissioner in London, thought Christie "will probably advise the Americans to keep out of the war and tell them how sorry he is that we got involved"; Hilliker, *Canada's Department of External Affairs*, 219; Skelton memorandum, 9 September 1939, NAC, RG25, vol. 1963, file 863; "Our Minister to Washington," *Toronto Financial Post*, 30 September 1939; and Massey diary, 6 October 1939, UTA, Massey Papers, vol. 310.

126. Cole, *Roosevelt & the Isolationists, 1932–45*, 281.

127. Christie to SSEA, no. 2061, 28 October 1939, NAC, King Correspondence, reel C3742, 225013–18.

128. Interestingly, that 1940 sampling found that only 54.4 and 36.8 percent of respondents supported military aid to Mexico and Brazil respectively; Wilfrid Hardy Callcott, *The Western Hemisphere: Its Influence on United States Policies to the End of World War II* (Austin: University of Texas Press, 1968), 384.

129. Christie to Skelton, 21 October 1939, NAC, RG25, vol. 807, file 581.

130. DEA Legal Advisor to Skelton, "U.S. Neutrality Legislation," 30 September 1939, in David R. Murray, ed., *Documents on Canadian External Relations. 1939–1941, Part II. Volume 8* (Ottawa: Department of External Affairs, 1976), 5–14; and Morgenthau memorandum of interview with J.L. Ralston, 22 December 1939, FDRL, Henry Morgenthau Jr. Papers, book 232, reel 62.

Chapter 3

Far Better to Trust in the Honor of the United States: Canada and the United States, 1939–1941

As 1939 bled into 1940, Prime Minister King held a particularly uncharitable view of the United States and American foreign policy. Although he accepted that President Roosevelt could not contemplate having his nation "going into a war at once," the Soviet Union's unprovoked invasion of tiny Finland on 30 November had prompted King to wonder if the United States was losing, "if it has not already lost—its one great opportunity and mission, which would be to become the leader of neutral nations, protecting their neutrality, and give courage to all those small nations to unite in defence of themselves."[1] James Cromwell's appointment as the new American minister in Ottawa had made matters much worse in King's mind. Complaining that Roosevelt should have consulted him first before taking that step, King wondered if the selection, given Cromwell's marriage to the tobacco heiress and socialite Doris Duke, would send the wrong signal to Canadians "at a time when we trying to hold to democratic ideals." Doubting too that Cromwell possessed the necessary judgment to hold the critical post of minister in a country that had become the "interpreter between Great Britain and the U.S.," King concluded that James Cromwell would "represent the wrong type of American influence in our Capital."[2]

The view from the American capital was not very much kinder. Although a prominent American newspaper had praised Prime Minister King as "the most astute politician the Dominion has possessed since Wilfrid Laurier,"[3] Berle held a quite different view. Greatly impressed with O.D. Skelton, "a singularly attractive, honest and high grade man," Berle thought Skelton was "working himself to death" because King also held the foreign affairs portfolio, "and the result is that the Under Secretary does all the work."[4] Even normally affable Franklin Roosevelt was affected by this spreading contagion of ill will. After meeting with King in late April at Warm Springs, Georgia, a "disgusted" president confided to Morgenthau that all his visitor had talked about "was what a great man he, Mackenzie King, was and how he pulled this trick and that trick to get re-elected" and that it took "two or three days to get Mackenzie King talking about the war."[5]

Although very divergent personalities had played some role in exacerbating the problems, these frustrations stemmed largely from the dissimilar circumstances facing Canadians and Americans in early 1940. After Poland had collapsed in the autumn of 1939, the Allies and Germany had traded the occasional shell or bomb on an otherwise inactive western front. Only in Finland's cold snows was the war truly hot, and some Canadians, like Minister of Agriculture T.A. Crerar, worried that that northern conflict presaged joint Soviet-German action in Scandinavia or further south in the Balkans. And even if the various belligerents chose "to talk peace" rather than continuing to fight, Crerar feared that the fears and suspicions the war had impressed "upon the face of Europe will not easily be rubbed out."[6] Adding to the concern was the presence of Canadian soldiers in Europe for the second time in a generation. Although King had hoped to avoid sending troops across the Atlantic to fight in France, both circumstances and the army had conspired against him. As the Polish crisis had sped to its unfortunate climax, the Canadian military dropped any pretense that it supported home defense. Denying that Canada faced any threat at home as long as the Royal Navy and the USN guarded the Dominion's maritime approaches, the chiefs of staff (COS) claimed on 29 August that Canada should despatch two divisions plus ancillary units (60,000 soldiers) to Britain. Though Skelton argued that home defense and safeguarding Britain's many Caribbean possessions were sufficiently big objectives "to require the organizing ability of men of experience and the enthusiasm of our young men," and King fumed that it was "clear that the Defence Department has been spending most of its time preparing for an expeditionary force,"[7] the matter assumed a momentum all its own. As the COS predicted, when Britain asked Canada on 6 September to provide troops and air crew for service overseas, Canadian public opinion compelled King's acquiescence, and a Canadian division arrived in Britain in early December.

Roosevelt faced a very different set of problems. Torn between demands that he should broker peace or prepare to meet any threats to national and hemispheric security, the president opted to try both. On 9 February 1940 he announced that he had decided to despatch Welles to Europe to meet with the leaders of Britain, France, Germany, and Italy. Declaring publicly that Welles had been ordered only to gather information about the deteriorating European situation, and not to seek any alliances, Roosevelt told Lothian privately that he wanted to satisfy himself and the American public that the United States had done everything possible to end the war. If Welles failed to get the parties talking, then Roosevelt would brand Germany an aggressor and the hindrance to peace. The Welles mission accomplished little. Unhappy with Welles's stubborn insistence that Europe's problems stemmed from a need for disarmament rather than territorial and political adjustments, Britain and France showed no enthusiasm for attending a peace conference with their German foe. Moreover, whereas Welles formed a far too-optimistic opinion of Benito Mussolini's ability to influence German thinking, the assistant secretary found Adolf Hitler and Germany personally distasteful (an opinion he had some trouble concealing), and Roosevelt's failure to contact Hitler prior to despatching Welles to Berlin did not help either. When Welles returned empty-handed in late March, the president reluctantly concluded that there was "scant immediate prospect" for peace in Europe. Less than two weeks later, German forces invaded Denmark and Norway.[8]

Addressing America's military needs proved no less frustrating. Having succeeded General Craig as the army's chief of staff, Major General George Marshall, believing that Americans "expect too much of machines" and that talk of air power efficacy "staggers the imagination,"[9] had sought permission to expand the army to 250,000 men, but Roosevelt agreed only to 227,000. Marshall got little support from Secretary of War Harry Woodring. Believing that American involvement in the war should be avoided at all costs and fearful that a large standing army would encourage militarism at home, Woodring felt certain that a small American army capable of expansion could be an effective combat force if it was well-armed and well-trained.[10] Deprived therefore of a strong cabinet advocate for the army's interests, Marshall had to deal with a president more naturally inclined to give air and sea power more attention, especially when the creation of a large army could prompt public fears that it might be employed overseas. So when Roosevelt decided to cut the army's 1941 appropriations in early 1940, Marshall recruited influential financier and Democratic Party adviser Bernard Baruch to seek the reinstatement of the military's funding. Germany's invasion of the Low Countries and France on 10 May helped too; although Roosevelt initially opposed Marshall's appeal, he canceled the cuts on 13 May.[11]

So when King made the long trip south to Warm Springs to meet Roosevelt on 23 April 1940, both leaders faced quite dissimilar problems and possessed little empathy for the other's position. And despite Roosevelt's claim that King did not want to discuss the war, King's diary reveals that the president experienced no such difficulty. Doubting that the Allies could do anything to save Norway from the invading German forces, Roosevelt expected Italy to soon join the German cause which would enable Hitler then to resort to "a totalitarian war at an early stage" against Britain. Should Germany succeed in driving Britain to defeat, then South America would be endangered, and if Mexico fell under German control, enemy aircraft could threaten the American Midwest. Noting as well Canada's weak defenses, which King agreed were inadequate but "that in the circumstances we were doing the best we could," Roosevelt offered a solution that would have chilled isolationists and not a few of his own supporters. Recalling that the United States had fought an undeclared eighteenth-century naval war with France, the president thought he might "find it desirable to send some destroyers and cruisers across the Atlantic to help" the Allies without benefit of a formal declaration of war.[12]

But any chance of speedily improving Canada's home defenses was lost after 10 May. As German armies roared through Holland and Belgium, and Britain's expeditionary force (BEF) reeled back to the English Channel to avoid envelopment and destruction at the hands of Germany's swiftly moving panzers, the prospect of an abject Allied defeat was all too real. All thought of a Canadian base in France, a project raised in late April, was abandoned as Canada rushed a second division to Britain, sent a battalion to the West Indies, and began mobilizing two more divisions immediately. On 22 May the RCAF's sole fully-equipped fighter squadron was bound for Britain, a brigade was ordered to Iceland, and the Royal Canadian Navy's (RCN) entire disposable force (four destroyers) began steaming at high speed for the eastern Atlantic battle zone. The dramatic and stunningly successful withdrawal of the BEF from Dunkirk at May's end, followed by France's request for an armistice on 17 June, only quickened the Canadian pace. The Canadian Cabinet War Committee (CWC), the government's real center of power, decided on 17 June to implement compulsory military service for home defense only. Four days later, that legislation, the National Resources Mobilization Act (NRMA), was approved by Parliament.[13]

But neither Canada nor the other British Dominions could do much to stop German forces from crossing the English Channel. Only one power seemed to possess that capability, and King was deluged by telegrams entreating him to approach Roosevelt for help. Australian Prime Minister Robert Menzies pleaded with King to compel the United States to release "every available aircraft" to the empire, and Vincent Massey, Canada's high commissioner to Britain, thought Roosevelt should be told plainly that unless American aid was immediately forthcoming, then Britain might be compelled to surrender the Royal Navy and the West Indies to the Germans. Britain's new leader, Winston Churchill (Chamberlain had resigned on 15 May), noting that "[e]very form of intimate appeal and most cogent arguments have already been sent to Roosevelt," thought that the president was doing his best "but must carry Congress and public opinion, still much diverted by impending Presidential election." Still, if King and other Dominion leaders were willing to issue a personal appeal to Roosevelt, "this would be very welcome to us."[14]

King had anticipated the requests. Asked by some of his ministers on 18 May to seek American aid, an initially reluctant King thought the situation now had become so desperate that Roosevelt and the American people had to be convinced that the danger facing Britain confronted Canada and the United States too. Because Christie was seriously ill, King charged Hugh Keenleyside with relaying his concerns directly to Roosevelt.[15] Receiving King's "almost incomprehensible" instructions by telephone at Ottawa's downtown train station, Keenleyside sped to Washington armed with the name and telephone number of General Edwin Watson, the gatekeeper of the president's appointment calendar. Within three hours of his arrival in the American capital on 19 May, Keenleyside found himself ushered into Roosevelt's office by Watson. Although very concerned by France's desperate military situation, Roosevelt had no planes to give to the Allies at present, but after new construction got underway, Canada or the Allies would share that output equally with the United States. But as Keenleyside prepared to leave, Roosevelt told him that King should visit Washington or Hyde Park to discuss "certain possible eventualities which could not possibly be mentioned aloud" for fear of being branded a "defeatist." Should King not understand the implication, Keenleyside should mention the words "British Fleet" to him.[16]

American warplanes indeed were in short supply, but even had they been more plentiful, some of Roosevelt's advisers would have resisted sharing them with the Allies. Having opposed since February selling even obsolete weapons to other nations as long as the American military's most basic equipment needs could not be met, Marshall supported Roosevelt's negative answer when Churchill asked for the transfer of 40 to 50 overage American destroyers to the Royal Navy on 15 May.

Telling Morgenthau two days later that "we have got to weigh the hazards in this hemisphere of one thing or another," Marshall said that meeting British arms requests would amount only "to a drop in the bucket on the other side, and it is a vital necessity on this side and that is that. Tragic as it is, that is that."[17]

Neither was Marshall keen to intervene militarily in the conflict, a sentiment widely shared by others in the administration. Even Harold Ickes, who had backed strong action against Germany in 1938, thought that there was no use now "crying over spilt milk" because the American people were "opposed to war, especially if that means sending a single soldier to Europe, and in this country the Government cannot be too far in advance of its people."[18] When Marshall told Welles, Roosevelt, and Admiral Harry Stark on 23 May that the American military currently was incapable of conducting "major operations" in the western Pacific or Europe because of "a lack of means at present" and that the United States would have to limit itself for at least a year to the Western Hemisphere's defense, Welles expressed his "complete agreement with every word." Roosevelt and Stark were in "general agreement."[19]

Whether that American defensive policy would prove successful, however, ultimately depended greatly upon the skill, bravery, and continued survival of the Royal Navy. According to the State Department's Stanley Hornbeck, the United States faced three scenarios if Britain collapsed: German control of the Royal Navy, in which case the United States would have to choose between "abandoning the Pacific to save the Hemisphere, or abandoning everything"; a sunken British armada, thus giving the United States time to build up its strength; or transferring Britain's ships to Canada.[20] Not surprisingly, Roosevelt found the latter option most appealing, especially after Lothian, though personally willing to withdraw the fleet to Canada and to consider a political union between the British commonwealth and the United States, declared in mid-May that British opinion would not tolerate relocating the fleet to a still-neutral United States.[21]

Unable to patiently await King's response, Roosevelt had Secretary of State Hull telephone the Canadian prime minister on 24 May to request that he send a senior official immediately to Washington for further political discussions. King needed no persuasion. Having given Britain all the military aid that he could provide, King, thinking it was time to reveal the true situation to the United States, and thus "give her time to give us aid as well," despatched Keenleyside again to the American capital.[22] This time Roosevelt clearly spelled out his intentions regarding the Royal Navy. Doubtful that France would last very much longer, the president feared that if (when) France collapsed, Germany, using French ships and air bases, would devote all of its strength against Britain. Believing that Britain could avoid devastation only if it surrendered its empire and navy to Germany, and that the pressure on the British government to accept a "soft" peace would be terribly hard to resist, Roosevelt said Churchill should move himself and the Royal Navy to Canada. In return, the United States would allow British warships to use American ports and would improve the capabilities of imperial harbors worldwide. But feeling that he could not put this case directly to Churchill, Roosevelt wanted King to do it for him.[23]

An appalled King, having never envisioned that his self-proclaimed role of interpreter between Britain and the United States might involve negotiating Britain's possible demise, thought that the Americans were intent on using Canada "to protect themselves in urging a course that would spare them immediate assistance to Britain and bring their own assistance too late to save the day for the British as well as themselves." Although willing to approach Churchill if that proved necessary, King contended instead that even limited American military aid might keep France fighting and deter Italian belligerence. Roosevelt disagreed. Americans were not yet ready to support intervention or to aid the Allies. Moreover, Roosevelt thought that British demands for assistance all seemed to carry "almost an explicit threat" that if aid was not forthcoming, "we will let the Germans have the Fleet and you can go to hell." But if King agreed to lobby Churchill about the fleet's disposition, Roosevelt promised to cooperate in the Atlantic at once, to defend the Pacific status quo, to participate soon in a continental blockade, and to bring the Allies ultimate victory.[24]

Roosevelt's promises had the desired effect. After hearing from Churchill on 27 May that France soon "was likely to give up altogether," King relayed Roosevelt's wishes to Churchill on 30 May.[25] The British leader delivered his response to the American request in a most dramatic form. Standing tall in the historic British House of Commons on 4 June and mustering all of his renowned oratorical skill, Churchill promised to fight on the beaches, in the streets, and in the hills. Britain would never surrender, and with a characteristic flourish, he concluded that "[e]ven if, which I do not for a moment believe, this island or a large part of it were subjugated and starving, then our Empire beyond the seas, armed and guarded by the British Fleet, would carry on the struggle, until, in God's good time, the New World, with all its power and might, steps forth to the rescue and the liberation of the Old."[26] Churchill's private communication to King on 5 June was far less moving and considerably more pointed. Confident that Britain could continue to resist the Germans even if France fell, Churchill warned against allowing the Americans to think that they would get the fleet and empire if Britain was defeated. If the United States entered the conflict and Britain then was "conquered locally," then perhaps such a transfer might occur. But if the Americans remained neutral "and we were overpowered," Churchill could not say "what policy might be adopted by a pro-German administration such as would undoubtedly be set up."[27]

The task of delivering that bluntly worded message to Roosevelt fell again to Keenleyside. Roosevelt, having had Lothian's assurance on 23 May that the present British regime would order the fleet moved to Canada even if Parliament "voted in a new government which would agree to surrender the fleet," found Churchill's warning most displeasing. Noting that even Germany had scuttled its navy in 1919 rather than hand it over to the Allies, Roosevelt thought the British "should at least show the same 'guts' as the Germans had shown when they were defeated." Keen to emphasize that the Royal Navy's proposed transfer was designed primarily "*to save the Empire*" so that Churchill would not be encouraged to "bargain" for immediate aid, Roosevelt wanted King to press the matter with London.[28] Firmly on the hot seat again but privately convinced that Britain's navy and government soon might require refuge in Canada, King wired Churchill on 17 June to say that Britain should lose no time in planning those transfers or in arranging for American military access to bases in Newfoundland, the West Indies, Greenland, and Iceland. Churchill's response a week later was cool. He would continue fighting, and doubting that much good would come from "dwelling" upon the Royal Navy's transfer, Churchill saw "no reason to make preparation or give any countenance" to such a plan. But repeating that he could not bind any future British government, he advised King to "impress this danger upon the President as I have done."[29]

Clearly an impasse had been reached, and King opted for another approach to safeguard Canadian security. Asking J. Pierrepont Moffat to see him on 14 June, King postulated that if Britain could not repel a German invasion, and if the Royal Navy came to Canada, the Dominion "would immediately be faced by many problems of a practical nature which could not be solved without American aid." Recalling the 1938 military discussions, King thought the time was ripe for another round of staff talks. But unsure if Roosevelt would welcome such a proposal, King asked Moffat to "feel out the situation and to let him know."[30] Moffat was the right man to approach. Having replaced Cromwell as the American minister to Canada in late May despite Morgenthau's attempt to send Woodring instead so as to rid Washington of the troublesome secretary of war, Moffat, described by American newspapers as "one of our crack diplomats" and "a statesman of demonstrated ability and good judgement," had been ordered personally by Roosevelt "constantly to emphasize" two things in all future discussions with Canadian officials: That Canada, "for its own sake," must seek assurances that the Royal Navy would not be surrendered to the Germans; and that a neutral United States could offer nearly as much military aid to Britain and Canada as a belligerent America.[31] Moreover, as Moffat remained philosophically opposed to American intervention in Europe (disagreeing with Henry Stimson's assertion that the European conflict was "our war," Moffat had responded that he knew of no American male under 45 years of age who wished to fight), King's offer of Canadian-American staff talks seemed to indicate to him that those Canadians favoring closer ties with the United States had bested those clinging to "the old Colonial mentality." Telling King that the president could do a great many things "short of actually declaring war," Moffat relayed the staff talk proposal to Hull on 16 June.[32]

Hull, however, found staff talks a particularly uninteresting subject. Twice in the previous five days, he had rejected calls—one by Lothian, the other from William Herridge—for discussions between the Allies and the United States, and when Canadian chargé d'affaires M.M. Mahoney made King's case for strictly bilateral discussions and asked for aircraft for Canadian use on 17 June, Hull agreed only to pass those requests on to the War and Navy Departments for their opinions.[33] The War Department, however, displayed considerably more interest in staff talks than did the secretary of state. Having already initiated studies of Canada's weakened defenses, the War Department had uneasily noted the Canadian army's poor state of mechanization, the presence of just one RCN destroyer and less than 70 warplanes (most obsolete) on Canada's East Coast, and Newfoundland's complete lack of defenses. Moreover, its Ottawa-based attaché, Major John Gullet, had reported that Canadian officers were making no attempts to conceal the fact that if Britain surrendered, they believed that Canada would require American military protection. On the assumption then that American forces might have to occupy Newfoundland, the War Plans Division (WPD) backed talks to reveal the extent to which Canada might cooperate to defend the East Coast.[34]

The implementation of closer ties with Canada also had political support in Washington. When Canadian journalist Bruce Hutchison, a man with close ties to

King's government, spoke to Berle and Senate Foreign Relations Committee chair Key Pittman in mid-June, he found that both men sanctioned an economic but not a political union between Canada and the United States. An unidentified MID officer put matters more bluntly. Telling Hutchison that the United States was currently "utterly impotent" militarily, the officer doubted that Britain would move its fleet because that would mean starvation for the British people. Yet, if the Royal Navy did not come to North America, it likely would be lost and then the United States might have to forfeit control of the Pacific and even Hawaii. Asked how Canada "fit into this picture," the officer replied that given that Germany could invade the Dominion via Iceland, Greenland, and Newfoundland, Canada had become America's "first line of defense." Large American bases were required in Newfoundland and near Halifax, and staff talks, not yet underway, "must be held soon."[35]

Most importantly, support for staff talks existed at the very top of the American political food chain. Buoyed by polls showing that 80 percent of Americans favored extending military aid to the Allies (a 23 percent rise in one week), Roosevelt had released 143 old warplanes to France on 7 June. Three days later, when Italy attacked France, a very angry president used a speech at the University of Virginia to attack isolationism as a "delusion" and to announce his determination to help the Allied cause. On 17 June Roosevelt informed Lothian that he desired staff talks with Britain, and two days later he dramatically replaced Woodring and navy secretary Charles Edison with proclaimed interventionist Republicans Henry Stimson and Frank Knox.[36] Though the president had said nothing about discussions with Canada, when the JPC reported on 26 June that the United States was so completely unprepared to meet German incursions into the Western Hemisphere that "so long as the choice is left to us, we should avoid the contest until we can be adequately prepared," Hull ordered Moffat to return to Washington to brief him on the Canadian situation.[37]

But before Moffat left Ottawa, King arranged for the American minister to meet with both C.G. Power and J.L. Ralston, the new defense minister (Ralston's predecessor, Norman Rogers, had been killed in a 10 June plane crash near Kingston, Ontario). Claiming that Canada feared no invasion "in force" as long as the Royal Navy ruled the north Atlantic, Power and Ralston thought that German forces might raid the Dominion's "very extended and much exposed" eastern coast. As to what the United States might be able to do to help the Canadian cause, they suggested placing powerful USN elements near New York or Boston to deter raids and having the American navy and air corps lease base sites in Newfoundland and Canada. No mention was made of the possibility of placing American ground troops in Canada, although the Canadian ministers felt that having American soldiers exercising near the border "also might have some moral effect." Most immediately, the Dominion needed fighter and reconnaissance planes, small arms, and ammunition.[38]

Moffat's various Washington meetings went well. Both Stark and Brigadier General George Strong strongly favored initiating staff talks with Canada, with Strong mentioning the need not only to discuss immediate defense measures, but "what help we could give Canada in her long-term preparations." Not so easily convinced, General Marshall thought that the holding of effective discussions would be hampered by the Roosevelt administration's inability to decide what it would do if the Royal Navy fell back on North America. Moreover, Marshall worried that an "entirely frank" exposition of the American military situation might discourage the Canadians, if the Canadians truly wished to talk Marshall would "be delighted" to see them, "but he feared under present conditions he would be more the talker than listener."[39]

Marshall, however, was less than delighted when he debated the issue with Morgenthau on 3 July. Worried that supplying Canada with arms would weaken his army, Marshall thought that it made more sense to keep those weapons at home and move American forces into Canada only during a crisis. But when he repeated his concern that substantive conversations seemed impossible until the administration had decided how it would handle a British collapse, Morgenthau retorted that talks would provide helpful information about Canada's military infrastructure and capabilities and could explore some potentially useful forms of cooperation. Siding with Morgenthau, Roosevelt authorized Moffat to invite "high-ranking" Canadian officers to come to Washington to discuss "matters of our respective interests in the field of defense" with Marshall and Stark with the definite understanding that no commitments would be asked for or given by the United States.[40]

Brigadier Kenneth Stuart (deputy chief of the general staff), Captain L.W. Murray (deputy chief of the naval staff), and Air Commodore A.A.L. Cuffe arrived in Washington on 11 July with general instructions from Prime Minister King to discuss the placement of American bases in Newfoundland, the coordination and financing of industrial production programs, and the possible adoption of American arms and equipment by the Canadian services. The briefing note prepared for the American delegation was somewhat more detailed. Noting that the despatch of American forces to Newfoundland and Canada would "involve the United States in the war," the note admitted that the lack of fully-equipped and well-trained American soldiers adequate to meet all possible "necessary commitments" elsewhere in the hemisphere "should demand that any protective forces allocated to Canada and Newfoundland be rigidly curtailed." Furthermore, any promise to train Canadian personnel, excepting perhaps pilots, would confront a lack of excess capacity in American facilities; moreover, the fact that Canadian military forces were accustomed to a training system "so foreign to the corresponding features of the United States Army" that Canadian reliance upon American instructors "would unquestionably be attended by confusion and lack of efficiency." But on the chance that the despatch of American forces to Canada and Newfoundland would be "deemed necessary" from a political or strategic standpoint, the American delegation was instructed to ascertain just what Canada required, the nature of Canadian and Newfoundland infrastructure, and to limit the potential American contribution to Canada's defense to two divisions and a composite air group.[41]

Opening the talks at Stark's home on the evening of 11 July, the Canadians sought to impress their American hosts that they were motivated, not by panic, but by a desire to explore the possibilities for common action. Moreover, asserting that they were "far from pessimistic about the outcome" of the war's present phase, the Canadians wanted no material aid if that assistance meant Britain would be deprived of vital items. And even though the discussions over the next few days went into great detail concerning Canadian facilities, it is difficult to dispute an American official historian's judgment that the "inconclusive" discussions had little impact on American military planning. Canada would continue to be solely responsible for the defense of its eastern coast plus Newfoundland with "such assistance as the United States can give in the way of equipment," although the Americans suggested that they might take over Newfoundland if the United States soon entered the war. Marshall seemed more concerned with the need for absolute secrecy, asserting that a leak, "because of its political consequences, might even force the [Roosevelt] Administration to cut some of his existing and contemplated appropriations."[42] After the talks ended, the War Department settled for sending Gullet to inspect Newfoundland, and Admiral Ernest J. King listed Canadian and Newfoundland security fifth on the navy's list of Western Hemisphere priorities.[43]

Though the military staff talks had done little to advance Canadian-American strategic cooperation, the pressure for some sort of formal understanding continued on both sides of the border. On 19 June the isolationist *Chicago Tribune* proposed an immediate military alliance with Canada, a suggestion echoed by the *New York Herald Tribune* and the *Montreal Standard*. On 22 June, Toronto magazine *Saturday Night* suggested an arrangement whereby the United States would protect Canada so that the Dominion could throw all of its military resources into Britain's defense.[44] External Affairs was not immune either from such sentiments. If Japan actively sided with Germany in the war, then Skelton informed King that there was "no possibility of our being able to defend ourselves without United States aid." In such circumstances, Canada would have little choice but to "contribute our share to the common pool in a way that would appeal to United States opinion."[45] Appealing to American opinion had its dangers though. Stating that the United States could no longer "be expected to be willing to accept responsibility for the results of a policy [defending Canada] over which the United States has no control," Keenleyside had apprised the prime minister that Roosevelt's government "will expect, if necessary demand, Canadian assistance in the defence of this continent and this hemisphere."[46]

Compulsory cooperation in hemispheric defense figured prominently in a document that emerged from a special CIIA conference held in Ottawa in mid-July. Given its belief that even right-wing and pro-imperial Canadians were showing "signs of transferring their allegiance from London to Washington,"[47] the CIIA sought an orderly shift in that allegiance that would do much to ensure Canada's continued independence. Therefore, with the help of some Liberal MPs as well as Hutchison and Keenleyside, the CIIA meeting produced "A Programme of Immediate Canadian Action." Arguing that Canada risked losing its national identity permanently if it ignored the implications of greater cooperation with the United States, the CIIA advocated a recognition that North America's strategic indivisibility demanded a substantial Canadian contribution under the rubric of "a new board of strategy in connection with the present general staff." But even if that binational agency emerged, "[s]uch extensive coordination of defence as is here contemplated will in fact require some political understanding," with both Canada and the United States wishing to know "the type of political relationship that may be established and the extent to which one country may influence or limit the policy of the other. Moreover, a political agreement with the United States would be necessary, in order to determine the extent of Canada's zone of defence and her function in the strategic sense."[48]

How much influence the CIIA recommendations had on King is hard to determine, but given Keenleyside's involvement, one can be certain that the prime minister had known about and had kept a careful watch over the CIIA effort. King also had an inkling that Roosevelt might be thinking along the same lines as the CIIA. Meeting with Christie on 13 July, the prime minister learned that noted presidential confidante Judge Felix Frankfurter had told Christie that Roosevelt wished King to journey to Hyde Park to discuss a common North American defense plan.[49] King, though, did not expect a call from the White House in the immediate near future. When the new CGS, Major General Crerar, recommended working out detailed defense plans with the Americans on 26 July, King thought that progress might not be possible until after November's presidential elections.[50]

But that call from the Oval Office came far sooner than King had expected. Given his cabinet's consensus that Britain's very survival might depend on American aid, Roosevelt agreed on 2 August to "sell directly or indirectly" 50 to 60 World War One-vintage destroyers to Britain. Concerned that Congress might not abandon an amendment forbidding any sale of military equipment unless Marshall or Stark certified that the items were "not essential for US defense," Roosevelt accepted Knox's proposal for a swap; Britain would get the ships in return for American leases of various British facilities in the Western Hemisphere. Though Churchill initially opposed the scheme, Britain's desperate need and his hope that the exchange marked the first steps towards America's entry into the war brought the British prime minister round by 4 August despite Foreign Secretary Anthony Eden's opinion that the deal was "a grievous blow to our authority and ultimately to our sovereignty." And after his advisers concluded that the deal legally could be made by an executive decision, Roosevelt saw no further reason to delay. Formally approved on 2 September, Britain received 50 old destroyers, the United States got 99-year leases for six bases in the Caribbean and one each on Bermuda and Newfoundland.[51]

Though Canada had not been directly involved in the Anglo-American destroyers-for-bases negotiations, the Canadian government had followed the issue with considerable interest. So when Roosevelt told Christie on 27 July that he still favored staff talks about common defense problems,[52] and then Lothian, worried that the destroyer deal might yet collapse given Churchill's attitude, told King on 12 August that Canada's influence in the United States might have "a decisive influence" now, Canada acted. On 13 August Christie met with Welles to say that King wished to talk over the destroyer-base deal with Roosevelt.[53] Moffat, too, pressed the White House to act. Noting in late July "an extraordinary recrudescence of optimism" in Canada regarding the war's outcome, Moffat thought that "all too many" Canadians had found it surprisingly easy to "refuse to admit the possibility of such a defeat." By August though, the American minister was putting matters far more plainly in his communications home. Canadian ambitions to build and crew modern warplanes and to field four army divisions in Europe, a manifestation of the Dominion's desire to "synchronously" fight in Europe and lay the foundations for the nation's future defense, "outran the possibilities of practical realization." Moreover, whereas both rabid imperialists (seeking aid for Britain) and left wing liberals and intellectuals (fearful that Britain would be defeated) supported an alliance with the United States, the Canadian government was quite hesitant to propose such a thing.[54] Successfully convincing Hickerson that the Canadians held a "spirit of optimism" unsupported by military facts,[55] Moffat also spurred the president to translate his staff talk notion into reality.

Receiving Moffat's despatch on 16 August (one day after he had told Loring Christie that he was considering obtaining American bases in Nova Scotia), Roosevelt called King to announce that he would be present in Ogdensburg, New York, the following evening to attend military maneuvers. The president invited King to meet him there to consider the "mutual defence of our coasts on the Atlantic." Very pleased, the prime minister accepted the president's invitation to meet in upstate New York, but declined Roosevelt's offer to send a car for him; King would drive himself to Ogdensburg.[56]

Arriving at the president's private railcar near Ogdensburg at seven in the evening on 17 August with Moffat in tow, King met with Roosevelt and a surprised Stimson just one day short of the two-year anniversary of the president's Queen's University address. Opening the discussions with a brief outline of the ongoing destroyer deal negotiations with the British, the president revealed that he had not yet formally decided which British possessions would be selected to receive American bases. As to the need for Canadian facilities, Roosevelt thought that two Nova Scotian sites might suffice, but that that would have to be negotiated with Canada. He then announced his key proposition: The creation of a Permanent Joint Board on Defense, comprised of four service people and one civilian from each country, to discuss and formulate defense plans for the northern half of the Western Hemisphere, with particular emphasis on Canada's northeast coast and the Gulf of St. Lawrence. King, "perfectly delighted with the whole thing" according to Stimson, accepted the board's creation "almost with tears in his eyes."[57]

Indeed delighted by the joint board suggestion, King also wholly agreed with Roosevelt's assertion that the word "permanent" made clear that the new agency was not just a measure designed for the needs of the moment but a step towards securing the continent "for the future." However, King had some objections. Explaining that Canada had allotted considerable funds to build airfields in Newfoundland, the prime minister thought that Canada had as much right as Britain or the United States to be involved in Newfoundland's defense. Moreover, if Ottawa granted the United States access to Canadian bases, the Dominion "would not wish to sell or lease any sites in Canada but would be ready to work out matters of facilities." Responding that "he had mostly in mind the need, if Canada were invaded, for getting troops quickly into Canada," the president then displayed what one Canadian historian has called "a Rooseveltian iron fist draped in the velvet of warmest good fellowship." Claiming that he was unable to comprehend Britain's reluctance to allow the United States access to imperial West Indian facilities, Roosevelt said that he had told Lothian that in the event of war with Germany in the absence of any pact with Britain, he would take those bases anyway if their possession was deemed necessary for American security. That is why, the president said, "it was much better to have a friendly agreement in advance."[58]

Roosevelt got his friendly agreement. That evening he and King signed a short document immediately creating the PJBD tasked with studying, "in the broad sense," all sea, land, and air problems including personnel and material, for "the defense of the north half of the Western Hemisphere."[59] Announced the next day, the PJBD found immediate public acceptance on both sides of the border. In the United States, where a full 87 percent of the population now favored defending Canada from attack, the PJBD was seen as "opening the way for an eventual defensive alliance" and an acknowledgment of the need for intelligent advanced planning. A Canadian poll taken in November found that 83.8 percent of the public approved of the PJBD, with just 5.2 percent of the respondents stating their opposition.[60]

Though Stimson believed that he had witnessed "the turning point in the tide of the war" on that fateful August evening, and Skelton called the PJBD's creation "the best day's work for many a year" and "the inevitable sequence of public policies and personal relationships, based upon the realization of the imperative necessity of close understanding between the English-speaking peoples,"[61] Conservative Senator Arthur Meighen nearly "lost his breakfast" at the news of the PJBD's creation. Although having no objection in principle to talks with the Americans, Meighen worried that such discussions would encourage Canadians "to get the idea that we don't need to exert ourselves." Moreover, he found it galling that King, having refused to sit on the British CID in the 1930s "for fear it might entangle us in war," had no objection to reaching such an arrangement with the United States. Renowned and feared for his acid tongue (especially by King, his long-time political rival), Meighen thought that there was no danger of the PJBD "entangling us in the war because there is no Spain left that the United States could lick."[62] Dominions Office Secretary Lord Cranborne, objecting to Ogdensburg because it constituted a defensive alliance between a British Dominion and a foreign country made "without any reference to or consultation with us," wanted Churchill to communicate that concern to Roosevelt and King. Instead, when King said that Canada still regarded Britain as North America's "first line of defence," Churchill icily responded that if Germany proved unable to best Britain, "all these transactions will be judged in a mood different to that while the issue still stands in the balance."[63]

Nonplussed by Churchill's reaction, when King presented the deal to the Canadian Parliament in November, he played up the linchpin analogy. Declaring that the PJBD deal, "in ultimate importance far surpasses the formation of the triple axis," and falsely claiming that he had kept Britain fully and "duly informed of what was taking place," King said that the "defence of the British commonwealth of nations as a whole" had been enhanced because Canada could now funnel resources to Britain secure in the knowledge that the United States would protect the entire hemisphere.[64] Nor was King alone in holding such sentiments. When Moffat met with CWC adviser Leonard Brockington, the Canadian official was enthused about the United States quickly formulating similar arrangements with Australia, New Zealand and Britain, whereas General Crerar plumped for an expanded board which would include just the British.[65]

The viewpoint in the United States was somewhat different. When Roosevelt telephoned Prime Minister King on 22 August to set the agenda for the PJBD's first meeting, aid to Britain was nowhere to be found. Instead, the president wanted to discuss Newfoundland, the defense of Canada's coasts, and material procurement. Furthermore, the American emphasis on hemispheric defense was made quite clear with Embick's appointment to the board.[66] But as the first meeting loomed on 26 August, confusion as to what the PJBD should do reigned. Embick thought that the board should agree to joint missions between Canada and the United States only "in their broad aspects"; the more-technical details should be left to "be worked out later by the proper agencies." John Hickerson, the American section's secretary, did not disagree, but the long-time Canadianist and State Department denizen thought that "while in reality the United States could expect little or no help from Canada," emphasizing the assistance that the Dominion might be able to give "would be a desirable gesture and morale factor for the Canadians." As to providing the Canadians with arms, whereas USN representative Captain H.W. Hill was willing to offer the RCN some coastal guns and other equipment, Embick thought that the weapons, given a lack of Canadian technical training, might better be employed in American hands. Moreover, in terms of priorities, he thought that safeguarding the approaches to the Panama Canal should come first, the defense of Newfoundland definitely second.[67]

Roosevelt provided some needed political guidance when the full American section (which also included Fiorello LaGuardia, Commander Forrest P. Sherman, and Lieutenant Colonel Joseph T. McNarney) came to the White House on 24 August. Asserting that his proposal to create the PJBD was completely unrelated to his plans to acquire leases to some British facilities in the Western Hemisphere, the president discussed getting American bases in Nova Scotia and acquiring the ability to quickly reinforce said facilities. According to Stimson, although the president was willing to consider aid to Britain (including allowing Americans to serve in the Canadian and British air forces), the PJBD's purpose was to prepare to counter an attack against the United States through Canada.[68]

That opinion was not unanimously held. After the PJBD's first rendezvous on 26–27 August in Ottawa, at which the participants decided to reinforce Canada's Newfoundland garrison, to improve defenses in Canada's eastern provinces, and to prepare "at once a detailed plan for the joint defence of Canada and the United States," Berle thought it "plain" that those efforts were being made to ensure that the Royal Navy continued fighting even if Britain succumbed.[69] But whether those plans were desirable was quite another matter. Almost alone among American commentators, Felix Morley of the *Washington Post* had warned that the Ogdensburg pact could severely strain the nation's neutrality given that Germany "unquestionably" saw the agreement as a hostile act. Berle concurred. If Britain collapsed, Canada likely would continue fighting, and in such circumstances, American arrangements with the Dominion would "force us either to talk with the Germans at that time or immediately to declare war ourselves." The fundamental consideration would be whether Germany invaded the Western Hemisphere or stopped before crossing Roosevelt's "Atlantic line."[70]

Germany indeed had noted the American initiatives with considerable alarm, with the German navy characterizing the destroyer-base deal as "an openly hostile act by the United States against Germany." Planning to seize the Canary, Azores, and Cape Verde islands was initiated on Hitler's orders "with an eye to the future war with America," but Hitler's inability to get Spanish support and his 22 June 1941 invasion of the Soviet Union ensured that such anti-American plans never came to fruition.[71] Roosevelt's desire for Canadian bases did not pan out either. Though the Canadians went ahead with the PJBD's recommended improvements and allowed American warships to use Nova Scotian installations, no deal was struck that would permit the United States to lease Canadian bases. Part of the reason was strong Canadian feeling against such a move. King had warned Roosevelt at Ogdensburg that he would prefer not to sell or lease bases, and C.G. Power told the Newfoundland government on 20

August that under no circumstances would Canada surrender sovereignty over any of its territory to the United States.[72] Yet it would seem that the Americans made no real effort to get their hands on Canadian sites. One American military historian has postulated that the initiative stalled because the American services had no real desire to obtain bases which they would then have to garrison when the required forces were badly needed elsewhere. Certainly that case has merit given a late September WPD assessment that the United States could expect no German attack until Britain had been defeated, an unlikely immediate prospect as winter approached with no sign of an imminent German invasion of the British Isles. As the WPD thought that the most probable threats over the next year would come from German political infiltration in Latin America or Japanese moves in the south Pacific, Nova Scotian bases certainly were not a major priority.[73] But as Marshall had not been much interested either in any formal pact with Canada, and Roosevelt had made that happen, one is left wondering if historians Fred Pollock and David Reynolds (and Berle) were correct in asserting that Roosevelt's sole motivation for creating the PJBD was to ensure American control of the Royal Navy if the British fleet fell back to Canada.[74]

If true, such an interpretation could explain Roosevelt's obvious reluctance to intervene in a dispute over command unity that plagued the PJBD's continental defense planning well into 1942. Initially, progress was smooth. By early October the PJBD's members had agreed to a tentative Basic Defense Plan No. 1 (in case Britain was defeated) and a number of defensive tasks for Canada and the United States, some to be carried out individually, others collectively. For Newfoundland's defense, the guiding principle would be mutual cooperation or unity-of-command by the prior consent of both governments or their designated commanders.[75] Such an arrangement, however, found little support within the American army. Embick had agreed in early September to station some American forces in Newfoundland and to augment British Columbia's defenses with an American division if Canada acquiesced to place its eastern maritime provinces under American strategic control, but as one WPD officer rightly complained, with Plan No. 1's adoption, "the whole issue of command has been side-stepped."[76]

Indeed it had, and General Strong happily welcomed that deliberate omission as the PJBD's tendency to formulate strategic plans and to arrange troop movements "was beyond its competence" and therefore likely to "later bring up vexing questions of command."[77] Still, such vexing questions could not be kept quiet for very long, and by early November, McNarney, now heading the WPD's plans and projects section, hoped to resolve this command question once and for all. Doubting that mutual cooperation or unity-of-command were either achievable or desirable, McNarney recommended that Newfoundland, Canada's maritime provinces, British Columbia, and Alaska should be incorporated as sectors within the American Atlantic and Pacific Coastal Frontiers. Canada would retain control of the British Columbia sector permanently and its eastern provinces and Newfoundland until American forces had moved into those regions in numbers.[78]

Doing nothing to shake the Canadian reluctance to surrender sovereignty, McNarney's "gloss of mutuality"[79] in fact encouraged the Canadians to amend existing agreements. Despite praising the PJBD as a "major step forward," General Crerar worried that its creation would strengthen the Canadian tendency "to look inward and think in terms of strict 'continental' defence." Believing very strongly that Britain constituted Canada's first line of defense and that the chances of Japan attacking North America were slight (except for Alaska but "such a remote possibility should not be allowed to exert a noticeable influence on the Board at this time"[80]), Crerar favored producing an army, five to seven divisions strong, capable of playing a major role in Germany's defeat. But knowing that Prime Minister King would be very reluctant to approve such a force (King had said on 1 October that he wanted Canada's greatest contribution to be made in the air, followed by the navy[81]), and concerned that any emphasis on continental defense could keep army resources from the war in Europe, Crerar opposed following through on an earlier guarantee to despatch forces to Alaska if Japan attacked there. Contending that the PJBD's Canadian section had made that promise because of a perceived "political need" to have Canada accept "a specific responsibility" to assist the United States, Crerar's insistence that there was no military reason for despatching Canadian troops to Alaska was reflected in the final version of the PJBD's continental defense scheme, Joint Canadian–United States Defense Plan No. 2 (ABC-22). If Alaska was assaulted, Canadian sailors and air crew, but not soldiers, would support American efforts in the north Pacific.[82]

Resolving the unity-of-command issue proved far more difficult. By January 1941, the Canadian army, charging that the strategic assumption that had prompted the adoption of Plan No. 1—that Britain would not survive—no longer held true, wanted to formulate a new scheme more firmly based upon current strategic reality. Moreover, American support for Plan No. 1 had alarm bells clanging, as Escott Reid noted in early March, in a Canada already concerned by the growing prospect of a "pretty tough and not very intelligent" American imperialism once the war had been won. So when O.M. Biggar, the PJBD's Canadian chair, asked King for guidance in advance of the board's next scheduled meeting, Biggar explained that the body's American members "may press for an arrangement having features which it might not be easy to justify to the public in Canada."[83]

The Canadian section did not wait for that guidance before acting on its own. Its 15 April draft proposal accepted American strategic direction over the Canadian army and RCAF only if Britain collapsed "subject to the proviso that any direction affecting the disposition or employment" of those forces would "not be given without prior consultation between the Chief of Staff, United States Army, and the Canadian Chief of Staff concerned, or their authorized representatives." This was not much of a concession, especially when Biggar admitted that the new definition would apply only to forces operating in certain areas at sea. Moreover, Biggar feared that even this compromise, given the rather vague definition of "strategic control," could permit the Americans to surrender Canadian territory "or to withdraw all Canadian forces from one coast and concentrate them on the other or even outside Canadian territory."[84] Crerar could not have agreed more. Concurring with a British assessment that as long as Britain stood unbowed and key places like Greenland, Iceland, Hawaii, and Alaska remained in friendly hands, no enemy, alone or in combination, had the wherewithal to mount a large-scale assault on North America, Crerar advocated no agreement unless the Americans accepted mutual cooperation rather than unity-of-command.[85] This the PJBD's American naval officers could not accept. As it provided the bulk of the forces in the western Atlantic and had recently struck a unity-of-command deal with Britain for that region (see Chapter 4), the USN felt that it should control all ships operating in those waters, a demand the RCN would not concede. The CWC did little to help resolve the matter. Fearing that there was "a real political danger" in the way defense plans were unfolding given the United States's overwhelming military power, King wanted no part in a process that conceivably might end in continental union. Therefore although the CWC concluded that it "might" be necessary to accept American strategic direction under Plan No. 1, that acceptance was contingent upon the board's failure to come to an agreement, thus setting the stage for an impasse.[86]

Not a man who could long tolerate a stalemate, and informed by the War Department that an acceptance of the Canadian point of view could lead to American forces being placed under "Canadian strategical and tactical command whenever they were serving in Canadian territory," Fiorello LaGuardia informed Biggar that the two nations were "getting dangerously apart" on the command unity issue. Canada's fears and suggestions, the "little flower" lectured, "would be all right" if one was trying to arrange a parade, but were not appropriate at a time when "we are engaged in the grim business of joint defense against a possible strong and ruthless enemy." Speaking very "frankly," LaGuardia told Biggar "that it is far better to trust to the honor of the United States, than to the mercy of the enemy." Though the Canadians liked LaGuardia (Prime Minister King, despite the mayor's pronounced and "unfortunate craze for publicity," thought LaGuardia "grows on one," while H.L. Keenleyside opined that LaGuardia, while he "resembled an ambulatory eggplant" was "one of the truly great Americans of his generation") an unmoved Biggar reminded his American counterpart that whereas Canada was "all out in the war," the United States was not in "yet," and thus it was a "very unpropitious" to suggest that Canada should surrender strategic control to the United States when the Dominion had refused to do exactly that with Britain.[87]

Thwarted, LaGuardia turned to the one person that he thought had the power to break the deadlock. Stating that the vital matter must be settled "without delay," LaGuardia maintained that wars against enemies as ruthless and efficient as Germany could be won only via centralized control, not "by consultation." But given Canada's stubborn refusal to relinquish strategic control even when the Americans had offered to allow Canada tactical command "in practically all of the Canadian territories and coastal waters," LaGuardia believed that the Canadian objections had been "created for political reasons." He therefore recommended that Roosevelt personally bring the matter to Prime Minister King's attention in the hope of resolving the matter in favor of the American position.[88]

LaGuardia's expectations that the president would see the link between the command unity problem and the American-British-Canadian [ABC] staff talks begun in February 1941, were largely frustrated. Although he agreed that strategic control over North America should rest with the United States "in view of the fact that in actual defense nine-tenths of the total effort will fall on the United States," Roosevelt suggested that LaGuardia make the case himself by emphasizing to the Canadians their devotion to the British cause overseas.[89] Left to their devices, the PJBD's American members adopted the same tack Roosevelt had employed with King at Ogdensburg. When Embick met with General Stuart on 12 May, he made it very clear that Biggar's proposals were unacceptable, "even as a basis for discussion." Moreover, if Canada could "not see her way to a continuation of discussions on a basis more in line with

U.S. views, then the U.S., very reluctantly, would be forced to either take up the matter with Great Britain, or to plan for unilateral action on her own part in order to safeguard her own interests."[90]

The tactic seemed to work. Stuart advocated letting the United States control the interaction between the American and Canadian operational zones, while Crerar, though worried that American troops in Canada "might endanger a situation, not assist it," thought that since the United States and Britain had agreed to command unity during the ABC talks, Canada should not now reject a similar arrangement. Claiming that it was "foolish to attempt to 'define the undefinable,'" the CGS thought the best that could be hoped for was "to establish broad and sound policies covering our respective relations and responsibilities in clearly definable *military situations*."[91] Brigadier Maurice Pope, Stuart's replacement on the PJBD, disagreed. Son of DEA founder Joseph Pope, Pope once was described as the Canadian army's best educated and most informed general and as possessing the most inquiring mind in the army.[92] Although Pope had long argued about the need to acknowledge American security concerns—during the 1930s when McNaughton had said Canada might remain neutral for 30 days in a war between the United States and Japan, Pope, estimating the time lapse to be 30 hours, warned that the United States "would be entirely justified" in making use of Canadian territory if Canada could not defend itself—he did not equate cooperation with allowing another nation to control Dominion affairs, especially when he believed that there had been no "*military* necessity whatever" for the PJBD's creation.[93] Asserting that a workable definition of strategic direction was obtainable, Pope strongly objected to having "a U.S. commanding-in-chief of either coast for that would mean not only the concession of strategical direction but also tactical command in our own country."[94]

The CWC, backing Pope, ruled that Canada would give the United States limited authority "subject to the determination of war policy by the governments of both countries," but the Dominion would not accept "unlimited authority over the disposition and employment of Canadian forces, in the circumstances contemplated." When two days of meetings on 27–28 May ("probably the most strained" in the PJBD's history[95]) failed to alter Canada's position, the American section, accepting a State Department assertion that given the RCN's small size and the fact that Canadian cooperation "would come about almost automatically" in a crisis, caved in despite Brigadier General L.T. Gerow's claim that the command provisions remained "defective."[96] When Rainbow Five received approval in June, the section outlining the command procedures for forces operating in Canada and Newfoundland said only that the responsibility for strategic direction and command "has not been fixed."[97] Using the joint command definition followed by the American services, the Americans agreed in July to allow mutual cooperation to govern continental defense except "when agreed upon by the Chiefs of Staff concerned," or in an emergency "when the commanders of the Canadian and United States forces concerned agree that the situation requires the exercise of unity of command, and further agree as to the Service that shall exercise such command." And after the need for command unity had been accepted, whereas the designated commander had the power to create task forces, designate objectives and tasks, and exercise the coordinating control "necessary to ensure the success of the operations," that officer could neither interfere with the other nation's forces nor transfer them "without authorization from the Chief of Staff concerned."[98]

Hopes that the unity-of-command issue finally had been resolved, however imperfectly, evaporated when Japan attacked Western outposts throughout Asia and the Pacific on 7 December. San Francisco was told to expect a possible air raid, and American army intelligence warned on 10 December that as Japan appeared to have "complete information not only of our dispositions but of the habits, customs and traits of the American Army, Navy and people," it expected that the enemy could strike as far afield as Alaska, the Panama Canal, or the American West Coast.[99] As the United States scrambled to meet its new foe, followed within days by German and Italian declarations of war, the War Department sought to maximize the punch American forces could deliver by any means possible, and unity-of-command, touted by some as the key to successfully combatting the perceived tight control Germany exercised over its allies,[100] was on the top of the American security agenda. Indeed, one WPD officer had recommended on 5 December that North America's entire West Coast from Alaska stretching south to the Mexican border, because it constituted a single physical theater of operations, should be governed by one headquarters. Gerow concurred. As Canada had few military assets in British Columbia, that region would have to be covered by American forces, and unwilling to waste time now that the United States was a full-fledged belligerent, Gerow asked the PJBD's American section on 15 December to broach the matter with the Canadians.[101]

Canada, however, had anticipated Gerow's recommendation. Having noted a *New York Times* despatch that said West Coast security was threatened by the lack of unity-of-command, Hugh Keenleyside, the PJBD's Canadian secretary, fumed that Embick likely had planted the story in the press to stampede Canada into agreeing to command unity. Whether such unity was militarily desirable Keenleyside did not profess to know, but he was certain that Canada had the definite right to "object very strenuously" to the American attempt "to scare us into accepting their wishes by publication in the press of inaccurate and coloured reports."[102] Canada's military, on the other hand, had absolutely no doubts that unity-of-command was both undesirable and unnecessary. Although the Allies had been badly weakened by a number of serious reverses in southeast Asia and the Pacific, the COS reported to the CWC on 10 December that even though those defeats had modified somewhat the assumption that American power would more than balance Japanese capabilities, it was "vitally important to ensure" that attention was not unduly diverted from the Atlantic Ocean and Europe where the real danger lay. All that Canada could expect were some raids for which the forces already in place in British Columbia were more than adequate to counter.[103]

Pope, having been recently promoted to the post of vice chief of the general staff (VCGS), and aware that Bruce Hutchison and T.A. Crerar were pushing King hard to add two divisions to British Columbia's defenses,[104] doubted that Japan could spare ships to send even one division against North America. More to the point, Pope could not possibly imagine what Japan might hope to accomplish by despatching valuable military assets to the eastern Pacific where they would be vulnerable to attack from superior forces based in North America's vastness. Given that Japanese raids, "apart from their effect on public opinion, can not possibly endanger national security," and concerned by the long-term impact American strategic dominance might have on Canada's national sovereignty (not to mention the Canadian army's more immediate plans for the war in Europe), the VCGS firmly asserted that "the need for a unified command over the land forces of the [United States and Canada] is not indicated nor can it be admitted."[105]

However, when the PJBD met again in New York City on 19 December, Pope's concerns seemed misplaced. Rather than simply demanding the institution of unity-of-command, Embick asked for the PJBD instead just to instruct local Canadian and American commanders to coordinate their operational activities on the Atlantic and Pacific coasts. Regarding this as a pleasing sign that the Americans were steadying after Pearl Harbor's shock, the Canadian section happily accepted this proposal (the PJBD's twenty-second recommendation).[106] Embick's failure to raise the command issue had not resulted from forgetfulness, nor a declining interest in the subject within the PJBD's American section. Rather, it reflected the inability of the American services to assent to command unity. Although the American army and navy had agreed in 1935 to govern joint operations by creating a theater commander with the power to oversee all military activities with the proviso that said appointee could neither "infringe upon the administrative and disciplinary functions of component services" nor direct "how a component commander could carry out his mission,"[107] the navy had demonstrated no enthusiasm for the idea in December 1941. When General Marshall asked the USN to assume command over Alaska and Hawaii, the USN, stating that unity-of-command had become a slogan, declined on the grounds that no commander, regardless of his service, was qualified to "make all decisions" for both arms in any particular situation. Moreover, whereas implementing unity-of-command might make sense for mixed task forces undertaking offensive operations, the navy thought mutual cooperation better suited for defensive campaigns.[108]

Dissatisfied with the American military's inability to put its own command unity house in order, LaGuardia again took matters into his own hands. Writing to Roosevelt in late December, he asked the president to convince Prime Minister King to institute unity-of-command on the West Coast. But Roosevelt again demurred, preferring instead that other channels be employed before he had to directly approach King.[109] LaGuardia was that other channel, and he wasted little time in making his case to Biggar. His 2 January note, which described British Columbia as "geographically an enclave within the Western Theater," insisted that the province's southern portion and Puget Sound "cannot be most effectively defended under the control of several commanders." Stating that Canadian forces in the region should come under the sway of Lieutenant General John L. DeWitt's Western Defense Command, but that DeWitt would have very limited powers regarding the transfer of Canadian units, LaGuardia concluded that "the problem presented is one of setting up, as a wise precautionary measure, in advance of an actual attack, that form of basic organization that will afford the greatest measure of protection against enemy operations."[110]

LaGuardia's plea met a Canadian stone wall. Convinced that the Americans simply were attempting to redraft ABC-22 to disguise their demand for command unity, Pope pointed out that the United States had refrained "as usual from stating any forms and scales" of attack that might justify such a step. Although it was fair to infer that the Americans believed that the West Coast was vulnerable to invasion, Pope, quick to point out that neither the Canadian army nor Britain's military agreed with that American view, therefore rejected LaGuardia's demand on the grounds that no evidence had been produced that suggested that existing West Coast cooperation was anything but satisfactory.[111] Canada's military chiefs made short work of LaGuardia's request too when they returned from Washington on 7 January. Stating that they had received assurances from their American counterparts that "they did not subscribe to the necessity of Unified Command either in Newfoundland or on the west coast," and ruling that they, and not the PJBD, were responsible for settling such matters, the Canadian service heads declined "to take any further action unless or until this matter [was] brought to their attention by the United States Chiefs of Staff themselves."[112]

Unwilling to accept this ruling, an unhappy Embick informed Pope on 14 January that as the USN might soon have to relinquish control of the north Pacific to the Japanese fleet, the United States had an obligation to explore every avenue of defense. As unity-of-command, especially over air and ground forces, was one of the most important means to improve defensive capabilities, Embick implored Pope to find a formula "for a unified command that will safeguard Canadian interests and yet provide for a more effective organization of the common defense."[113] Embick did not get the desired response. Ruling that there was no reason for unified command as long as mutual cooperation had not broken down, the COS instructed the PJBD's Canadian section, if the matter came up at the next board meeting (scheduled for 20 January), to ask the Americans "to produce concrete evidence" that such cooperation was unsatisfactory. Pope put matters even more bluntly. Complaining about "the propriety of an officer of the War Department writing *in the name of his Government* to an officer of the Department of National Defence on a matter of this kind may be open to question," Pope accused Embick of being too "vague in stating the premise on which his demand is based." As Japan could and would not conduct large-scale operations against North America, Pope said firmly that Embick's plea must be denied.[114]

Embick did raise command unity at the PJBD meeting on 20 January, but he was wasting his time. Pope's response was that if the United States military really desired unity-of-command, ABC-22's provisions demanded that General Marshall take the matter up directly with the Canadian chief of staff. Stymied, the American section gave up, asking only that its position be placed on the official record. Pope and his colleagues agreed, and the official PJBD journal recorded that in the opinion of the board's American members, the Canadian refusal to permit unity-of-command on the West Coast subjected that region "to an unnecessary hazard."[115] The matter was not raised again.

Canada thus had defeated what Norman Robertson, Skelton's successor to the post of USSEA (Skelton had died in January 1941 from a stroke while at the wheel of his car), would later call an "absurd and mischievous" notion that "the local defences of one sector of front could be strengthened by the transfer of responsibility from one party to another,"[116] but the reasons behind that Canadian victory are unclear. One might argue that Canada's determined and unrelenting resistance to American pressure had been the deciding factor, but that answer is not particularly satisfying given that Canada proved unable to block renewed American demands for an Alaskan highway just weeks later. Perhaps the most appropriate explanation lies with the American leadership's lack of commitment to unity-of-command. Favored by the army, the notion enjoyed little USN support, but most importantly, it failed to fire President Roosevelt's imagination. Asked twice by LaGuardia to personally intervene to overcome the Canadian opposition, the president declined to enter the fray even when King was in Washington in late December 1941. Had he elected to intervene, the unity matter may have turned out very differently because just the possibility that Roosevelt might want to discuss the matter had left King in a tizzy in the new year. Reading over Biggar's summaries of what had transpired to that point, the prime minister was happy to record in his diary on 14 January that no such call from the White House had come, as well as his hope that a compromise might resolve the issue.[117] Perhaps Pollock's case that Roosevelt created the PJBD solely as a means of acquiring the Royal Navy has merit, for the president certainly demonstrated little interest in what had proved to be the board's most controversial issue. And as the Canadians soon would discover, getting the president to pay attention to causes that little interested him, in this case, Canada's participation in new Allied war policy boards, was no easy task.

NOTES

1. King diary, 1 December 1939 and 15 January 1940, NAC.

2. Ibid., 5 January 1940.

3. "Mantle of Laurier," *Cleveland Plain Dealer*, 29 January 1940.

4. Berle diary, 11 January 1940, FDRL, box 211, Diary January–March 1940.

5. Morgenthau diary, 29 April 1940, FDRL, fiche 5.

6. T.A. Crerar diary, 13 December 1939, QUA, T.A. Crerar Papers, box 155, Diary 1939.

7. Chiefs of Staff, "Canada's National Effort (Armed Forces) in the Early Stages of a Major War," 29 August 1939, NAC, Privy Council Office, Memoranda of Defence Council and Emergency Council, 1938–1939, RG2 7c, vol. 1; Skelton, "Canadian War Policy," 24 August 1939, NAC, King Memoranda and Notes, vol. 228; and King diary, 5 September 1939, NAC.

8. Gellman, *Secret Affairs*, 172–73 and 201; and Offner, *The Origins of the Second World War*, 173.

9. Quoted in Michael S. Sherry, *In the Shadow of War: The United States since the 1930s* (New Haven: Yale University Press, 1995), 35.

10. Marshall to Harry Woodring, 7 September 1939, in Larry I. Bland, ed., *The Papers of George Catlett Marshall. Volume 2:"We Cannot Delay," July 1, 1939–December 6, 1941* (Baltimore: The Johns Hopkins University Press, 1986), 52–53; Marshall, "Subject: Increases in the Army," 8 September 1939, Ibid., 53–54; and McFarland, *Harry H. Woodring*, 115.

11. War Department, "Outline of War Department Program for National Defense," 13 April 1940, NARA, RG165, Entry 281, file WPD 3674–16; Morgenthau diary, 13 May 1940, FDRL, Fiche 5; Marshall to Bernard M. Baruch, 14 May 1940, in Bland, *The Papers of George Catlett Marshall*, 212; and Forrest C. Pogue, *George C. Marshall: Ordeal and Hope, 1939–1942* (New York: Viking Press, 1966), 16–32.

12. King diary, 23–24 April 1940, NAC.

13. CWC minutes, 10, 17, 22, and 23 May, and 14 and 17 June 1940, NAC, Cabinet War Committee Minutes and Records, RG2 7c, vol. 1. The French base is discussed in "Record of Visit to United Kingdom of Canadian Minister of National Defence (Mr. Norman McL. Rogers) April 18th to May 9th, 1940," QUA, Norman Rogers Papers, box 8, file III Departmental Papers.

14. Prime Minister Robert Menzies to King, 22 May 1940, NAC, King Memoranda and Notes, reel H1557, C281473–74; Massey to King, no. 669, 23 May 1940, Ibid., C281477–80; and Prime Minister Winston Churchill to King, no. M.29, 24 May 1940, Ibid., C281481–82.

15. King diary, 18 May 1940, NAC.

16. Hugh L. Keenleyside, *Memoirs of Hugh L. Keenleyside. Volume 2: On the Bridge of Time* (Toronto: McClelland and Stewart, 1982), 30–31; and Keenleyside to King, "Report of Discussion with President Roosevelt," 23 May 1940, NAC, King Memoranda and Notes, reel H1558, C282902–4.

17. Lowenthal, *Leadership and Indecision*, 179; and David G. Haglund, "George C. Marshall and the Question of Military Aid to England, May–June 1940," *Journal of Contemporary History*, 15 (October 1980), 748.

18. Harold Ickes to Professor Paul Perigold, 15 May 1940, LC, Harold L. Ickes Papers, box 371, file War (3).

19. Marshall, "Subject: National Strategic Decisions," 22 May 1940, NARA, RG165, Entry 281, file WPD 4175–7; and Marshall to the WPD, 23 May 1940, Ibid., file WPD 4175–10.

20. Berle diary, 21 May 1940, FDRL, box 211, Diary April–May 1940.

21. Fred E. Pollock, "Roosevelt, the Ogdensburg Agreement, and the British Fleet: All Done with Mirrors," *Diplomatic History*, 5 (Summer 1981), 206–7; and Stimson diary, 15 May 1940, YU, vol. 29.

22. King diary, 24 May 1940, NAC.

23. Keenleyside, "Report of a Discussion of Possible Eventualities," 26 May 1940, NAC, King Memoranda and Notes, reel H1558, C281907–10.

24. King diary, 26 May 1940, NAC; Keenleyside, "Discussion of Possible Eventualities," 29 May 1940, King Memoranda and Notes, reel H1558, C281914–19; and Keenleyside, *On the Bridge of Time*, 36–37.

25. King diary, 27 May 1940, NAC; and King to Churchill, 30 May 1940, NAC, RG25, vol. 779, file 381.

26. Winston Churchill, *The Second World War: Their Finest Hour. Volume 2* (Boston: Houghton Mifflin, 1949), 118.

27. Churchill to King, 5 June 1940, in Murray, *DCER, Volume 8*, 85–86.

28. Welles memorandum of conversation with Lothian, 23 May 1940, FDRL, Welles Papers, box 162, file Great Britain Jan–May 1940; and Keenleyside, "Report of a Discussion Held on the 7th of June 1940," 8 June 1940, in Murray, *DCER, Volume 8*, 95–97.

29. King diary, 17 June 1940, NAC; King to Churchill, 17 June 1940, NAC, RG25, vol. 779, file 381; and Churchill to King, 24 June 1940, Ibid., vol. 819, file 674.

30. Moffat memorandum of conversation with King, 14 June 1940, NARA, RG84, file 711 1940 Memoranda of Conversations.

31. Moffat diary, 10 June 1940, HL, MS Am 1407, vol. 46. Though William Castle thought that Moffat would prove ideally suited to repair the damage done in Ottawa by past American mistakes, he feared that Moffat's "sound and sane" judgment was more sorely needed in Washington; M.M. Mahoney to SSEA, no. 1078, NAC, King Correspondence, reel C4571, 246607–9; Morgenthau diary, 13 May 1940, FDRL, fiche 5; and Castle diary, 28 May 1940, HHL.

32. Moffat to Welles, 26 June 1940, FDRL, Welles Papers, box 63, file 2; King diary, 14 June 1940, NAC; Moffat to Hull, 16 June 1940, NARA, RG59, Decimal File 1940–44, 711.42/194; and Moffat diary, 3 May 1940, HL, MS Am 1407, vol. 45.

33. Hull to Mahoney, 15 June 1940, NAC, RG25, vol. 824, file 711; Hull memorandum of conversation with Lothian, 11 June 1940, LC, Hull Papers, box 58, file Great Britain, 1939–40; King to Mahoney, no. 110, 16 June 1940, NAC, King Memoranda and

Notes, vol. 428, file Canadian-American Relations War Purchases 1940–1941; and Hull memorandum of conversation with Mahoney, 17 June 1940, LC, Hull Papers, box 57, file Canada 1933–44. Herridge had made his request through Skelton, who forwarded it to Washington with King's approval; Herridge to Skelton, 8 June 1940, NAC, RG25, vol. 824, file 711; and Skelton to Herridge, 11 June 1940, Ibid.

34. Major J.S. Gullet, "Notes on Canadian Defense—Atlantic Sector," NARA, RG165, MID Correspondence, file 2694–72/1; and Brigadier General Sherman Miles, "Data on Newfoundland and Greenland," 22 May 1940, NARA, RG165, Entry 281, file WPD 4300. Canada despatched its first military attaché, an air force officer, to Washington in February 1940, followed by army and navy representatives in August. In turn, the United States sent Gullet in April, and a naval officer in August; Dziuban, *Military Relations between the United States and Canada*, 71–72.

35. Bruce Hutchison memorandum, 12 June 1940, NAC, King Memoranda and Notes, reel H1557, C281501–5; and Hutchison memorandum of conversation with Senator Key Pittman, 16 June 1940, NAC, RG25, vol. 2789, file 703–40, pt. 1.

36. Dallek, *Franklin D. Roosevelt and American Foreign Policy*, 228 and 232; and Lothian to the Foreign Office no. 1019, 17 June 1940, PRO, FO371, vol. 24240, file A3582/131/45.

37. JPC, "Views on questions propounded by the President on the war situation," 26 June 1940, NARA, RG165, Entry 281, file WPD 4250–3; and Moffat diary, 27 June 1940, HL, MS Am 1407, vol. 46.

38. King diary, 27 June 1940, NAC; Power, "Memorandum of conversation with the American Minister, Mr. Moffat, June 29th 1940," 30 June 1940, QUA, Power Papers, box 69, file D–2018; and Moffat diary, 29 June 1940, HL, MS Am 1407, vol. 46.

39. Moffat memoranda of conversations with Stark, Marshall, and Strong, 2–3 July 1940, HL, Moffat Papers, MS Am 1407, vol. 46.

40. Dziuban, *Military Relations between the United States and Canada*, 15–16; and Hull to Marshall, 3 July 1940, LC, Hull Papers, box 47, file July 1–15, 1940.

41. Keenleyside, "Summary of Points Suggested for Discussion with the United States," 30 June 1940, NAC, RG25, vol. 2789, file 703–40 pt. 1; and War Department, "Decisions Required if Military Assistance is to be Afforded to Canada in the Immediate Future," 5 July 1940, NARA, RG59, Decimal File 1940–44, 842.20/150 ½.

42. Dziuban, *Military Relations between the United States and Canada*, 17; and Stuart, "Report of Conversations in Washington, D.C.," 15 July 1940, NAC, RG25, vol. 2459, file C–10.

43. Moffat to Welles, 26 July 1940, FDRL, Welles Papers, box 63, file 2; Admiral King, "Control of Western Hemisphere," 15 July 1940, LC, King Papers, box 21, file General Board 1940.

44. Simmons to Hull, no. 90, 3 July 1940, NARA, RG59, Decimal File 1940–44, 842.00 P.R./181; "A Treaty with the U.S.," *Montreal Standard*, 3 August 1940; and "In Defense of the United States," *New York Herald Tribune*, 7 August 1940.

45. Skelton to King, no. 274, 1 July 1940, in Murray, *DCER, Volume 8*, 449–50.

46. Keenleyside to King, "An Outline Synopsis for a Reconsideration of Canadian External Policy with Particular Reference to the United States," 17 June 1940, NAC, RG25, vol. 781, file 394.

47. CIIA National Secretary John R. Baldwin to Reid, 5 July 1940, NAC, Reid Papers, vol. 27, file 8. Edgar Dean of the Council of Foreign Relations agreed that even Toronto "Imperialists" might now welcome a political connection with the United States, but that many Canadians feared public discussions of the issue for fear of being branded defeatists; Moffat memorandum of conversation with Edgar Dean, 7 August 1940, NARA, RG84, Entry 2195A, file 711 1940 Memoranda of Conversations.

48. "A Programme of Immediate Canadian Action Drawn Up by a Group of Twenty Canadians, Meeting at the Chateau Laurier, Ottawa, on July 17–18, 1940," copy in NAC, King Correspondence, vol. 286, file Church to Colquhoun.

49. King diary, 13 July 1940, NAC.

50. CWC minutes, 26 July 1940, NAC, RG2 7c, vol. 2; King diary, 26 July 1940, NAC.

51. Roosevelt memorandum, 2 August 1940, FDRL, Roosevelt PSF, file Navy: Destroyers & Naval Bases; Reynolds, *The Creation of the Anglo-American Alliance*, 125–32; and Eden quoted in Charmley, *Churchill's Grand Alliance*, 21.

52. Christie to King, 29 July 1940, NAC, RG25, vol. 2989, file B–79.

53. Lothian to King, 12 August 1940, NAC, King Memoranda and Notes, reel H1558, 282235–37A; and Welles memorandum of conversation with Christie, 13 August 1940, NARA, RG59, Decimal File 1940–44, 841.34/370.

54. Moffat to Welles, 26 July 1940, FDRL, Welles Papers, box 63, file 2; Moffat to Hull, no. 199, 1 August 1940, NARA, RG84, Entry 2195A, file 711 1940 Canada's War Effort; and Moffat to Hull, no. 239, 8 August 1940, University of Virginia Archives [UVA], Charlottesville, Edward R. Stettinius Papers, box 631, file Canada.

55. Hickerson to Moffat, 8 August 1940, State Department Records, RG59, Office of European Affairs (Matthews-Hickerson File) 1934–1947, M1244, reel 5.

56. Christie to King, 15 August 1940, in Murray, *DCER, Volume 8*, 129; and King diary, 16 August 1940, NAC.

57. Stimson diary, 17 August 1940, YU, vol. 30.

58. J.L. Granatstein, "Mackenzie King and Canada at Ogdensburg, August 1940," in Joel J. Sokolsky and Joseph T. Jockel, eds., *Fifty Years of Canada–United States Defense Cooperation: The Road from Ogdensburg* (Lewiston: The Edwin Mellen Press, 1992), 21; and King diary, 17 August 1940, NAC.

59. "Declaration by the Prime Minister of Canada and the President of the United States of America regarding the Establishment of a Permanent Joint Board on Defence Made on 18 August 1940," in C.P. Stacey, ed., *Historical Documents of Canada. Volume V: The Arts of War and Peace 1914–1945* (Toronto: Macmillan, 1972), 650–51.

60. Callcott, *The Western Hemisphere*, 384; "Says Defense Plan Opens Way to Pact," *New York Times*, 19 August 1940; and Dziuban, *Military Cooperation between the United States and Canada*, 25. Other favorable views of the PJBD are: "U.S. Wins Military Benefits by Canadian Defense Pact," *Christian Science Monitor*, 9 September 1940; "Together for Defense," *Boston Globe*, 19 August 1940; "Wise Foreign Policy," *Providence Journal*, 19 August 1940; and "Insurance against Invasion," *Washington Herald*, 20 August 1940. A poll asking what Canada should do if Britain fell, found that over 40 percent of Americans favored annexation, 36 percent thought that Canada should become independent, while almost 20 percent said that Canada should become the seat of Britain's government; "36 Per Cent Believe Area Should be Separate Nation," *Washington Herald*, 1 September 1940.

61. Stimson diary, 17 August 1940, YU, vol. 30; and Skelton to King, 19 August 1940, NAC, King Memoranda and Notes, reel H1516, C220892–94.

62. J.L. Granatstein, "The Conservative Party and the Ogdensburg Agreement," *International Journal*, 22 (Winter 1966–67), 74.

63. Lord Cranborne to Churchill, 6 March 1941, PRO, Prime Minister's Papers, PREM 11/43A/12; King to Churchill, 18 August 1940, NAC, King Memoranda and Notes, vol. 428, file Ogdensburg Agreement 1940; and Churchill to King, no. 96, 22 August 1940, Ibid., reel H1558, C282290.

64. King statement, 12 November 1940, *Debates*, House of Commons, 54–59.

65. Moffat memorandum of conversation with Leonard Brockington, 19 August 1940, NARA, RG59, Matthews-Hickerson File, reel 5; and Hickerson to Welles and Hull, 23 October 1940, HL, Moffat Papers, MS Am 1407, vol. 46. Canberra instructed its minister in the United States to determine if President Roosevelt favored reaching a similar arrangement with Australia and New Zealand. After hearing from Welles that the pact was "solely connected with Western Hemisphere defence," R.G. Casey reported that he thought it "inadvisable" to seek a deal because the "American public mind has not yet advanced that far." But when Berle stated in early September that an agreement with Australia, although presently "unwise," might be "possible" if it was "arranged quickly and confidentially," Casey advised waiting until after the presidential elections; Minister of External Affairs John McEwen to Casey, no. 131, 20 August 1940, Australian Archives [AA], Canberra, Department of External Affairs Records, Series A3300/7, Item 38; Casey to DEA Canberra, no. 215, 21 August 1940, Ibid.; and Casey to McEwen, RGC no. 14, 17 September 1940, Ibid.

66. King diary, 22 August 1940, NAC.

67. "Summary of meeting of Canadian Staff Conference Members, held in Room 2705, Munitions Building, August 23, 1940," NARA, RG165, Entry 281, file WPD 4330-2.

68. Stimson diary, 24 August 1940, YU, vol. 30.

69. PJBD, "Journal of Discussions and Decisions," 26–27 August 1940, NAC, King Memoranda and Notes, reel H1516, C220909–17; and Berle diary, 31 August 1940, FDRL, box 212, Diary June–August 1940.

70. Felix Morley, "Canadian-American Defense Pact Is Severe Strain on U.S. Neutrality Pact," *Washington Post*, 25 August 1940; and Berle diary, 28 August 1940, FDRL, box 212, Diary June–August 1940.

71. Holger H. Herwig, *Politics of Frustration: The United States in German Naval Planning, 1889–1941* (Boston: Little, Brown and Company, 1976), 210–15.

72. Quoted in David Mackenzie, *Inside the Atlantic Triangle: Canada and the Entrance of Newfoundland into Confederation, 1939–1949* (Toronto: University of Toronto Press, 1986), 44.

73. Dziuban, *Military Cooperation between the United States and Canada*, 49–50; and WPD, "The Problem of Production of Munitions in Relation to the Ability of the United States to Cope with Its Defense Problems in the Present World Situation," 25 September 1940, NARA, RG165, Entry 281, file WPD 4321–9.

74. Pollock, "Roosevelt, the Ogdensburg Agreement," 219; and Reynolds, *The Creation of the Anglo-American Alliance*, 183.

75. PJBD, "First Report," 10 October 1940, in FDRL, Roosevelt PSF, File Canada: Permanent Joint Board on Defense.

76. Embick to Marshall, "Joint Defense Plan, Canada-US," 7 September 1940, NARA, RG165, Entry 281, file WPD 4330–4; and Colonel F.S. Clark to Marshall, "Joint Canadian-United States Basic Defense Plan—1940 (First Joint Draft)," 17 September 1940, Ibid., file WPD 4330–5.

77. Moffat diary, 6–10 October 1940, HL, MS Am 1407, vol. 46.

78. McNarney to Embick, "Joint Canadian–United States Basic Defense Plans, 1940," 9 November 1940, NARA, RG165, Entry 281, file WPD 4330–5.

79. Stetson Conn and Byron Fairchild, *The Framework of Hemisphere Defense* (Washington, D.C.: Department of the Army, 1959), 381.

80. Crerar to McNaughton, 9 September 1940, NAC, H.D.G. Crerar Papers, vol. 1, file 958C.009 (D12); and Crerar to Stuart, 14 September 1940, DHH, Kardex file 82/196.

81. King diary, 1 October 1940, NAC; and CWC minutes, 1 October 1940, NAC, RG2 7c, vol. 2. See also Crerar to Ralston, "Canadian Army Programme for 1941," 24 September 1940, NAC, King Memoranda and Notes, vol. 257, reel H1483, C173329–33.

82. Crerar to Ralston, 14 October 1940, NAC, Privy Council Records, RG2, vol. 4, file D–19–2 1940; and "Joint Canadian–United States Basic Defense Plan No. 2 (Short Title ABC–22)," 28 July 1941, in Murray, *DCER, Volume 8*, 250–51.

83. Stuart, "Memorandum on J.D.B. Plans for 1941," 16 January 1941, DHH, Kardex file 112.11 (D1A); Reid to Christie, 5 March 1941, NAC, Reid Papers, vol. 32, file 6; and O.M. Biggar to King, 13 March 1941, NAC, King Correspondence, vol. 300, file Beau–Bjar.

84. Canadian Section, "Joint Operational Plan No. 1 United States, Army–Canada, Army & Air Force," 15 April 1941, DHH, Kardex file 112.11 (DNA); and Biggar to King, 22 April 1941, Ibid.

85. Crerar, "C.G.S. Memo re Basic Plan No. 2," 22 April 1941, DHH, Kardex file 112.3M2 (D497); COS to the CWC, 22 April 1941, NAC, RG2 7c, vol. 4; and "Possible Scale of Japanese Attack on the American Coast," COS (40) 970, 22 November 1940, PRO, Chiefs of Staff Committee Records, CAB80/23.

86. Captain H.E. Reid, RCN, to Chief of Naval Staff [CNS], 19 April 1941, NAC, RG24, vol. 2724, file HQS 5199–Q–1–B; King diary, 23 April 1941, NAC; and CWC minutes, 23 April 1941, NAC, RG2 7c, vol. 4.

87. Brigadier General Harry J. Maloney to Senior Army Member PJBD, 7 May 1941, NARA, RG165, Entry 281, file WPD 4330–25; LaGuardia to Biggar, 2 May 1941, NARA, State Department Records, RG59, Permanent Joint Board on Defense Files, box 8, file Correspondence on PJB on Defense no. 2; King diary, 26 August 1940, NAC; and Keenleyside, *On the Bridge of Time*, 55–56; and Biggar to LaGuardia, 3 May 1941, NAC, RG24, vol. 2724, file HQS 5199–W–1–B.

88. LaGuardia to Roosevelt, early May 1941, FDRL, Roosevelt PSF, file Permanent Joint Board on Defense.

89. Roosevelt to LaGuardia, 16 May 1941, Ibid., file Canada: Permanent Joint Board on Defense.

90. Stuart to Crerar, 14 May 1941, DHH, Kardex file 112.11 (D1A).

91. Ibid.; and Crerar to Brigadier Maurice Pope, 16 May 1941, Ibid.

92. Jack Pickersgill quoted in J.L. Granatstein, *The Generals: The Canadian Army's Senior Commanders in the Second World War* (Toronto: Stoddart, 1993), 207.

93. Maurice A. Pope, *Soldiers and Politicians: The Memoirs of Lt.-Gen. Maurice A. Pope* (Toronto: University of Toronto Press, 1962), 91 and 150.

94. Pope to Biggar, 22 May 1941, DHH, Kardex file 112.11 (D1A).

95. Stacey, *Arms, Men and Governments*, 352.

96. CWC minutes, 27 May 1941, NAC, RG2 7c, vol. 4; PJBD minutes, 28–29 May 1941, DHH, Kardex file 82/196; Moffat, "Notes on Visit to Washington July 10–July 12, 1941," HL, Moffat Papers, MS Am 1407, vol. 47; and L.T. Gerow to Senior Army Member, 17 June 1941, NARA, RG165, Entry 281, file WPD 4330–21.

97. Rainbow No. 5, June 1941, NARA, Adjutant General's Office Records, War Plans "Color" 1920–1948, RG407, box 98, file AG381–A.

98. "Joint Canadian–United States Basic Defense Plan No. 2, (Short Title ABC–22)," 28 July 1941, in Murray, *DCER, Volume 8*, 250–51.

99. "Army Warns West Coast to Prepare for Bombing," *New York Herald Tribune*, 10 December 1941; Lt. Colonel P.M. Robinett, "Brief Estimate of the Situation in the Pacific," NARA, RG165, Entry 281, file WPD 4544–28.

100. General Frank McCoy, Hanson W. Baldwin, and Major George Fielding Eliot, "War Planning," *Council of Foreign Relations Report No. A-B 35* (New York: Council of Foreign Relations, 15 December 1941), 1.

101. Lt. Colonel Nelson M. Walker, "Report of Observation—Alaska—General," 5 December 1941, NARA, RG165, Entry 281, file WPD 3512–146; and Gerow to Marshall, "Defensive Preparations in Western Canada," 15 December 1941, NARA, Operations and Plans Division Records, Executive Files, RG165, Exec file 8, book 1.

102. Keenleyside, "Unity of Command on the Pacific Coast," 10 December 1941, NAC, RG2, vol. 4, file D–19–2; and "Joint U.S.–Canada Defence Plans Incomplete As Japan Opens War," *Montreal Gazette*, 10 December 1941.

103. COS, "Appreciation," 10 December 1941, NAC, RG2 7c, vol. 6; and CWC minutes, 10 December 1941, Ibid.

104. Bruce Hutchison, "Jap Bombs Shocked U.S. into Sudden and Bitter Discovery," *Vancouver Sun*, 8 December 1941; and Grant Dexter memorandum, 8 December 1941, QUA, Grant Dexter Papers, vol. 2, file 20.

105. Pope, "Note on Question of United States–Canada Unity of Command," DHH, Kardex file 72/145.

106. Pope, "Note on Meeting of Permanent Joint Board on Defence held at New York, 19th–20th Dec. 41," 22 December 1941, DHH, Kardex file 112.11 (D1A); and PJBD minutes, 20 December 1941, Ibid., file 82/196.

107. "Joint Action of the Army and Navy," 1935, quoted in Major Charles B. Breslin, *World War II in the Aleutians: The Fundamentals of Joint Campaigns* (Newport: Naval War College, 1994), 9.

108. CNO to Marshall, "Unity of command over joint operations," December 1941, NARA, RG165, Entry 281, file WPD 2917–35; and Larry Bland, ed., *George C. Marshall Interviews and Reminiscences for Forrest C. Pogue* (Lexington: George C. Marshall Foundation, 1991), 595.

109. LaGuardia to Roosevelt, (late) December 1941, NARA, RG59. PJBD, box 8, file Correspondence of PJB on Defense, no. 2; and Dziuban, *Military Relations between the United States and Canada*, 120.

110. LaGuardia to Biggar, 2 January 1942, DHH, Kardex file 112.11 (D1A).

111. Pope to Stuart, 3 January 1942, Ibid.

112. COS minutes, 7 January 1942, NAC, RG24, vol. 8081, file NSS 1272–2.

113. Embick to Pope, 14 January 1942, NARA, RG59, PJBD box 8, file Correspondence of PJBD 1942 Jan–March.

114. COS minutes, 17 January 1942, NAC, RG24, vol. 8081, file NSS 1272–2; and Pope, "Southern British Columbia—Puget Sound U.S. Request for Institution of Unity of Command," 16 January 1942, DHH, Kardex file 112.11 (D1A).

115. Pope to Stuart, 21 January 1942, DHH, Kardex file 112.11 (D1A); and PJBD minutes, 20 January 1942, NAC, King Memoranda and Notes, vol. 319, file F3369.

116. Robertson to Brockington, 4 April 1942, NAC, N.A. Robertson Papers, vol. 2, file Personal Correspondence 1940–1943.

117. King diary, 14 January 1942, NAC.

Chapter 4

Not a Particularly Heroic Role:
Canada Confronts the United
States, 1941–1942

The unity-of-command wrangle in 1941–1942 clearly had demonstrated that though Canada remained fully committed to a cooperative approach to continental defense planning in tandem its American ally, such cooperation did not amount to a surrender of Canadian national sovereignty, no matter the size of the power disparity in the bilateral relationship. Unfortunately, as Canadian officials soon discovered to their considerable dismay, size sometimes makes all the difference (at least in diplomacy), and victories like the command unity debate proved far harder to achieve, especially as both the stakes and the number of players increased.

Just six days after President Roosevelt's unprecedented re-election to a third term on 6 November 1940, the USN's Admiral Harold Stark composed one of the war's most influential planning documents. Assuming that if Britain lost its battle with Germany, that the military problems that the United States would have to face "would be very great," and that "while we might not *lose everywhere*, we might, possibly, not *win anywhere*," Stark thought that American national strategic objectives, beyond the preservation of the territorial, economic, and ideological integrity of the United States and the Western Hemisphere, included preventing the disruption of the British empire and the diminution of Japan's offensive military power. Believing that the British were "over-optimistic as to their chances for ultimate success," Stark doubted that having the United States provide naval assistance to the Royal Navy in the Atlantic would assure Britain's final victory over Germany; that potential triumph could be achieved only by initiating a land offensive in Europe, an option Britain could not adopt given its insufficient manpower reserves. Faced with such daunting challenges, Stark offered four basic strategic alternatives for the United States: Strict hemispheric defense;

concentrating on Japan at the expense of the Atlantic front; splitting American resources equally between the Pacific and the Atlantic; and assaulting Germany alone while remaining on the defensive against Japan. Because Stark thought that the latter of his options, "Plan Dog," offered the United States the best hope for victory, he recommended initiating immediate technical discussions with the Royal Navy, the Canadians, and the Dutch (the colonial masters of the Netherlands East Indies) "to reach agreement and to lay down plans for promoting unity of allied effort should the United States find it necessary to enter the war."[1]

Though the WPD disagreed with Stark's definition of vital national interests and doubted that the United States possessed the ability to sustain all those three goals simultaneously, it did accept that Britain's only hope for defeating Germany and Italy lay in going on the offensive. But most reluctant to commit the United States to all-out participation in such an assault, the WPD recommended limiting any national military commitment to reinforcing the Royal Navy's European blockade and to supplying resources and material so that Britain could establish a strong air offensive over the European continent and in the Mediterranean. Marshall, too, favored meetings with the British, but he wanted to ensure as well that the USN would transfer the bulk of its forces from the Pacific after an offensive in Europe got underway.[2]

Roosevelt had considerably more sympathy for Admiral Stark's proposal. Faced with increasing British requests for American arms and other supplies, on 7 November the president tentatively had floated the idea of allocating Britain half of his nation's military production, including the new B-17 Flying Fortress. And when Secretary of War Stimson reported that he could find no way around congressional limitations regarding the export of such key weapons, Roosevelt suggested letting the British "test" the planes under combat conditions. Clearly these notions were stopgap measures at best, especially because Britain's ability to pay for any American arms currently was doubtful, but Roosevelt had another suggestion for solving that problem. Speaking to Morgenthau on 17 December, the president proposed "lending" Britain arms in return for a promise that those items would be returned to the United States at war's end. A presidential press conference held later that day put the case to the American people in a fashion almost everyone could understand. Using the analogy of a household fire, Roosevelt said that if his neighbor asked to use his garden hose to douse the flames, he would not say that the neighbor could obtain the hose only after first paying for the item. Rather, Roosevelt would lend it with the understanding that "I want my garden hose back after the fire is over." When polls showed that 80 percent of Americans favored the idea, on 11 January Roosevelt had congressional Democrats introduce a bill authorizing him "to sell, transfer title to, exchange, lease, lend, or otherwise dispose of any defense article" to any nation whose defense he deemed "vital to the defense of the United States."[3]

Though the amended Lend-Lease Act passed Congress on 11 March, that "most unsordid act" as Winston Churchill so famously described it,[4] did not address the Alarger strategic problem raised by Stark; Britain's inability to quickly bring the war to a decisive and successful conclusion without direct and substantial American military intervention. But at a White House conference on 16 January 1941, Roosevelt told Stimson, Knox, Hull, Marshall, and Stark that he was committed to Britain's survival, and that not even hostile action against the United States by both Japan and

Germany would curtail the shipment of American supplies to Britain. And though the president did not formally approve Plan Dog, for the time being the United States would stand on the defensive in the Pacific while the navy prepared to convoy supplies to Britain. The army would "not be committed to any aggressive action until it was fully prepared to undertake it."[5] Thirteen days later the ABC staff talks began in Washington, and by March the discussions had produced an "extremely loose" defensive pact known as ABC-1.[6] Although the British had sought a firm American promise to base some warships at Singapore and to intervene militarily in the Pacific if Japan made trouble, having clearly stated before the talks had begun that "no specific commitments can now be made except as to technical methods of coopera-tion," the United States delegation refused to send any ships to an exposed Singapore or to guarantee it would intervene militarily if Japan attacked only British and Dutch outposts.[7] Facing the unhappy prospect that the talks might bog down over the Singapore issue, Churchill felt compelled to remind his representatives in Washington that "[o]ur object is to get the Americans into the war." Once that had happened, then the British leader was quite certain that "the proper strategic dispositions will soon emerge." The resulting hypothetical agreement pledged that a belligerent United States would endeavour to support Britain's position in the southwest Pacific, but maintained that the USN's main effort would take place in the Atlantic and Mediterranean so that the Royal Navy could shift most of its ships to Singapore. Moreover, the western Atlantic region and the Western Hemisphere as a whole, including all British possessions and forces therein, but not Canada, would come under American strategic control.[8]

Canada's initial reaction to these initiatives was most favorable; King termed the Lend-Lease program "an open challenge to Hitler" and hoped that American plans to seek eventual repayment from Britain soon would be dropped. But as Malcolm Macdonald, Britain's high commissioner in Ottawa, reported to the Dominions Office in March, such approval masked a deeper Canadian resentment that the Dominion, despite having made a significant contribution to the war from its very beginning, now felt unjustly overshadowed by a still-neutral United States. And although Macdonald agreed that this situation was "very unjust," he laid much of the fault for this situation squarely upon King's failure to properly promote Canadian activities both in Britain and the United States. Now clearly alarmed by the American propaganda effort, King seemed intent on rectifying that situation.[9]

But more than just poor publicity was troubling the Canadian war effort. Convinced that the costly financial errors of World War One—insufficient financing and poor planning that had led to chaotic production and soaring inflation—had to be avoided in the new global conflict, Canada's Department of Finance had hoped to fight and pay for the war on a "pay as you go basis" that would limit borrowing and thus prevent the economy from overheating.[10] Unfortunately, France's collapse in June 1940 and Canada's subsequent and rapid abandonment of its limited war strategy had played mayhem with such prewar designs, and as Britain ran short of funds to finance purchases, Canada, having traditionally relied on British sales to balance its persistent American trade deficit, found itself in potentially disastrous financial straits as its American purchases soared. Prohibiting the importation of products from outside the sterling bloc and slapping heavy duties on some American goods helped, but even those drastic steps saved only $70 million (U.S.) at the cost of angering the United States. Selling Canadian securities held in the United States or borrowing from American lenders were possibilities, but Canadian officials feared that adopting either or both of those options likely would have a long-term deleterious impact on Canada's postwar solvency, not to mention what might occur in the immediate future.[11]

Forced to consider abandoning the axiom that "what should be provided is what is physically possible [and that] what is physically possible, is financially possible,"[12] Keenleyside had suggested approaching the United States about the need "for the coordination and rational integration of the war industries of Canada and the United States." Warmly received by the CWC and the State Department, King and his ministers approved the idea on 20 January, but both Hickerson and Berle thought that Roosevelt first should appoint a small committee to examine Canadian-American economic integration. "Given the political dynamite in both countries inherent in any study of the possible integration of industry, however desirable, or even essential, this may be from the standpoint of efficiency," Hickerson cautioned that the proposed committee should do its work with as little publicity as possible.[13]

Lend-Lease added some new dimensions to the Canadian problem. Not only did the bill's debate push Keenleyside's notion aside, as Britain now could meet most of its military supply needs from the United States and defer costs until the war's end, it no longer had much incentive to make Canadian purchases, particularly as Britain's deficit with Canada had reached $795 million (CDN) by March. Faced with British requests for a substantial sterling overdraft (a dollar loan) if the Canadian government wished for Britain to continue buying Canadian-made products, and with federal government expenditures approaching $2.8 billion (well over half of the national income[14]), Canada's financial situation seemed dire. A desperate CWC twice sent Deputy Finance Minister W.C. Clark to Washington in March 1941 to explore the possibility of obtaining American approval for Canada's inclusion in the new Lend-Lease program. But Prime Minister King and his senior advisers, worried that the United States would seek to use Lend-Lease debts "to compel open markets or return of materials, etc.,"[15] did not want to place Canada in such an unhappy position. Rather than seeking American financial aid, they sought a provision that would allow Britain to "spend" some of its Lend-Lease dollars in Canada rather than exclusively in the United States. The Treasury Department's answer to this Canadian query was not especially pleasing. Although one of Morgenthau's aides said that he would seek the secretary's opinion, his personal view was that before the United States would allow Britain to make any Lend-Lease purchases in Canada, the Dominion would have to liquidate its American securities. Faced with Clark's considered recommendation that it would be a "mistake to ask, at present, for the application of the Lend-Lease Bill to Canada," the CWC therefore decided on 13 March to put the matter directly to Roosevelt.[16]

It was a good choice. When Clark met with Morgenthau on 18–19 March, the treasury secretary repeated that American securities held by Canadians had to be sold off first before he would consider altering Lend-Lease's rules, a not unexpected rebuff that compelled Clark to conclude unhappily that Morgenthau remained the chief obstacle to Canada getting what it wanted, and that only direct representations to Roosevelt would overcome that obstruction. Agreeing, King announced his intention to visit Washington in mid-April.[17] King suffered from no shortage of advice as he prepared for his trip. Norman Robertson wanted the Canadian prime minister to emphasize to the president at every opportunity that a wide-ranging economic deal could make many American imports from Canada very much cheaper and "prevent uneconomic and unnecessary industrial expansion" in both countries. American-born C.D. Howe, Canada's "Super Minister" of Munitions and Supply, put matters more bluntly. An engineer who had speedily amassed a sizeable fortune building grain elevators in Canada, Howe, described by Moffat as ruthless "man of substance, used to thinking in big terms," said that unless the United States chose to put more American dollars in Canadian hands, it would "be impossible to finance purchases in that country without serious disturbance to our post-war relations, which demand that we trade together on the basis of equality, and not as between debtor and creditor." W.C. Clark, not surprisingly, had the most to say. Submitting lengthy analyses of Canada's financial position, and noting that Canada's balance of payment deficit with the United States would reach $478 million by March 1942, Clark told King that as nearly half of Canada's annual military imports from the United States went to fill British orders already ($244 million from $428 million), British purchases of Canadian products through Lend-Lease would do much to solve Canada's dollar woes.[18]

Still, when King finally met with Franklin Roosevelt on 16 April, economic arrangements took a back seat to other matters. The president seemed far more interested in discussing his plans to send USN vessels on patrols and convoy duty as far as Iceland, extending American military protection to Greenland and the Azores, and using American aircraft to coordinate the running down of German U-boats and surface raiders by the Royal Navy. No doubt quite eager to hear such evidence of the deepening American involvement in the conflict, and wanting to take up financial matters in private, King refrained from bringing up the Lend-Lease issue on the first day of discussions with Roosevelt.[19] However, he showed no such hesitation the next day while meeting with renowned free trader Cordell Hull. Emphasizing that without an agreement soon a financially dependent Canada might opt for nationalist economic policies in the postwar period, King made his case for allowing Britain to purchase Canadian items via the Lend-Lease program. Hull had no objections and indeed noted that the committees suggested by Keenleyside could begin their work immediately. Morgenthau proved a harder sell. Mentioning continued congressional reluctance to extend much aid to a still-solvent Britain, the treasury secretary thought Canada would be fine financially until at least year's end, a claim King quickly disputed. But when King suggested instituting some sort of barter system between Canada and the United States, Morgenthau demonstrated some interest and therefore agreed to meet with Clark the next day to discuss the issue in more detail. That meeting also went well. Saying that Roosevelt liked the barter notion, Morgenthau proposed placing American orders in Canadian factories and shipyards.[20]

Extremely pleased with this turn of affairs, Clark produced a draft agreement for presentation to King on 20 April before the prime minister visited Roosevelt at Hyde Park. Clark's short document—seven paragraphs long—outlining Canadian industrial overcapacity and the Dominion's ability to speedily produce munitions, ships, and other vital items urgently required by the United States, committed the

United States to purchasing at least $200 million worth of Canadian goods over the next year. Moreover, as so much of Canada's defense purchases from American sources were components that went into finished goods later exported to Britain, the pact would allow Britain to use Lend-Lease credits to finance goods bought in Canada. Amended in places by King (he raised the amount to $300 million), the document accompanied the prime minister to Hyde Park. Though Roosevelt showed some initial reluctance to approve the provision that would allow the United States to lend Canadian-made goods, the president, striking out only a phrase that explicitly linked the Canadian agreement to the Lend-Lease Act, signed the document after reading the provisions to Morgenthau over the telephone.[21]

King's diary records that he "was never more surprised in his life than when [Roosevelt] accepted the statement as a whole without a word."[22] And surprised he should have been, for the Hyde Park Declaration was a stunning achievement for the Canadian prime minister and his nation. Facing possible financial ruin, Canada came away with an accord that permitted it to sell any defense item it could produce to the United States, a right no other Allied nation ever possessed. The results were easily apparent; after 1942, Canada ran trade surpluses with the United States that exceeded $1 billion (CDN) annually for the rest of the war.[23] It has been claimed that Canada would have accrued the same financial advantages without the agreement once the United States became a belligerent in December 1941, and that the pact's effective integration of the Canadian and American economies "made an independent Canadian course ever more unlikely."[24] Perhaps so, but facing financial ruin in the here and now, and possibly the onset of severe damage to his nation's war effort, King quite simply lacked the luxury in 1941 of looking to the war's eventual end, let alone to the years beyond that unknown date. Even Malcolm Macdonald, hopeful that the new ties would not weaken pro-British sentiment in Canada, cautioned Lord Cranborne that given geography, not only was it "natural and inevitable that Canada and the United States should come closer and closer together," it was "to the general advantage of the English-speaking peoples and of the world that they should do so."[25]

Far more puzzling is why Roosevelt plumped for the deal. The United States really did not need Canadian arms and munitions as its own military production had expanded quite considerably since 1939 (and would grow even more). Moreover, the president had declined to make any reciprocal demands from Canada in return for his sending substantial dollars north of the border. Cynics and Canadian nationalists might suggest that Roosevelt knew that the pact would weld Canada's economy to that of the United States at the obvious expense of the Dominion's ties to Britain, but if that was the president's motivation, it remained unspoken. Perhaps Roosevelt thought the sums involved with Canada quite paltry given that the Lend-Lease Act had appropriated $7 billion; perhaps the president worried that American investors might suffer if financial stringency forced Canadian action against foreign holdings. He may have wished as well to guarantee a secure access to Canadian resources, or perhaps he agreed with Berle's comment "that Canadian defense comes so close to our own that we have to consider Canadian needs as though they were to a considerable extent the needs of the American armed forces."[26] One might also see the Hyde Park Declaration's origins in terms of Roosevelt's largely ad hoc approach to foreign policy issues, his tendency to act without seeking either advice or serious contemplation of possible long-term consequences, and a strong attachment to the conduct of personal diplomacy.[27]

King counted on Roosevelt's attachment to personal diplomacy to solve two other Canadian concerns. First, having been firmly and repeatedly rebuffed by the Americans in attempts to have an official military observer present at the ABC talks, on 17 April King expressed to Hull the need for the Dominion to be represented at conferences where Canadian interests were involved.[28] Additionally, Britain recently had established in Washington a Joint Staff Mission (BJSM) officially charged with the task of interpreting British military thinking to the joint chiefs of staff, keeping the ABC plans up to date, and maintaining the free flow of information, planning, and intelligence between Washington and London. Unofficially, the BJSM, which would quickly grow to well over 200 officers by October 1941, sought to guide "the young, inexperienced, self-conscious and rapidly expanding" American military while simultaneously drawing "off a proportion of the aircraft, supplies and equipment" that Britain so badly needed.[29] Believing that the creation of an independent Canadian Joint Staff Mission (CJSM) charged with coordinating Canada's place in Anglo-American planning would be highly "desirable," Crerar and his fellow service chiefs formally proposed that notion to the CWC on 20 May.[30]

Despite having given the idea "general approval" in late April, reluctant to move too quickly on the matter, the CWC decided on 21 May to get Britain's opinion before taking any further action. But by 5 June King, amazed by how completely Canada's part in Allied planning seemed to have been shunted aside and forgotten by the British and Americans, made clear to Malcolm Macdonald his intention to reject any anticipated British recommendation to abandon the establishment of a CJSM in favor of simply attaching a Canadian officer to the BJSM.[31] British opinion on the matter, however, was far from unanimous. Although the Dominions Office viewed a CJSM as the logical result of Prime Minister King's "traditional desire to ensure the fullest recognition of Canada's status especially in relation to the United States," and therefore counseled against intervening in Canada's attempt to get American approval, the BJSM strongly opposed the formation of a separate Canadian mission. Not only would a new CJSM greatly complicate "the transaction of business and increase the difficulties of ensuring security," the BJSM also expressed doubts that Canada could find "officers of sufficient experience" to form a separate mission. Most importantly, believing that Canadian interests would be better served by a united imperial mission that included just one Canadian officer equal in rank to his British counterparts, the BJSM argued, perhaps not without foundation, that its current "close and friendly relations would certainly suffer if the relations between the Canadian Mission and the United States staffs did not in fact prove as close and friendly as the Prime Minister of Canada hopes."[32] But when Macdonald reported that the compromise probably would not satisfy King, the British COS decided on 14 June that Canada, "on political grounds," must be allowed to approach the Americans about the CJSM.[33]

Getting American approval for the mission proved far more difficult. When Hume Wrong spoke to Hickerson on 1 July, he learned that Welles, though "generally favourable" to the idea, thought that the matter should be handled by the War and Navy Departments. So did General Embick and Captain Hill as the proposal, in their opinions, went "considerably beyond" the PJBD's scope. But the American services, upon receiving Canada's formal request to establish a CJSM in Washington (plus an offer to allow the United States to establish its own military mission in Ottawa) on 3 July,[34] proved quite unenthusiastic. From the War Department's considered point of view, as it stubbornly continued to see Canada's ability to interact with "the world at large" restricted by its imperial ties, a CJSM not only made little sense given the existence of the PJBD and the BJSM, it would encourage the other Dominions (especially Australia and New Zealand) and some of the Latin American states to demand the same treatment, thus precluding the chance for "effective deliberation and incisive action." However, if Canada established permanent offices for its PJBD section in Washington, both the army and navy would support that step.[35] Faced with such strong opposition, and personally convinced that the American services had made a good case against allowing the Canadian mission, Hickerson told Wrong on 25 July that the State Department, although it could welcome the creation of a CJSM "from the standpoint of general policy," was "disposed to defer" to the military's judgment.[36]

Although the American opposition did not surprise Pope (he had advised his superiors to delay the mission request until after the command unity problem had been resolved[37]), Wrong took the rejection hard. Noting that Canada's service attachés rarely received invitations to important USN meetings, that the Americans normally contacted only the BJSM whenever they wanted information regarding Canada, and that Canadian attachés had little or no knowledge of the extent of Anglo-American military planning, Wrong asserted that the American authorities, especially the Navy Department, "do not appear to recognize Canada as a separate free nation within the British Empire." Unwilling to let the BJSM handle Canadian affairs, Wrong suggested creating a de facto staff mission by putting the PJBD's headquarters in Washington and then having the Canadian attachés attached to the legation cross-appointed to the board.[38]

Though the always blunt Wrong, given his charges that Leighton McCarthy, Canada's minister to the United States (Loring Christie had died early 1941) lacked regular personal contact with Hull, Welles, and the British ambassador at a time when Washington had become the world's diplomatic center, obviously had an axe to grind,[39] even King recognized that Wrong's concerns had merit. However, maintaining that any move to combine the CJSM with the PJBD "would be unsatisfactory" given that the PJBD's mandate to examine and report recommendations did not jibe with the mission's executive and command functions, the prime minister ordered under-secretary Robertson and the chiefs of staff on 31 July to study Canada's options.[40] But any doubts about the course of action vanished after King learned on 6 August that Roosevelt and Churchill already were on their way to a secret rendezvous at an isolated Newfoundland cove. Greatly displeased that he had not been invited (Liberal Senator—and renowned party bagman—Norman Lambert said that King's rage upon learning of the Roosevelt-Churchill meeting had been "unbounded"), convinced that Britain and the United States were intent on "leaving Canada completely to one side" in the war, and worried that his much prized position as an Anglo-American interpreter had been sorely compromised, King decided on two things: He would travel to Britain in late August to publicize Canada's war effort; and noting that Robertson and the Canadian military remained intent on creating the CJSM as originally envisioned regardless of the American attitude, he agreed to take the matter up with Moffat as soon as possible.[41]

Meeting with Moffat on the eve of his belated departure to Britain, King did not exactly take the American minister to task for his nation's refusal to accept the creation of the CJSM. Stating that the CJSM issue was the only "seriously troubling" matter in relations with the United States, the prime minister, urging the Americans to give as much weight to political considerations as they did to military objections, said the mission's quick approval would place relations between Canada and both Britain and America "on a sounder basis" and generate Canadian public confidence. Though King declined to say just what other considerations might be at work, Moffat told the State Department that some Canadians held the opinion "that the British in Washington had been consciously sidetracking" them and that the "cumulative effect" of perceived British and American snubs since the ABC talks was taking its toll on the Canadian psyche.[42]

But the American answer, delayed until 20 October, perhaps because the American services had hoped "to use the mission question as a *quid pro quo*" to force Canadian capitulation over unity-of-command,[43] remained the same. Although the CWC, prompted by Moffat to accept the PJBD headquarters notion, had agreed to consider a special three-officer technical delegation rather than a CJSM, the War and Navy Departments, agreeing "that foreign political considerations inimical to our military interests should not be allowed to determine" their attitudes, rejected that approach too. Only the PJBD's permanent relocation to a Washington office would be acceptable.[44]

Although Wrong thought that Canada now could either accept the American suggestion or forget completely about forming a CJSM, his superiors adhered to their original path. On 22 October, Robertson and Lester Pearson presented Moffat with the Canadian military's view "that there was a distinction between a body which made plans and a body which passed them on," but as Moffat recorded in his diary that the DEA officials "were inclined to agree with us that this distinction was theoretical," one is left to wonder just how strongly Robertson and Pearson had made the case to the American minister. Instead, claiming that Canada could not afford to have its senior military advisers serving permanently on a Washington-based PJBD, Robertson and Pearson pushed for allowing the attachés already in Washington to serve as PJBD alternates. Although Moffat thought much would depend on the quality of the officers involved, if Canada felt that its current attachés had carried inadequate weight with American and British authorities, he doubted that the new option would help matters very much. The COS disagreed, deciding on 27 October to appoint the attachés as alternate or associate PJBD members, a step tentatively approved two days later by the CWC.[45] King, however, agreeing with Moffat, thought that the PJBD's Canadian officers could be transferred to Washington, and for the first time raised the subject with Roosevelt while in Hyde Park in early November. According to King, Roosevelt agreed that Canada should "be adequately represented in Washington by appropriate Service officers." Canada's Defence Council, chaired by Ralston, broke with the prime minister. If Canada agreed to place the headquarters for its PJBD section somewhere in the American capital, then the Council thought that the attachés would have to suffice as alternate board members.[46]

But as the United States had not managed to approve even this compromise course of action when the Pacific crisis exploded on 7 December, it seemed that

Canada's ersatz staff mission might never get off the drawing board. Given Pearson's considered worry that a weak and ineffectual mission might "be worse than none at all,"[47] the Canadian legation, concerned that Canadian interests might be lost in the shuffle if a rumored Allied supreme council proved true, recommended abandoning King's weak compromise proposal in favor of a joint Commonwealth mission composed of British and individual sections from all of the Dominions. Unable to make any decision, the DEA and DND sought instead to determine the American attitude from Moffat.[48] The Americans had much bigger fish to fry. They were indeed exploring the possibility of a supreme Allied war council capable of not only directing operations and planning, but the creation and distribution of key weapons and strategic materials. And though competing visions of the proposed council produced by the State Department included American, British, Soviet, Chinese, and even Dutch participation, none of those proposals deigned to grant Canada or the other Dominions independent status or membership. When Lord Halifax pointed this out, Hull simply replied that too many participants would render the supreme council "unwieldy and ineffective."[49]

But even these tentative and limited membership formulae would not survive Winston Churchill's much anticipated arrival in the United States on 22 December for the Arcadia Conference. Although that lengthy meeting produced the broad outline of the Allied strategy with its acceptance of the dictum that Germany's defeat was the primary goal, it is perhaps best known for the creation of the combined chiefs of staff (CCS), the powerful military body that would direct the Western powers' war efforts until ultimate victory in 1945. Suggested by the British, the CCS included the three top American commanders and three high-ranking British officers to be left behind in Washington, although the CCS's tendency to hold conferences overseas usually allowed the British chiefs of staff to take a very active part in its deliberations. Most importantly, membership in the CCS excluded all but Britons and Americans so as to prevent the creation of the unwieldy multinational organization the American officials so dreaded. Even so, CCS meetings, particularly in 1942–43, very often were quite lively and fractious affairs, the British complaining that their American counterparts were "completely dumb and appallingly slow," whereas the Americans found the British patronizing and elusive, especially when an early European invasion was up for discussion.[50]

Though Canadian officials knew of the Arcadia discussions—in fact, King and the Canadian service chiefs had made a special trip south to Washington in case their opinions might be needed—not one Canadian official or officer was invited to participate in the complex and wide-ranging Anglo-American discussions. More to the point, the Canadian government was not even officially notified of the creation of the combined chiefs of staff; King learned about that body's birth in the headlines of an American newspaper.[51] Such exclusionary tactics obviously did not make for very many happy Canadians. For Norman Robertson, putting his pen to paper on 22 December, the United States's domination of the failed 1941 negotiations with Japan, the growing American hegemony in Newfoundland, the subordination of the PJBD's defense plans to the new ABC agreement, the refusal to allow the CJSM, a State Department veto against any Canadian participation in the upcoming Pan-American conference in Brazil, and an American tendency to talk only to the British about war issues all were symptomatic of the increasing aggressiveness and high-handedness demonstrated by most American officials. Although Robertson thought it should be expected that American belligerence and its leadership of the democratic cause would allow Roosevelt little time to spend on exclusively Canadian matters, that transition, in the USSEA's opinion had "been rather abrupt and not too tactfully handled" south of the border. Robertson partly blamed bureaucratic struggles as the State Department battled to gain control the nation's foreign policy against a plethora of grasping and competing departments and agencies. But the primary reason for the deteriorating relations between Canada and the United States was the sea change in the American attitude after 7 December. No longer confined to just exhorting the other powers to follow its guiding path, the United States clearly was demonstrating a new and conscious sense of its "'manifest destiny' and a corresponding disposition to take decisions and accept responsibilities."[52]

Keenleyside's 27 December memorandum pulled fewer punches. Citing a recent *Fortune* magazine poll that had found that 71 percent of Americans displayed an "unblushedly imperialist attitude" in regards to their nation's foreign policy goals, it seemed to Keenleyside that Robertson's complaints as well as the unity-of-command problem had demonstrated that Americans "were ready for Canadian 'cooperation' so long as that meant Canada would follow the American lead and subordinate the policies of Ottawa to Washington." This tendency to ignore Canada—"in startling contrast to our own punctilious care to keep the United States informed and to secure United States approval before we take any action which might affect United States policy"—could worsen dramatically if the United States and Britain set up an Allied supreme war council that included Canada only as a British empire member. Unable to say how this problem might be resolved, Keenleyside was certain of one thing: Although Canada could not risk harming the war effort, that effort would not be helped "if the authorities in Washington feel they can consider us as almost a colonial dependency."[53]

Escott Reid had some possible solutions. Unless Canada responded to the American pressure, Canada would lose its reason to exist, and although Reid thought that Canada should willingly commit national suicide if that course best served its people, he doubted that many Canadians believed that an American government had a better idea of where Canada's interests lay than a Canadian administration. Advising that there was no sense "being indignant about what the United States is doing," Reid concluded that Canadians were "being treated as children because we have refused to behave as adults" in the realm of foreign policy. Included in his prescription was the strengthening of the Washington legation (also sought by Robertson), regular contact with Hull and his principal State Department assistants, the reform of the DEA, the separation of the posts of prime minister and secretary of state for external affairs, and making "the construction of an effective collective system the main goal of our policy."[54]

Though Prime Minister King declined to act on any of these proposals (he resented the DEA's attempts to alter the legation as an usurpation of prime ministerial powers[55]), some of Reid's spirit had rubbed off on the normally conservative Canadian leader. Having already expressed his considerable displeasure to Welles before the Pearl Harbor attack about the way the United States had excluded Canada from Hull's failed negotiations with Japan,[56] King brought up the subject of the CJSM when Prime Minister Churchill visited Ottawa in late December. Noting that a Canadian mission had existed in Washington in World War One, King expressed displeasure that the Dominion was being shut out by Britain and the United States. Churchill was not very supportive. Though he said Canada should have some form of representation in Washington, Britain's leader hoped that King's government "would take a large view of the relationships of the large countries" and thus avoid any action that would cause antagonism. The surest "way to lose the war," Churchill maintained, was for every Allied nation to be represented "on all the councils and organisations which have been set up and to require that everybody is consulted before anything is done." Very anxious to "keep the United States to the fore, and avoid anything in the nature of partisanship," Churchill said "it was his responsibility to see that the Canadian government were fully informed."[57]

As it became clear that the new CCS agencies aimed to control such key sectors as munitions, shipping, and raw materials production without Canada's input or approval, Canada's new CGS, Lieutenant General Kenneth Stuart, though claiming that Canada "should not press for representation in planning unless our own interests are vitally concerned," thought that Canada had a right to know what was happening and definitely must take "a leading part" in any discussions where Canadian interests were likely to arise. As the Americans probably would continue to oppose the creation of a CJSM, Stuart revived the previously rejected idea of a Canadian contingent operating within a joint commonwealth mission.[58] Although Ralston was willing to consider this option, King, complaining that informal messages from British officials about what the CCS was doing hardly amounted to "adequate consultation," ordered the legation to determine what form the joint machinery was likely to take.[59]

Initial indications were not good. Having secured reliable information as to what the new combined agencies would be doing, Robertson reported on 28 January that Canada faced three alternatives: "Full and separate" Canadian membership on all combined boards and committees; "full and complete representation on those Boards where our interests and importance justifies such a request"; or the far more likely option given expected American opposition, accepting the status quo and dealing with issues affecting Canada as they came, perhaps by setting up an independent Canadian COS in Washington (likely to be opposed by the United States), attaching Canadian officers to the BJSM, or sending a high-ranking officer to represent the CWC. King had already opted for the third approach, having despatched Major General Maurice Pope to Washington in early 1942 in anticipation of the CJSM's creation[60] though the prime minister had not abandoned hopes that Canada might yet plant its foot in the joint machinery door. Howe had a quite different idea. Obviously concerned with turf protection, he told the CWC on 4 February that Canada should refrain from seeking spots on the Combined Raw Materials and Munitions Assignment Boards (RMB and MAB) given that Canadian resources (so far) were excluded from their mandates. In addition, Howe had ordered his senior officials to decline any invitations to sit on any combined subcommittees.[61]

Given that Roosevelt had confirmed on 26 January that the combined boards would only confer with representatives from the other Allied powers, not accept them as equal members,[62] the chance of getting Canadians any seats at any of the committee tables seemed very unlikely. However, Roosevelt, under considerable pressure from Australia to recognize its right to be represented in Allied decision-making regarding the Pacific war, finally relented on the issue of allowing Dominion missions in early February. All of the British Dominions and the Dutch government-in-exile would be permitted to establish formal joint staff missions in Washington, but although those missions would be allowed and expected to have "normal contacts" with American military authorities, the BJSM would be held responsible for evolving "a co-ordinated British Commonwealth point of view." Moreover, when the CCS discussed questions affecting the Dominions, their staff mission heads would be invited to sit in on those meetings, although the right to make any decisions would remain with the combined chiefs.[63]

This breakthrough re-energized the Canadians. On 14 February the COS, arguing that Canada was (and should be) responsible for properly equipping its forces at home and abroad, recommended seeking equal representation on the MAB. If Britain and the United States rejected that claim, then Canada should retain the right to allocate as it saw fit all Canadian-made arms regardless of where the original orders originated. Howe, however, told W.L. Batt, the RMB's American member, that though he supported Canadian participation in any fact-finding commission studying Allied raw material needs, he thought that the Americans could "appreciate our difficulty in turning over control of our raw materials to a committee formed outside Canada on which we have neither representation nor a proper channel through which to present the facts of our raw material position."[64]

Moffat received a much more detailed picture of Canadian concerns when he met with Robertson on 19 February. Stating that the problem had arisen from the natural Anglo-American inclination to keep top-level consultations as streamlined as possible, the under-secretary thought that Prime Minister Churchill, by purporting to speak for the British empire as a whole, and that the American military, by treating Canada as "a nuisance" much better handled "as a part of Britain," had made matters very much worse. And though Robertson said that the Canadian services' inability to decide "just what they wanted" had not helped very much, he had found the entire situation, especially as it pertained to the ongoing raw material problem, to be both highly "unsatisfactory" and clearly "intolerable." Struck both by the vehemence of Robertson's comments and by the fact that almost every Canadian official excepting Prime Minister King had raised the matter with him on numerous occasions, Moffat lobbied Welles to add one Canadian member to the RMB.[65]

Though Welles advised President Roosevelt to consider the proposal, Batt, having worked out his own side deal with Howe to handle Canadian matters via a separate channel not involving Britain, opposed formal RMB membership for Canada. Furthermore, by mid-March, Howe and Ralston had managed to convince the CWC that such informal arrangements with the Americans better suited Canadian interests than formal RMB membership.[66] As to whether Canada should have an official voice in the CCS itself, as it was clear that neither the United States nor Britain intended to approve any other nation's application to the combined chiefs of staff, Canada, opting instead for the right to have "full representation" before the CCS when Canadian issues were on the agenda, notified Welles on 25 March that Maurice Pope would be the CWC's official representative to the combined chiefs.[67] As Canada's official army historian has noted, this appointment put General Pope "in the peculiar position" of representing a Canadian civil authority (the CWC) to the purely military CCS.[68] But this "ingenious" solution, as Moffat so aptly described it, soon demonstrated serious drawbacks. The CWC had chosen Pope with the express purpose of emulating Field Marshal Sir John Dill's position as head of the BJSM, but the Canadian navy and air force resented an army officer representing their positions. Furthermore, on the very day the Canadian government informed Welles of Pope's appointment as its personal representative to the combined chiefs, Pope was informed by a BJSM member that the Americans were reluctant to release any command arrangement information "to diplomatic representatives."[69] Though the liaison situation soon improved, especially as General Pope proved an extraordinarily able advocate and leader for the CJSM (officially approved by the United States in July 1942), at no time did the holders of the "big battalions" ever give Canadians the "opportunity to proffer advice as to how the war should be directed," and if they had, Pope wondered "if our knowledge of the general situation and our limited experience in matters of this kind would have made us competent to give it effectively."[70]

But with the Canadian appetite for compromise apparently sated, and thanks to Hume Wrong, the Dominion now had a new weapon with which to battle for full membership on the MAB. Although Wrong worried about damaging the efficacy of the combined boards, in late January 1942 he had penned an influential memorandum centered on his growing concern that Canada, confronted by 27 Allied governments all clamoring for attention and input, might see its voice go unheeded in Washington power circles. Unwilling to see the unique Canadian viewpoint lost in a multinational jostling for position, Wrong suggested "that each member of the grand alliance should have a voice in the conduct of the war proportional to its contribution to the general war effort," and "that the influence of the various countries should be greatest in connection with those matters with which they are most directly concerned." As Canada ranked third in the alliance as a supplier of arms and munitions and stood fifth or sixth as a provider of fighting men, Wrong thought that the Dominion should "seek representation only on those combined boards with whose activities Canada is most vitally concerned."[71]

Wrong's advocacy of this so-called "Functional Principle," quite possibly "the first independently derived Canadian position in international politics,"[72] was not entirely original. Prime Minister Arthur Meighen had said much the same thing at a 1921 imperial conference when he stated that "in spheres in which any Dominion is particularly concerned that view must be given a weight commensurate with the importance of the decision to that Dominion."[73] But Wrong's 1942 restatement was certainly the right thing spoken at the right time, although Wrong worried that the Canadian government, given its adoption of "a semi-colonial position" prior to December 1941, had waited too long to make its case for a stronger voice in Allied strategy formulation.[74]

Wrong may have been correct, but King's government, having awoken from its semi-colonial slumber, set its sights on gaining membership on the MAB. Canada thought it had a good case. Canadian munitions output, although only 5 percent of the Anglo-American total, was nearly five times larger than the contributions made by the other Dominions and India combined.[75] After some dithering as to whether Canada would seek a seat on the London or Washington MAB council, by April the CWC had decided upon the American-based branch and then set out to convince the Americans to let Canada join. The petition surprised few in Washington with any real interest in Canadian affairs. The Coordinator of Information (the precursor to the Office of Strategic Services) had warned in late March that Canadian-American relations, given Canadian displeasure about the treatment meted out to the Dominion since December 1941 and an American propensity to overlook the Canadian war effort, threatened to become "less cordial than they have been." Moffat thought that much of that anger had subsided, but as he made perfectly clear to Welles, because Canada was the only one of the three exporting Allies without any say in munitions policy, the Dominion was most anxious to get an MAB seat, especially if the war effort demanded that Canadian industry had to be transformed so that the other Allies could be supplied with military materials.[76]

So anxious were the Canadians that Prime Minister King himself intended to bring the matter directly to Roosevelt's attention when he arrived in Washington on 15 April to attend a meeting of the fledgling Pacific War Council (PWC). Convinced that an invitation to stay overnight at the White House reflected his growing status as a spokesperson for the other self-governing Dominions,[77] King found his room to maneuver in Washington severely limited by the presence of H.V. Evatt, Australia's external affairs minister. Having just visited Ottawa on a quest to get Canadian troops for Australia's defense, a pilgrimage brought on by an ill-considered offer of aid by Canada's high commissioner in Canberra, Evatt had also sought Canadian support for an Australian place at the MAB's table. Though King had not promised Australia any troops and would anger Evatt further by declining to give a definite answer until late April, Evatt came to the 15 April PWC meeting convinced that Canada not only would be sending help down under, but that King happily would support Australia's bid for MAB membership.[78] That did not happen. Though Evatt pushed for a Canadian place on the MAB, King told the PWC that even though a Canadian seat was desirable, Canada "would not wish this representation on the score of being there to protect the interests of any particular part of the Empire."[79]

Having thus squandered his one good chance to placate the Australians, King pushed Canada's position concerning the MAB in a private chat on 16 April with Roosevelt. Though King thought that the MAB would function best with dual boards sitting in both London and Washington, he told the president that Canada required a membership only on the Washington-based entity. And though Roosevelt apparently could not tell King the names of the officials assigned to the board excepting Harry Hopkins, he would tell Hopkins that he felt that Canada should be allowed to have a representative sitting on the Washington board.[80] Yet when Leighton McCarthy asked the State Department on 13 May if there had been progress, the American answer stunned the Canadian minister. Contrary to the impression received by King, Hopkins said the president felt certain that "he had not made any definite commitment that Canada would become a full member of the Board." Still, Hopkins said he was working hard on a scheme that would allow for Canadian participation in the MAB's work, although he declined to outline what he had in mind to McCarthy.[81] Though Roosevelt subsequently explained to McCarthy simply that he had forgotten to inform Hopkins about his conversation with Prime Minister King, Brigadier General Henry

S. Aurand told Pope that while the American military had no problem with Canadian membership, that the difficulties existed on the political level. If Canada did not press the matter for a day or two, Aurand counseled Pope that "everything would work out satisfactorily."[82]

But the matter failed to work out satisfactorily, at least from Canada' point of view. Canada waited in vain for Hopkins's answer, and when King, at another PWC meeting on 25 June, finally got an explanation from the influential man once referred to as "Roosevelt's own, personal Foreign Office,"[83] it was not to the prime minister's liking. Hopkins firmly opposed Canadian membership on the MAB for fear of setting a precedent and because he did not want to risk having the United States outvoted by Canada and Britain. If Canada had dealings with the MAB, then Hopkins favored allowing its representatives opportunity to meet with MAB officials when needed.[84] Finding that answer completely unacceptable, the CWC ordered McCarthy again to see Hopkins, and if necessary, Secretary Hull, Welles, and even President Roosevelt, to protest Canada's "undue subordination" and the transfer of Canada's entire military production over to the United States without a proper Canadian voice in the decision.[85]

Though Berle and Hickerson thought that Canada had a good case, the State Department had not been consulted about the MAB controversy, and when the MAB convened on 10 July, Hopkins made it clear that granting full membership to Canada would encourage Australia, New Zealand, and China to seek similar status, thus rendering the board unwieldy. Lieutenant General Gordon MacReady, head of the British Army Staff Mission, offered a possible compromise; Canada could be given membership, but the Canadian representative would have a voice only in decisions regarding Canadian production. With Hopkins's approval, Major General James H. Burns of the MAB made this proposal to the Canadians on 8 August.[86] The Burns proposal prompted a mixed response. Pope thought that the compromise was a good one given that the United States had conceded almost all of Canada's original points except that the Dominion would have no voice in determining how production bids for other nations were handled. Howe, however, was opposed. If Canada accepted the Burns compromise, Howe charged it would surrender control of domestic production to the United States, thus leaving his ministry unable to guarantee its ability to equip Canadian forces. Unable to decide, the CWC chose instead on 19 August to defer the matter until it could be determined just how dependent Canada's military had become on American sources of supply. Not until 16 September did the CWC act. Arguing that the Burns compromise did not meet Canadian needs, the CWC instructed Pope to tell the Americans that Canada would stick with the informal munitions pooling procedures currently in operation. Canada, however, wanted full membership in the Combined Production and Resources Board (CPRB).[87]

Canada got its seat on the CPRB in November 1942 and later the Combined Food Board, but as those agencies were relatively unimportant, one cannot escape concluding that Canada's attempt to gain a real voice in Allied strategy-making had failed miserably. Pope and the CJSM, however well they might have performed, were no substitute for a real Canadian say in the combined chiefs, though it is hard to argue with Pope's conclusion that Canada did not possess enough battalions to gain access to the CCS, especially when neither the Soviet Union nor China managed to gain membership either to that exclusive Anglo-American cabal. But the surrender on the

MAB issue when Canada had received nearly all that it had asked for is less easy to accept. Pope blamed that defeat on Howe's refusal to allow any change to the cozy relationship he had with the Americans, a charge supported by Wrong.[88] Moffat had a more picturesque analogy. Likening the entire process to watching a Roman legion march up a hill, only to see that formation turn on its heels to go back down before it had reached the summit, Moffat thought the result had been a "general realization here that Canada's role in asking for something and then declining it, when to a large degree it was offered, has not been particularly heroic."[89] Perhaps had King pushed Roosevelt harder to accept or at least acknowledge the Canadian position, the results might have more closely resembled those the prime minister had gained at Hyde Park in April 1941. But because King, in the opinion of Australian politician Robert Menzies, was "no war leader" as well as "a politician who possibly prefers to lead from behind,"[90] he obviously had not wished to risk his special relationship with the president over the MAB. Caution, not heroism, always was King's watchword.

NOTES

1. Stark to Knox, 12 November 1940, FDRL, Roosevelt PSF, file Navy Department: Plan Dog.

2. Colonel Jonathan W. Anderson to Marshall, "National Policy of the United States," 13 November 1940, NARA, RG165, Entry 281, file WPD 4175–15; Marshall to Stark, "Tentative Draft, Navy Basic War Plan—Rainbow No. 3," 29 November 1940, in Bland, *The Papers of George Catlett Marshall, Volume 2*, 360–61; and Marshall to Stark, "Joint Basic War Plans, Rainbow Nos. 3 and 5," 2 December 1940, Ibid., 362.

3. Dallek, *Franklin D. Roosevelt and American Foreign Policy*, 252-58.

4. Lend-Lease's origins are discussed in Warren Kimball, *"The Most Unsordid Act" Lend-Lease, 1939–1941* (Baltimore: The Johns Hopkins University Press, 1969).

5. Marshall to Gerow, "White House Conference of Thursday, January 16, 1941," 17 January 1941, NARA, RG165, Entry 281, file WPD 4175–18.

6. W. David McIntyre, *The Rise and Fall of the Singapore Naval Base, 1919–1942* (London: Macmillan, 1979), 182.

7. "Statement by the Chief of Naval Operations and the Chief of Staff," 27 January 1941, NARA, RG165, Entry 281, file WPD 4202–1; Embick, Miles, Gerow, and McNarney to Marshall, "Dispatch of United States Forces to Singapore," 12 February 1941, Ibid; and Halifax to the Four Dominion High Commissioners, 14 February 1941, PRO, FO371/27887.

8. Churchill minute, 17 February 1941, PRO, Admiralty Records, ADM116/4877; and ABC-1 report, "United States–British Staff Conversations," 27 March 1941, PRO, CAB122/1582.

9. King diary, 6 January 1941, NAC; and Malcolm Macdonald to Dominions Office, March 1941, PRO, Prime Minister's Papers, PREM4/44/10.

10. Paul Marsden, "The Costs of No Commitments: Canadian Economic Planning for War," in Hillmer et al., *A Country of Limitations*, 199–200.

11. J.L. Granatstein, "Free Trade between Canada and the United States: The Issue That Will Not Go Away," in Denis Stairs and Gilbert R. Winham, eds., *The Politics of Canada's Relationship with the United States* (Toronto: University of Toronto Press, 1985), 34–35.

12. Skelton to King, "Re Defence Expenditures," 11 October 1940, NAC, King Memoranda and Notes, reel H1483, C173453–54.

13. Keenleyside, "The Integration of War Industry in Canada and the United States," 27 December 1940, NAC, King Memoranda and Notes, reel H1525, C240057–61; CWC minutes, 20 January 1941, NAC, RG2 7c; Berle to Welles, 7 January 1941, NARA, RG59, Decimal File 1940–44, 842.20 Defense/82; and Hickerson to Berle, 13 January 1941, Ibid.

14. J.L. Granatstein and R.D. Cuff, "The Hyde Park Declaration 1941: Origins and Significance," *Canadian Historical Review*, 55 (March 1974), 62. King thought that government expenditures could hit 65 percent of national income; King diary, 13 March 1941, NAC.

15. King diary, 13 March 1941, NAC.

16. Cochran to Morgenthau, 4 March 1941, FDRL, Morgenthau Diary, book 378, reel 104; and CWC minutes, 13 March 1941, NAC, RG2 7c, vol. 3.

17. W.C. Clark, "Report on Visit to Washington, March 17–21," 21 March 1941, in Murray, *DCER, Volume 8*, 295–303; and CWC minutes, 21 March 1941, NAC, RG2 7c, vol. 3.

18. Robertson to King, "Recent Trends in Economic Relations between Canada and the United States," 7 April 1941, NAC, King Memoranda and Notes, reel H1562, C287996–288005; C.D. Howe to King, 8 April 1941, Ibid., C288010–12; and W.C. Clark to King, 9 April 1941, Ibid., C288013–33. Moffat also described Howe as ambitious "more for the privilege of exercising power, than for honors or emoluments," and a ruthless but not "faultless administrator" who had accelerated Canada's war output tremendously while perhaps spreading the Dominion's industrial capacity too thin. "In many respects the ablest man in the Canadian government," though his "growing" dictatorial tendency stood him well in running his massive ministry, Howe's political inexperience proved "a liability in his relations" with the Canadian cabinet; Moffat to Hull, no. 1117, 26 February 1941, NARA, RG59, Decimal File 1940–44, 842.002/107. Howe's life is explored in Robert Bothwell and William Kilbourn, *C.D. Howe: A Biography* (Toronto: McClelland and Stewart, 1979).

19. King diary, 16 April 1941, NAC. For Roosevelt's deepening interest in the battle of the Atlantic, see Waldo Heinrichs, *Threshold of War: Franklin D. Roosevelt & American Entry into World War II* (New York: Oxford University Press, 1988).

20. King diary, 17 April 1941, NAC; and J.E. Coyne, "Memorandum of Meeting with Morgenthau, April 18, 1941," 18 April 1941, in Murray, *DCER, Volume 8*, 321–23.

21. Hyde Park Agreement text in King to Cranborne, no. 62, NAC, RG25, vol. 781, file 394; and King diary, 20 April 1941, NAC.

22. Ibid.

23. Bothwell, *Canada and the United States*, 20.

24. Granatstein and Cuff, "The Hyde Park Declaration," 75; and Granatstein, "Free Trade between Canada and the United States," 35.

25. Macdonald to Cranborne, 29 April 1941, Durham University Archives [DUA], Durham, Malcolm Macdonald Papers, file 14/4/2–5.

26. Granatstein and Cuff, "The Hyde Park Declaration," 77; and Berle to Hull, 28 February 1941, NARA, RG59, Decimal File 1940–44, 842.20 Defense/71. Ironically, Berle was "very much upset" that Roosevelt had agreed to the Hyde Park Declaration without taking into account Berle's ongoing discussions with Keenleyside about a joint economic committee to oversee industrial integration; Kasurak, "The United States Legation at Ottawa, 1927–1941," 220.

27. Kimball, *The Juggler*, 5; and Cecil V. Crabb, Jr., and Kevin V. Mulcahy, *Presidents and Foreign Policy Making: From FDR to Reagan* (Baton Rouge: Louisiana State University Press, 1986), 93–94.

28. The CWC had decided on 20 January to send a naval officer to the ABC talks, but like his counterparts from Australia and New Zealand, he was denied official status by the American services; they preferred to deal with the British services alone. The British had to brief

the Dominions about the discussions; CWC minutes, 20 January 1941, NAC, RG2 7c, vol. 3; and Dziuban, *Military Cooperation between the United States and Canada*, 57.

29. "Chiefs of Staff Directive to the Joint Staff Mission in Washington," COS (41) 312 (Final), 19 May 1941, PRO, CAB80/28; and Alex Danchev, *Very Special Relationship: Field-Marshal Sir John Dill and the Anglo-American Alliance 1941–44* (London: Brassey's Defence Publishers, 1986), 19–20.

30. COS minutes, 12 and 20 May 1941, NAC, RG24, vol. 8081, file NSS 1272–2; COS to the Ministers, 20 May 1941, NAC, RG2 7c, vol. 4.

31. CWC minutes, 23 April and 21 May 1941, NAC, RG2 7c, vol. 4; King diary, 5 June 1941, NAC; and King to Macdonald, 6 June 1941, Ibid.

32. Dominions Office minutes, 9 and 14 June 1941, PRO, DO35/1010, file WG 476/4/6; and BJSM to COS, GLEAM no. 62, 5 June 1941, Ibid.

33. Macdonald to Dominions Office, no. 893, 13 June 1941; and COS (41) 212th meeting minutes, 14 June 1941, PRO, Chiefs of Staff Committee Records, Minutes, CAB79/12.

34. Wrong to SSEA, no. 1917, 3 July 1941, NAC, RG25, vol. 2902, file 2341–40C; Hickerson to Welles, 2 July 1941, NARA, RG59, Decimal File 1940–44, 842.20/192; Welles to Stimson and Knox, 3 July 1941, Ibid.; and Canadian Legation to the Department of State, 3 July 1941, NARA, RG59, Decimal File 1940–44, 842.20/192.

35. MID, "Canada Estimate of the Political Situation," 23 June 1941, NARA, RG165, MID Regional File 1922–44, file 3000; Gerow to Marshall, "Proposed Establishment of Canadian Military Mission in Washington," 17 July 1941, NARA, RG165, Entry 281, file WPD 4543–1; and Knox to Hull, 21 July 1941, NARA, RG59, Decimal File 1940–44, 842.20/196.

36. Hickerson memorandum of conversation with Wrong, 25 July 1941, NARA, Decimal File 1940–44, 842.20/198; and Canadian Minister Leighton McCarthy to SSEA, no. 308, 25 July 1941, NAC, J.L. Ralston Papers, vol. 39, file Canadian Army Mission (Gen).

37. Pope to Crerar, 30 June 1941, NAC, RG25, vol. 2902, file 2341–40C.

38. Wrong, "Future Communications between Canada and the U.S.A. on Defence Matters," 26 July 1941, Ibid.

39. Wrong, "Notes on Some Legation Problems," 15 August 1941, NAC, RG25, vol. 2961, file 56. Ironically, McCarthy had asked for Wrong to replace Escott Reid because he thought Reid to be too left wing in his sympathies. The elderly McCarthy had been selected for Washington because of his long-standing relationship with Roosevelt, begun when McCarthy's son sought relief from his own battle with polio at Warm Springs. McCarthy stayed in Washington, and Wrong was posted back to Ottawa; John English, *Shadow of Heaven: The Life of Lester Pearson. Volume One: 1897–1948* (Toronto: Lester & Orpen Dennys, 1989), 249–50.

40. CWC minutes, 31 July 1941, NAC, RG2 7c, vol. 5.

41. King diary, 7 August 1941, NAC; "Record of Meeting of Chiefs of Staff with Under-Secretary of State for External Affairs," 11 August 1941, DHH, Kardex file 193.009 (D3); and CWC minutes, 13 August 1941, NAC, RG2 7c, vol. 5. Lambert also said that King was so worried about the blow to his linchpin reputation that he overcame a serious fear of flying to make the trip to Britain; Dexter memorandum, 16 September 1941, QUA, Dexter Papers, box 2, file 20.

42. Moffat to Hull and Welles, no. 218, 18 August 1941, NARA, RG59, Decimal File 1940–44, 842.20/197; and Moffat to Hickerson, 5 September 1941, Ibid., 842.20/203.

43. Dziuban, *Military Cooperation between the United States and Canada*, 74.

44. Moffat memorandum of conversation with Keenleyside, 29 August 1941, HL, Moffat Papers, MS Am 1407, vol. 47; CWC minutes, 2 September 1941, NAC, RG2 7c, vol. 5; Stimson to Hull, 8 October 1941, NARA, RG59, Decimal File 1940–44, 842.20/201; and

United States Legation to the DEA, 20 October 1941, NAC, RG2 7c, vol. 5.

45. Wrong, "Canadian Military Mission," 14 October 1941, NAC, RG25, vol. 2902, file 2341–40C; Moffat memorandum of conversation with Robertson, 22 October 1941, HL, Moffat Papers, MS Am 1407, vol. 47; Lester Pearson to King, 28 October 1941, NAC, RG2 7c, vol. 5; and CWC minutes, 29 October 1941, Ibid.

46. Wrong memorandum, 5 November 1941, NAC, RG25, vol. 2902, file 2341–40C; CWC minutes, 6 November 1941, NAC, RG2 7c, vol. 6; and Defence Council minutes, 28 November 1941, DHH, Kardex file 112.1 (D80).

47. Pearson to Robertson, "Canadian Military Mission, Washington," 8 December 1941, NAC, RG25, vol. 2902, file 2341–40C.

48. McCarthy to SSEA, no. 567, 11 December 1941, Ibid.; record of DEA-DND discussion, "Canadian Military Mission in Washington," 12 December 1941, Ibid.; and Robertson to Moffat, 13 December 1941, NAC, RG24, vol. 2687, file HQS 5199.

49. Berle to Hull, 16 December 1941, FDRL, Berle Papers, box 213, Diary December 12–31 1941; Carlton Savage to Hull, 17 December 1941, LC, Hull Papers, box 87, file Supreme War Council; and John Allan English, "Not an Equilateral Triangle: Canada's Strategic Relationship with the United States and Great Britain, 1939–1945," in McKercher and Aronsen, eds., *The North Atlantic Triangle in a Changing World*, 168.

50. Richard Overy, *Why the Allies Won* (London: Pimlico, 1995), 250.

51. Stacey, *Canada and the Age of Conflict, Volume 2*, 327.

52. Robertson to King, 22 December 1941, in John F. Hilliker, ed., *Documents on Canadian External Relations. Volume 9: 1942–1943* (Ottawa: Department of External Affairs, 1980), 1125–31.

53. Keenleyside, "Recent Trends in United States–Canada Relations," 27 December 1941, NAC, RG25, vol. 5758, file 71 (s).

54. Reid, "The United States and Canada. Domination, Cooperation, Absorption," 12 January 1942, NAC, Reid Papers, vol. 13, file US and Canada.

55. King diary, 28 December 1941, NAC.

56. Welles memorandum of conversation with Wrong, 25 November 1941, FDRL, Welles Papers, box 161, file Canada. Moffat said that although other Allied representatives constantly sought information from the State Department, McCarthy "never appeared there at all"; Keenleyside to Robertson, "Representation in Washington," 13 March 1942, NAC, RG25, vol. 5699, file 4–AH (s).

57. King diary, 29 December 1941, NAC; and CWC minutes, 29 December 1941, NAC, RG2 7c, vol. 6.

58. Stuart draft memorandum, 12 January 1942, NAC, RG24, vol. 2687, file HQS 5199.

59. CWC minutes, 14 January 1942, NAC, RG2 7c, vol. 8; King to McCarthy, no. 30, 14 January 1942, NAC, King Correspondence, vol. 327, reel C6808, 278334–35.

60. Robertson to King, "United States–United Kingdom Combined War Boards," 28 January 1942, NAC, King Memoranda and Notes, reel H1531, C243537–44. Pope's formal instructions were issued in March. Retaining his place on the PJBD, Pope was to be the CWC's personal representative in Washington, charged with maintaining continuous contact with the CCS and presenting the Canadian point of view to that body; King to McCarthy, 24 March 1942, Ibid., 278443–44.

61. CWC minutes, 4 February 1942, NAC, RG2 7c, vol. 8.

62. Roosevelt to Churchill, 26 January 1942, FDRL, Roosevelt Map Room Files [MRF], file FDR-Churchill Jan–Feb 1942.

63. Stark and Marshall to Roosevelt, 4 February 1942, FDRL, Roosevelt PSF, file American-British Chiefs of Staff. Roosevelt and Churchill formally approved the measure on 10 February. Australia's effort is described in D.M. Horner, *High Command: Australia & Allied*

Strategy 1939–1945 (Sydney: George Allen & Unwin, 1982).

64. COS to the Ministers, 14 February 1942, DHH, Kardex file 112.1 (D82); and Howe to W.L. Batt, 10 February 1942, FDRL, Roosevelt OF, file OF4752.

65. Moffat memoranda of conversations with Robertson and Welles, 19 February and 3 March 1942, HL, Moffat Papers, MS Am 1407, vol. 47.

66. Welles to Roosevelt, 3 March 1942, FDRL, Welles Papers, box 81, file MO; Batt to Roosevelt, 18 March 1942, FDRL, Roosevelt OF, file OF4752; and CWC minutes, 11 March 1942, NAC, RG2 7c, vol. 8.

67. McCarthy to Welles, no. 203, 25 March 1942, NARA, RG59, Decimal File 1940–44, 842.01BLL/53.

68. Stacey, *Arms, Men and Governments*, 165.

69. Moffat memorandum of conversation with Robertson, 31 March 1942, HL, Moffat Papers, MS Am 1407, vol. 47; and Pope diary, 25 March 1942, NAC, Maurice Pope Papers, vol. 1.

70. Pope, *Soldiers and Politicians*, 175.

71. Wrong to Robertson, 20 January 1942, NAC, RG25, file 3265–A–40. Wrong's concern about the efficacy of the combined boards is explored in Wrong, "Canada, the United Nations, and the Combined Boards," 8 August 1942, NAC, Wrong Papers, vol. 4, file 20.

72. J.L. Granatstein, *Mackenzie King: His Life and His World* (Toronto: McGraw-Hill Ryerson 1977), 185.

73. C.P. Stacey, *Canada and the Age of Conflict: A History of Canadian External Relations. Volume 1: 1867–1921* (Toronto: University of Toronto Press, 1977), 339. See also A.J. Miller, "The Functional Principle in Canada's External Relations," *International Journal*, 35 (Spring 1980), 309–28.

74. Wrong to Pearson, 3 February 1942, NAC, RG25, file 3265–A–40.

75. Stacey, *Arms, Men and Governments*, 167.

76. British Empire Section, Coordinator of Information, "Changing Canadian-American Relations," 5 March 1942, NARA, RG59, Decimal File 1940–44, 711.42/241; Moffat to Welles, 1 April 1942, FDRL, Welles Papers, box 81, file MO; and Moffat, "Notes of Visit to Washington, April 4–11, 1942," 13 April 1942, HL, Moffat Papers, MS Am 1407, vol. 47.

77. King diary, 9 April 1942, NAC.

78. H.V. Evatt to Prime Minister John Curtin, 14 April 1942, AA, Frederick Shedden Papers, Series A5954/1, Item 581/16. Major High Commissioner General Victor Odlum had rashly promised aid to Australia. This sad story's impact on Canadian-Australian relations is explored in R.G. Haycock, "The 'Myth' of Imperial Defence: Australian-Canadian Bilateral Military Co-operation, 1942," *War & Society*, 2 (May 1984), 65–84; and Galen Roger Perras, "'The parties with whom we have been estranged so long can scarcely be brought into a close relationship at a moment's notice:' Canada's Failure to Provide Military Aid to Australia, 1942–1945," paper presented at the annual meeting of the Australian Studies Association of North America, Vancouver, 7–9 March 1996.

79. PWC minutes, 15 April 1942, FDRL, Roosevelt MRF, file Naval Aide's Files Pacific War Council April–August 1942; and King memorandum, 15 April 1942, NAC, King Diaries.

80. King diary, 16 April 1942, NAC.

81. McCarthy to Hull, no. 317, 13 May 1942, NAC, King Correspondence, reel C6808, 278567–72; and Pearson to Robertson, "Munitions Assignment Board," 29 May 1942, NAC, King Memoranda and Notes, reel H1531, C243554.

82. Pearson to Robertson, 1 June 1942, Ibid., C243557.

83. Robert E. Sherwood, *Roosevelt and Hopkins: An Intimate History* (New York: Harper & Brothers, 1948), 202.

84. King diary, 25 June 1942, NAC; Moffat memorandum of conversation with Robertson, 26 June 1942, NARA, RG59, Matthews-Hickerson File, reel 2; and CWC minutes, 26 June 1942, NAC, RG2 7c, vol. 9.

85. King to McCarthy, no. EX1402, 2 July 1942, NAC, King Correspondence, reel C6808, 278711–17.

86. Hickerson to Berle and Hull, 16 July 1942, NARA, RG59, Matthews-Hickerson File, reel 2; Berle to Hull, 17 July 1942, FDRL, Berle Papers, box 58, file Hull, Cordell Jan–Aug 1942 Memoranda to; McCarthy to SSEA, no. WA–1680, 11 July 1942, NAC, King Correspondence, reel C6808, 278739–40; and Stacey, *Arms, Men and Governments*, 169.

87. CWC minutes, 19 August and 16 September 1942, NAC, RG2 7c, vol. 10.

88. Pope, *Soldiers and Politicians*, 201–2; and Wrong to King, 4 September 1942, NAC, King Memoranda and Notes, reel H1532, C243627.

89. Moffat memorandum of conversation with Keenleyside, 18 September 1942, NARA, RG59, Matthews-Hickerson File, reel 2.

90. Robert Menzies diary, 8 May 1941, in A.W. Martin and Patsy Hardy, eds., *Dark and Hurrying Days: Menzies' 1941 Diary* (Canberra: National Library of Australia, 1993), 124.

Chapter 5

Terribly Serious About the Wrong Things: Roosevelt and the Decline of American Interest in Canada, 1942–1945

In 1974 Canadian historian J.L. Granatstein commented that the linking of Canada's economy to the United States during World War Two "might have been marginally acceptable to Canada if there had been an accretion of influence in Washington to offset it, but if such an intangible as influence can be measured, after mid-1941 there was probably an absolute decline."[1] Granatstein was correct. Canada's influence in the United States, never substantial, had declined dramatically after 1941; perhaps far more importantly though, American interest in the Dominion had fallen even more precipitously. Though Moffat warned in February 1942 that the American military's desire to keep "Canada outside their counsels is going to cost us dear for decades," and the American consul in Winnipeg cautioned that many Canadians believed that the United States had formulated secret plans to occupy much of northern Canada,[2] few Washington decision-makers heeded such concerns. Hickerson dismissed allegations of an American conspiracy to control Canada as "saddening," and though the State Department's veteran Canadianist expected to witness the rise of "some degree" of anti-Americanism occurring in Canada at war's end, in May 1943 he definitely thought that his nation's relations with Canada were "excellent."[3]

Senior American officers heartily agreed with this assessment, although few were inclined to ponder Canada's strategic future even when prompted. In July 1942 Assistant Secretary of War John McCloy had distributed within the War Department an anonymously written memorandum that argued that because they had "devoted too little thought to our Northern neighbor," Americans had not recognized the existence of a "*Canadian mind*." Postulating that this continued American failure to cultivate

Canada's military leadership might result in even tighter Anglo-Canadian political and military relations, the document proposed immediate close cooperation with Canada so as to "condition [Canadian] minds for future understanding of our mutual community of interest."[4] But the document was not well received by much of the War Department. Embick criticized the memorandum's failure to comprehend the nature of the PJBD's work, whereas other officers pointed out that the document's definition of the so-called "Canadian mind" resembled only Canadian Tory imperialist opinion at the considerable expense of quite different views held by western Canadians (sympathetic to the United States) and Quebeckers (self-centered and provincial). Major General Thomas Handy's impression, like that of Hickerson's, was that "our relations with Canada are and have been pretty good."[5]

Although McCloy's document abjectly failed to alter the complacency of a War Department preoccupied by the more pressing demands of the bitter struggle in the Pacific, the North Africa campaign, and an anticipated invasion of Europe perhaps as early as 1943, its demand for the recognition of Canada's future strategic value did not go unheeded in some circles. By 1942 Adolf Berle, President Roosevelt's point man for the contentious postwar civilian aviation negotiations, had concluded that in the postwar period both commercial and military air power would "have a greater influence on American foreign interests and American foreign policy than any other non-political consideration."[6] Having told Congress in February 1943 that the vast American expenditures on airfields outside the United States, "to the extent that they have permanent utility represent an item of equity which can and should be urged in the ensuing negotiation" for the postwar use of such facilities,[7] and regarding Canada as "a first line territory in case of any air attack on this hemisphere from Europe or Asia," in January 1944 Berle proposed to make permanent existing American rights to use Canadian military bases.[8]

Canada had different ideas about this subject. Canadian officials initially had been slow to acknowledge American activities in their nation's northwest. When the PJBD had recommended the creation of a Northwest Staging Route in late 1940 to facilitate the transfer of aircraft and supplies to Alaska, the King government had quickly agreed. Canadian support for an Alaskan highway was even forthcoming, albeit somewhat reluctantly. When Hull raised the matter again in April 1941, King, arguing that the staging route superseded a road at this time, held out little "hope for immediate cooperation."[9] And although Germany's surprise June 1941 invasion of the Soviet Union compelled both American services to view an Alaskan road as "valuable in a long term defense program," they had no immediate strategic need for the route.[10] But by 11 January 1942, believing that conditions now justified active support for an Alaskan overland route, Gerow suggested studying the project's feasibility. Five days later President Roosevelt asked Ickes, Knox, and Stimson to "agree on the necessity for a road and a proper route." Although some officers objected to expending considerable effort and money on a road that likely would not be operational before 1944, the WPD had decided that an Alaskan highway was worthwhile. Despite Admiral Ernest King's protest that the American navy could adequately safeguard sea communications to Alaska, on 11 February Roosevelt sanctioned the immediate construction of the Alaskan road.[11]

Though the Canadian chiefs of staff doubted that an Alaskan route would directly influence the war's outcome, the CWC was willing to allow the survey team to do its job as long as the United States understood that surveying northwest Canada did not imply Canadian acceptance of the need for the road's construction. However, when the State Department reassured the Canadian government that permitting the survey to go ahead did not constitute approval of the road itself, the Canadians agreed to transfer the highway matter from the contentious political sphere to the PJBD's purview.[12] In late February, having determined that an inland highway route would provide an important alternate avenue should sea communications be disrupted and might "be of great value in the event of an offensive against Japan projected from Alaska," the PJBD recommended construction. On 5 March the Canadian government acceded, and the first American workers began to arrive in northwest Canada by month's end.[13]

Canada's acceptance of an American-built highway on its soil in early 1942 after expending so much effort in the 1930s to prevent just such a thing was surprising and might be explained away by King's refusal in 1942 to guarantee that the American military would have postwar access to the highway; instead, the prime minister and his government agreed only to "give due consideration" to any proposal the PJBD might put forward.[14] Far more astounding is that Canada did so little to monitor the scale of American activities in northwest Canada, an effort that involved 33,000 personnel by June 1943. One might blame this stunning omission on the Canadian government's preoccupation with the far more pressing demands of the brutal war with Germany, but for western Canadians, especially those living in the remote and sparsely populated northwest portion, such neglect was nothing new; in early 1942 for example, British Columbia newspapers had spouted bitter accusations that the far-off federal government in Ottawa was content to leave the nation's exposed West Coast to Japan's not-so-tender mercies.[15] Malcolm Macdonald did much to end that neglect in the spring of 1943. Having recently toured Canada's northwest and then Alaska, he had found the situation there "alarming." Maintaining that King and his ministers were exercising far too little influence upon the "colossal" American projects on Canadian soil, Macdonald worried that the powerful American army was operating in northwest Canada without proper control or direction from the Canadian government or the State Department. Regardless of whether the various projects would benefit Canada—and Macdonald felt certain that the many enterprises were promoting development in an isolated and underdeveloped portion of the country—the high commissioner feared that those projects were being built solely with American needs and goals in mind. Concerned that Congress would seek to extract guarantees from Canada in return for such a massive economic investment, Macdonald wanted King to appoint a special commissioner to safeguard Canada's interests in the region.[16]

To Vincent Massey in London, the report revealed a "disturbing picture of American encroachment" carried out by the War Department's "Army of occupation," a popular turn of phrase among Canadian nationalists and historians.[17] Lester Pearson, by now a minister-counsellor at the Washington legation, had warned that American officials tended "to consider us not as a foreign nation at all, but one of themselves." Though "flattering" and sometimes quite helpful, that tendency often led the United

States to make casual demands of Canada that no American would "dream of showing towards Brazil or any other Latin American State." Escott Reid put the case more strongly. Too long accustomed to thinking "of foreign policy as being concerned with relations with Europe, the Far East or Latin America," Canadians and Americans had to begin to see each other once again as peoples from separate nations. Arguing that war had not integrated the two economies but only fostered "the growth of habits and institutions for the cooperative solution of common problems," Reid declared that the United States government might expect Canada "at least" to grant American military access to the Alaska highway and the airfields in northwest Canada, if not outright belligerency, in a future Soviet-American conflict.[18]

Modern devotees of the peripheral dependence school of Canadian foreign policy history, a viewpoint that gives "critical emphasis to Canada's lack of domestic socio-economic and external political independence from the United States and the world centered upon it,"[19] have tended to see Canada's military cooperation with the Americans as the logical culmination of the "continentalist" policies of King and a Department of External Affairs devoid of even "an ounce" of anti-Americanism, or have castigated King for failing to appreciate that the grasping United States was no less imperialist than Europe's competing powers.[20] Always cautious in his many dealings with Americans, King worried that permitting the United States to have too prominent a role in Canada's defense would encourage Canadians to conclude that the British connection constituted "a liability instead of an asset, and that the plain facts of the situation showed that Canada was an American country dependent on the United States for protection and security."[21] Having strenuously objected in December 1942 to allowing American participation in a study of the Canadian territory opened up by the Alaskan highway project on the grounds that the United States would try "to control developments in our country after the war, and to bring Canada out of the orbit of the British Commonwealth of Nations into their own orbit," in April 1943 King and the CWC, declaring that all American projects and joint defense undertakings in Canada's northwest had to be the "subject of specific agreement between the two governments," appointed Major General W.W. Foster as a special commissioner. His job was to ensure that all American requests to initiate new projects were cleared first by the DEA or the PJBD, and to make certain "that no commitments are made and no situation allowed to develop as a result of which the full Canadian control of the area would be in any way prejudiced or endangered."[22]

Left unresolved by the special commissioner's appointment was the status of the many American projects already underway in northwest Canada. Keenleyside, having initially thought that Macdonald's case had been somewhat overstated, soon reversed his position after undertaking his own tour of northwest North America in 1943. Disturbed by "the disparity between the American and Canadian contributions to defence operations in the Northwest" and greatly impressed by the scale, intensity, and permanence of the American effort, in late July 1943 Keenleyside, aware that the Cabinet War Committee already had committed a brigade to the recapture of the Aleutian island of Kiska (slated for mid-August), suggested allocating more troops to additional north Pacific operations. Not only would such action counter the perception that Canada's role in continental defense was too passive, Keenleyside hoped that an expanded Canadian presence in the Pacific would gain the Dominion a say in Japanese affairs after Japan's defeat had been achieved.[23]

Reid's outlook was much less optimistic. Having already pointed out in April 1943 that Canadians had "not won from London complete freedom to make our own decisions on every issue—including that of peace and war—in order to become a colony of Washington," by August, Reid fretted that the United States was seeking to safeguard itself from any future assaults from Europe or Asia by acquiring "bases not only in Alaska and perhaps the Japanese Kuriles but also across northern Canada." If Canada allowed the United States to construct "a Maginot Line of air defenses in the Canadian North," then the Dominion would face the "danger of being involved in a future war either by a direct attack on our own territory or by an attack launched against one of our neighbours over our territory."[24] King took a middle ground. Having risked much political capital in sending 5,000 conscripts to Kiska only to have those men assault a deserted island (the Japanese had left Kiska three weeks before 35,000 Canadian and American troops stormed its beaches), King was no longer willing to engage in further Pacific adventures. Some combat-ready troops would be maintained in Pacific Command in case they might be needed at some future point, but Canadian troops would not be used in the Pacific anytime soon if the prime minister could help it.[25] In December 1943 the CWC decided that it would no longer accept or request any additional American funds for the construction or improvement of any airfields in the northwest; furthermore, Canada would pay the United States for all the permanent facilities it had constructed on Canadian soil excepting the Alaska highway (completed in November 1943). By 1946 all American-built facilities on Canadian soil had been formally handed over to Canadian control.[26]

Roosevelt's role in Canadian-American defense relations over the last three years of the war is most notable only for his virtual absence. With his responsibility as commander-in-chief of the massive American military effort, Roosevelt had his hands full, and as historian Kent Roberts Greenfield has shown, the president took those military duties very seriously.[27] But it is also clear that after 1941's Hyde Park Agreement, Roosevelt had little time for Canadian issues. He visited Quebec City in August 1943 and September 1944, but did so in order to meet with Churchill and the combined chiefs. In fact, when Prime Minister King protested in 1943 against the exclusion of the Canadian service heads from the Quebec meetings, though Churchill supported a Canadian presence at least at the plenary sessions, citing concerns that China and Brazil would demand CCS membership, Roosevelt refused to make the alteration. Though such rebuffs were seen by Escott Reid as proof not only that "Mr. Roosevelt's peculiar virtues as a war-maker unfit him for the task of peacemaking" but also that a mentally and physically overtired president had "inevitably been corrupted by power,"[28] Roosevelt stood like a monolith shadowing Ottawa's halls of power. When Canadian generals coerced their reluctant government into despatching troops to the Aleutians, their effort very well might have flopped except that King, worried that a refusal to countenance the project might damage his relationship with President Roosevelt, gave in. And just over a year later, when King sought to include a Canadian Army Pacific Force (CAPF) in the final operations against Japan, he managed to overcome American military resistance to the notion by going directly to Roosevelt.[29]

Historian Frank Freidel has argued that Roosevelt, as a believer in collective security, was compelled to slowly build a foreign policy by trial and error because he led a nation that was "fundamentally isolationist."[30] Such a statement does much to explain Roosevelt's Canada policy prior to December 1941. Unable to offer concrete security agreements to any foreign powers, Roosevelt seized opportunities when they presented themselves in order to encourage other nations to deter aggression from the revisionist powers. This is not to say that the president had a plan from the very start, whatever Sumner Welles's claim. Asked by an admirer in 1934 if he could give some permanency to American foreign policy, Roosevelt frankly replied that he did not know how to do that.[31] What Roosevelt did know how to do was to encourage, and if necessary—as he demonstrated in 1936 at Quebec and at Ogdensburg in 1940—to push. Moreover, even when confronted by some advisers who demonstrated little enthusiasm and sometimes outright opposition to presidential initiatives regarding Canada, Roosevelt most often prevailed. This was no small achievement. Not only did the strong-willed General Marshall give way to the president's wishes regarding aid to Canada and Britain in 1940, Roosevelt dealt most effectively with numerous subordinates most likely to share Dean Acheson's acid view of Canadians as "a tribal society, naive, terribly serious about the wrong things, and not at all aware of their real problems." Speaking perhaps with a bitterness that only the beloved son of expatriate Canadian parents could muster, Acheson thought that the best move Canadians could make "would be to ask us to take them over; and our best move would be to say, no."[32]

In November 1941 Roosevelt wrote to say that he hoped King indulged as he did in the "thoroughly sanctimonious and pharisaical thought that it is a grand and glorious thing for Canada and the United States to have the team of Mackenzie and Roosevelt at the helm at times like these." Though Roosevelt felt that "probably both nations could get along without us, but I think we may be pardoned for our thoughts, especially in view of the fact that our association has brought some proven benefits to both nations."[33] Roosevelt was right; Canada and the United States could and did get along without King and him, but one doubts that the Canadian-American alliance would have had so promising a start in the 1940s without those two political giants. When John F. Kennedy visited a decidedly stodgy Ottawa in July 1961, that doomed and tragic president told Canadian parliamentarians that "geography has made us partners. History has made us allies. These whom nature hath so jointed together, let no man put asunder." Fine words well-spoken, but many nationalist Canadians likely would agree with a far less romantic statement that the Canadian-American alliance, "like the long relationship from which it grew, was predicated upon geopolitical and economic realities more than cultural affinity."[34]

Theorists of alliance formation and political scientists have contended that nations ally to oppose a common threat, to accommodate such a threat through a pact of restraint, to provide great powers with a mechanism to manage weaker nations, or that small powers seek military pacts not only because they are weak, but because through such agreements they gain the "right" to be consulted by their great power ally.[35] The American alliance with Canada after 1940 fits this expanded definition perfectly. Although some Canadian historians have suggested that Roosevelt's interest in Canada may have stemmed simply from many idyll summers spent on Campobello Island,[36] the geopolitically-minded Roosevelt, facing a quite serious military threat from Germany in 1940, through the PJBD's creation gained a tool of management over Canada and its hitherto neglected and weak home defense forces. By ensuring that America's potentially vulnerable maritime and aerial approaches to the north were more properly guarded, Roosevelt did his job as commander-in-chief and reassured nervous compatriots that he sought hemispheric security, not foreign adventure. That Roosevelt weaved in and out of Canadian affairs, especially after 1941, might have reflected his wandering attention span or a realization that there were far greater issues to occupy his limited and valuable presidential time. Moreover, with the PJBD's formation and expanding ties on a multiplicity of levels between official Canada and the United States, relations between Washington and Ottawa had become highly institutionalized; thus Roosevelt doubtless felt he had little need to personally consider Canadian matters at length.

Things were somewhat different north of the forty-ninth parallel. There can be no doubt that Canada benefited greatly from the American security umbrella or that it profited magnificently from the Hyde Park Agreement. Indeed, it has been argued that Ogdensburg's real significance lay in King's recognition that British weakness demanded that he accept American strategic guardianship, not just so Canada would survive, but because aid to Canada was aid as well to Britain.[37] Furthermore, given the realization that Roosevelt would have organized continental defense with or without Canadian approval, King gained Canada at least a voice, and possibly an important one, in the formulation of hemispheric defense, no small achievement for a nation only one-tenth as large as its neighbor. Though an anonymous Canadian had observed in the pages of the noted journal *Foreign Affairs* in 1932 that the Dominion's material inferiority compared to the United States would be balanced by Canadian moral superiority—"you are big, but we are better; you are great but we are good"—it did not hurt that the Canadian cause that a great power often must support a small ally "with a certain amount of deference, merely because it is an ally—and the disruption of an ally is a political, if not a military loss."[38] As the unhappy argument over West Coast unity-of-command demonstrated, Canada could hold its own sometimes against the United States when viewpoints did not converge, although one might conclude that the story might have been very much different had LaGuardia been able to convince Roosevelt to intervene more forcefully, or had more vital American interests been at stake. Fortunately for Canadians, the Americans have possessed for some time "a strong conscience that restrains them from forcing their will on us."[39] Many other peoples bordering great powers—the Finns, the Poles, or the Latin Americans for example—have not been so fortunate.

But even the most benevolent elephant can crush a tiny mouse when it rolls over, and for many Canadian officials, keeping a proper distance from an elephantine America was problematic. Lester Pearson, soon to become ambassador to the United States and then Canada's prime minister in the 1960s, had considerable affection for Americans. Yet in February 1943, fearing that postwar American foreign policy was "not going to be much more intelligent than it was after the last," Pearson thought that Canadians "were in for a sticky time."[40] It was a common sentiment within the DEA.

Arguing that many Canadians feared they were on the verge of becoming part of the United States "without the formalities of annexation," Escott Reid advised Norman Robertson in March 1943 that as many Americans seemed to think their participation in the war was "a favour which the United States is conferring on humanity and which carries with it the right to run things their own way," Canada therefore should steel itself for "energetic, aggressive and at times inconsiderate policies on the part of the Administration in Washington and as close neighbours we may see more of this than most people."[41]

Though the Canadian government used such concerns to buttress its support for multilateral international organizations and to avoid being caught between Britain and the United States,[42] the Canadian army, so long suspicious of American motives, by 1944 saw its role in guaranteeing national security as linked intimately with the American ally. Not only did Maurice Pope oppose attaching the CAPF to British forces in the Pacific, recalling that Canada had not done enough in the 1930s to assure the United States that it would or could defend itself, by early 1944 Pope was certain that "what we have to fear is more a lack of confidence in [the] United States as to our security, rather than enemy action. If we do enough to assure the United States we shall have done more than a cold assessment of that risk would indicate to be necessary." To this end, the Post-Hostilities Problems Committee, formed in 1943 by the CWC to determine Canada's postwar policy goals, recommended in 1945 that as the Soviet Union loomed as the most likely threat to North American security, "the defences of Canada should be closely coordinated with the United States after the war."[43]

Already gratified "by the degree of frankness in Canadian-American relations," the State Department's Office of British Commonwealth and Northern European Affairs regarded the PJBD's continued existence as "a recognition of the interdependence" of Canadian and American defense interests. Major General Guy V. Henry of the PJBD's American section had similar hopes for the agency. Interested in putting the vast defense infrastructure in northwest Canada and Alaska to good use but concerned that Canadian public opinion might not yet be ready to accept closer military ties with the United States and the standardization of the Canadian and American armed forces, in June 1945 Henry proposed talks to determine the Canadian position.[44] Though the Canadian members of the PJBD initially reacted favorably to the standardization proposal, the lack of any Canadian studies on the strategic value of the Dominion's vast northern regions made any meaningful discussions with the Americans difficult. But by September the Canadian view had changed. Although the Canadian government was quite happy to retain both the PJBD and the Northwest Staging Route, Pope told the PJBD that given a conclusion that Canada's north faced no invasion threat "over the next one or two decades" and that major operations likely would not occur on or near Canadian territory in that time frame, there was no present need for "complete uniformity of equipment, organization and training of the Forces of our two countries." The door, however, was left open to having meetings "for the purpose of making a broad survey of the requirements of North American joint defence."[45]

The document had King's fingerprints all over it. Having decided at war's end that it was time to bring Canada back "to the old Liberal Principles of economy, reduction of taxes, anti-militarism etc.," King cut the military's budget for fiscal year 1946 from $290 million down to $172 million.[46] And with Roosevelt dead, King's second thoughts about closer military and political ties with the United States only intensified. Informing an aide"that it was the secret aim of every American leader, including Franklin Roosevelt, to dominate Canada and ultimately to possess the country,"[47] in 1948, just months before his retirement after 40 years of public service, King scuttled a free trade agreement with the United States on the grounds that the pact had been too hastily arranged, that it could bring down the his government, and that provisions for a customs union could fulfil "the long objective of the Americans to control this Continent."[48]

    But even the wily and highly-determined King could not permanently block the development of much closer security ties between Canada and the United States, especially as relations with the Soviet Union worsened after the discovery of a Soviet spy ring in Canada in September 1945. Although Henry's attempts to reach a series of joint principles for defense cooperation and to create a Canada–United States joint chiefs of staff met with a cool response from the American joint chiefs and Canada in 1946, in February 1947 the two nations agreed to issue a "Joint Statement on Defence Collaboration." Both parties retained control over all military activities taking place in or over their respective territories as well as the right to determine the extent of future cooperation, but they agreed as well to exchange military personnel, cooperate in exercises and tests, encourage the standardization of equipment and practices, and make available military facilities to the other nation on a case-by-case basis. As to rumors of American bases in Canada's north, King "emphatically" denied talk of Maginot Lines or any other large-scale projects in northern Canada, labelling such rumors "unwarranted" and "fantastic."[49]

    After King's final retirement in 1948 and his subsequent death in July 1950 (just as Canadian leaders were approving the despatch of troops to Korea), much of the caution he had shown regarding defense ties with the United States went by the board. As the Cold War heated up, so did Canadian military budgets and often virulent anti-Communist sentiment. With the advent of long-range Soviet bombers and then missile technology in the 1950s, the threat to North America's northern approaches that had seemed impossible in September 1945 had arrived. Ironically, when Ottawa approved the North American Air Defense Command in 1957, a military system that demanded a type of very close defense cooperation far exceeding anything King had envisioned, the reigning government was a Conservative one led by John Diefenbaker, an Anglophile renowned for his distrust of things American. Although the Cold War likely did more than Roosevelt ever could have done to ensure the Canadian-American military alliance's survival beyond 1945, given the disparity between the American and Canadian security contributions and an American tendency to expect Canada's collaboration no matter what the situation, few Canadians could not help but agree with Pearson's World War Two comment that from the vantage point of imperial Washington, countries like Canada were "necessary, but not necessary enough."[50]

NOTES

1. J.L. Granatstein, "Getting On with the Americans: Changing Canadian Perceptions of the United States, 1939–1945," *The Canadian Review of American Studies*, 5 (Spring 1974), 3.

2. Moffat to Ray Atherton, 2 February 1942, NARA, RG84, Entry 2195A, file 800; and A.W. Klieforth to Hickerson, 6 May 1943, NARA, RG59 Decimal File 1940–44, 711.42/5–643.

3. Hickerson to Klieforth, 1 June 1943, Ibid.; and Hickerson to Hull, 20 May 1943, Ibid., 711.42/255.

4. "Northward the Course of Empire," July 1942, NARA, RG165, War Department Records, Office of the Director of Plans and Operations [OPD], Entry 418, file OPD 336 Canada.

5. Embick to Major General Thomas T. Handy, 24 July 1942, Ibid.; draft memorandum by Brigadier General A.C. Wedermeyer, 29 July 1942, Ibid.; and Handy to McCloy, 30 July 1942, Ibid.

6. Quoted in Shelagh D. Grant, *Sovereignty or Security? Government Policy in the Canadian North 1936–1950* (Vancouver: University of British Columbia Press, 1988), 101.

7. Quoted in Keenleyside to Robertson, "Evidence Relating to United States Efforts to Obtain Post-War Advantages from Wartime Expenditures in Canada," 11 December 1943, NAC, King Memoranda and Notes, reel H1530, C241909–14.

8. Berle memorandum of interview with Hutchison, 9 February 1943, FDRL, Berle Diary, box 214; and Berle to Hull, 12 January 1944, Ibid., Berle Papers, State Department File 1938–45, box 59, file Hull, Cordell—1944 Memoranda to.

9. Hull memorandum of conversation with King, 17 April 1941, LC, Hull Papers, box 57, file Canada 1933–44.

10. Minutes of the Alaskan International Highway Commission, 6 August 1941, FDRL, Roosevelt OF, file OF 1566; and Bureau of the Budget to General Watson, 8 September 1941, Ibid.

11. M.V. Bezeau, "The Realities of Strategic Planning: The Decision to Build the Alaska Highway," in Kenneth Coates, ed., *The Alaska Highway: Papers of the 40th Anniversary Symposium* (Vancouver: University of British Columbia Press, 1985), 27–30; and Admiral King to Marshall, 5 February 1942, LC, King Papers, box 13, file George Marshall.

12. COS to Ministers, 4 February 1942, DHH, Kardex file 112.1 (D82); CWC minutes, 12 February 1942, NAC, RG2 7c, vol. 8; and Moffat memorandum of conversation with Robertson, 13 February 1942, HL, Moffat Papers, MS Am 1407, vol. 47.

13. LaGuardia to Roosevelt, 7 March 1942, FDRL, Roosevelt PSF, file Permanent Joint Board on Defense; and CWC minutes, 5 March 1942, NAC, RG2 7c, vol. 8.

14. Dziuban, *Military Relations between the United States and Canada*, 221.

15. See Perras, "Stepping Stones on a Road to Nowhere?" Chapter 4.

16. Macdonald to Clement Attlee plus "Notes on Developments in North-Western Canada," 7 April 1943, PRO, DO35/1645, file WG 533/7.

17. Massey diary, 29 April 1943, UTA, Massey Papers, vol. 311. See K.S. Coates and W.R. Morrison, *The Alaska Highway in World War II: The U.S. Army of Occupation in Canada's Northwest* (Toronto: University of Toronto Press, 1992).

18. Pearson to McCarthy, "Certain Developments in Canada–United States Relations," 18 March 1943, NAC, RG25, vol. 5758, file 71(s); and Reid, "Some Problems in the Relations between Canada and the United States," 16 April 1943, NAC, Reid Papers, vol. 6, file 10.

19. David B. Dewitt and John Kirton, *Canada as a Principal Power: A Study in Foreign Policy and International Relations* (Toronto: Wiley, 1983), 29.

20. John W. Warnock, *Partner to Behemoth: The Military Policy of Canada* (Toronto: New Press, 1970), 313; and George Grant, *Lament for a Nation: The Defeat of Canadian Nationalism* (Toronto: McClelland and Stewart, 1965), 50.

21. Macdonald to Attlee, 3 February 1942, no. 63, attached to WP (42) 103, 28 February 1942, PRO, Cabinet Office Records, CAB 66/22.

22. King diary, 30 December 1942, NAC; CWC minutes, 16 April 1943, NAC, RG2 7c, vol. 12; and King to W.W. Foster, 20 May 1943, NAC, RG2, vol. 27, file D–19–D–5 1943–45.

23. Keenleyside to King, "Canadian-American Relations in the Northwest," 29 July 1943, NAC, King Correspondence, vol. 337, file BA–BL 1943.

24. Reid, "Some Problems in the Relations between Canada and the United States," 16 April 1943, Reid Papers, vol. 6, file 10; and Reid, "Canada's Position on the Main Air Routes between North America and Northern and Central Europe and Northern Asia: Some General Political and Security Considerations," 2 August 1943, Ibid.

25. CWC minutes, 8 September 1943, NAC, RG2 7c, vol. 13.

26. Stacey, *Arms, Men and Governments*, 381; and John W. Holmes, *The Shaping of Peace: Canada and the Search for World Order 1943–1957. Volume 1* (Toronto: University of Toronto Press, 1979), 175. Canada paid just over $93 million to the United States to settle the outstanding project accounts; Dziuban, *Military Relations between the United States and Canada*, 334.

27. From 1938 until 1945, Roosevelt made 22 major decisions "against the advice, or over the protests, of his major advisers," and personally instigated 13 more including aid to Britain in 1940, the creation of Lend-Lease, choosing General Dwight Eisenhower to lead the European invasion, and authorizing Douglas MacArthur to retake the Philippines; Kent Roberts Greenfield, *American Strategy in World War II: A Reconsideration* (Baltimore: The Johns Hopkins University Press, 1963), 80–4.

28. Churchill to Macdonald, no. 1783, 23 July 1943, NAC, King Correspondence, reel C7035, 290701; Roosevelt to Churchill, no. R–323, 24 July 1943, in Warren F. Kimball, ed., *Churchill & Roosevelt: The Complete Correspondence. II. Alliance Forged November 1942–February 1944* (Princeton: Princeton University Press, 1984), 344; and Reid, "The United States and the Peace-Making," 16 June 1944, NAC, Reid Papers, vol. 13, file United States June 1944.

29. King diary, 30 May 1943, NAC; and Ibid., 14 September 1944, NAC. The CAPF is discussed in Galen Roger Perras, "Once Bitten, Twice Shy: The Origins of the Canadian Army Pacific Force, 1944–1945," in Greg Donaghy, ed., *Uncertain Horizon: Canadians and Their World in 1945* (Ottawa: Canadian Committee for the History of the Second World War, 1997), 77–99.

30. Freidel, *Franklin D. Roosevelt*, 106.

31. Quoted in Edward M. Bennett, *Franklin D. Roosevelt and the Search for Security: American-Soviet Relations, 1933–1939* (Wilmington: Scholarly Resources Inc., 1985), xvii.

32. Dean Acheson to Jane A. Brown, 15 July 1963, in David S. McLellan and David C. Acheson, eds., *Among Friends: Personal Letters of Dean Acheson* (New York: Dodd, Mead & Company, 1980), 250.

33. Roosevelt to King, 5 November 1941, FDRL, Roosevelt PSF, file PSF 1 Diplomatic Correspondence—Canada.

34. Kennedy quoted in R.F. Swanson, ed., *Canadian-American Summit Diplomacy, 1923–1973* (Toronto: McClelland and Stewart, 1975), 201; and John Herd Thompson and Stephen J. Randall, *Canada and the United States: Ambivalent Allies* (Montreal: McGill-Queen's University Press, 1994), 128.

35. Paul Schroeder quoted in Stephen M. Walt, *The Origins of Alliances* (Ithaca: Cornell University Press, 1987), 7; and Robert L. Rothstein, *Alliances and Small Powers* (New York: Columbia University Press, 1968), 49.

36. Stacey, *Canada and the Age of Conflict, Volume 2*, 231; and Thompson and Randall, *Canada and the United States*, 143–44.

37. J.L. Granatstein, *How Britain's Weakness Forced Canada into the Arms of the United States* (Toronto: University of Toronto Press, 1989), 3.

38. "R," "Neighbours, A Canadian View," *Foreign Affairs* X (April 1932), 422; and Rothstein, *Alliances and Small Powers*, 120.

39. Holmes, *Life with Uncle*, 105.

40. Pearson diary entry, 8 February 1943, NAC, Lester Pearson Papers, vol. 8.

41. Reid, "Certain Developments in Canada–United States Relations," 18 March 1943, NAC, RG25, vol. 5758, file 71 (s).

42. See Brooke Claxton, "The Place of Canada in Post-War Organization," *Canadian Journal of Economics and Political Science* X (November 1944), 412.

43. Pope to Lieutenant Colonel J.H. Jenkins, 4 April 1944, NAC, RG25, file 52–C (s); and Post-Hostilities Problems Committee, "Post-War Canadian Defence Relationships with the United States: General Considerations," 2 March 1945, Ibid.

44. "Policy and Information Statement on Canada," 2 June 1945, NARA, Records of the Office of British Commonwealth and Northern European Affairs 1941–1953, RG59, box 6, file Canada—General; Major General Guy V. Henry, "Continental Defense Value of Canadian Northwest," 8 June 1945, NARA, RG59, Decimal File 1945–49, 842.20 Defense/6–2745; and Henry, "Canada–United States Post-War Collaboration," 8 June 1945, USMHI, Guy V. Henry Papers, box 2, file Autobiography.

45. J.G. Parsons to Hickerson, 27 June 1945, NARA, RG59, Decimal File 1945–49, 842.20 Defense/6–2745; and Pope, "Note on General Henry's Statements," 3 September 1945, DHH, Kardex file 314.009 (D17).

46. Jockel, *No Boundaries Upstairs*, 14.

47. J.W. Pickersgill, "Mackenzie King's Political Attitudes and Public Policies: A Personal Impression," in John English and J.O. Stubbs, eds., *Mackenzie King: Widening the Debate* (Toronto: Macmillan, 1978), 18.

48. Robert Cuff and J.L. Granatstein, "The Rise and Fall of Canadian Free Trade, 1947–8," *Canadian Historical Review* 58 (December 1977), 478.

49. Jockel, *No Boundaries Upstairs*, 15–29.

50. Quoted in Bothwell, *Canada and the United States*, 23.

Bibliography

PRIMARY SOURCES

1. Records and Manuscript Groups

A. AUSTRALIA

Australian Archives, Canberra

Department of External Affairs Records, Series A3300
Frederick Shedden Papers, Series A5954

B. CANADA

British Columbia Archives and Records Service, Victoria

T.D. Pattullo Papers

Directorate of History and Heritage, National Defence, Ottawa

Kardex Files

National Archives of Canada, Ottawa

R.B. Bennett Papers
Cabinet War Committee Minutes and Records, RG2 7c

Loring Christie Papers
H.D.G. Crerar Papers
Department of External Affairs Records, RG25
Department of National Defence Records, RG24
C.F. Hamilton Papers
William Lyon Mackenzie King Papers, Correspondence
William Lyon Mackenzie King Papers, Diaries
William Lyon Mackenzie King Papers, Memoranda and Notes
Ian Mackenzie Papers
A.G.L. McNaughton Papers
Lester Pearson Papers, Diaries
Maurice Pope Papers
Privy Council Office Records, RG2
Privy Council Office Records, Memoranda of Defence Council and Emergency Council,
        1938–1939, RG2 7c
J.L. Ralston Papers
Escott Reid Papers
N.A. Robertson Papers
O.D. Skelton Papers
Hume Wrong Papers

                        Queen's University Archives, Kingston

J. Sutherland Brown Papers
John Buchan Papers
T.A. Crerar Papers
Grant Dexter Papers
Charles Gavan Power Papers
Norman Rogers Papers

                        University of Toronto Archives, Toronto

Vincent Massey Papers

                        C. GREAT BRITAIN

                        Durham University Archives, Durham

Malcolm Macdonald Papers

                        Public Record Office, Kew

Admiralty Records, ADM116
Cabinet Office Records, CAB66
Cabinet Office Records, CAB122
Chiefs of Staff Committee Records, Minutes, CAB79
Chiefs of Staff Committee Records, CAB80
Dominion Office Records, DO35
Foreign Office Records, FO371
Maurice Hankey Official Papers, CAB63

Prime Minister's Papers, PREM4
Prime Minister's Papers, PREM11

D. UNITED STATES

Duke University Archives, Durham

John Jackson McSwain Papers

Herbert Hoover Presidential Library, West Branch

William R. Castle Papers
Herbert Hoover Presidential Papers, Subject File
Hanford MacNider Papers
Ferdinand Mayer Papers

Houghton Library, Harvard University, Cambridge

J. Pierrepont Moffat Papers

Library of Congress, Manuscript Division, Washington, D.C.

Raymond L. Buell Papers
Josephus Daniels Papers
Cordell Hull Papers
Harold L. Ickes Papers
Ernest J. King Papers
William Leahy Papers
William Mitchell Papers

George C. Marshall Library, Lexington

George C. Marshall Papers

National Archives and Records Administration, Washington, D.C.

Adjutant General's Office Records, "Color" Plans 1920–1948, RG407
Army Air Forces Central Decimal Files 1917–38, RG18, Entry 166
Joint Board Records, RG225, 1903–1947
Navy Department Records, Office of the Secretary, RG80
State Department Post Records, RG84, Canada, Entry 2195A
State Department Post Records, RG84, Canada, Vancouver, Series 2238
State Department Records, RG59, Decimal File 1930–39
State Department Records, RG59, Decimal File 1940–44
State Department Records, RG59, Decimal File 1945–49
State Department Records, RG59, Office of British Commonwealth and Northern European
        Affairs 1941–53
State Department Records, RG59, Office of European Affairs (Matthews-Hickerson File)
        1934–47, M1244
State Department Records, RG59, Permanent Joint Board on Defense

War Department Records, Military Intelligence Division, RG165, Entry 77
War Department Records, Office of the Director of Plans and Operations, Executive Files,
       RG165
War Department Records, Office of the Director of Plans and Operations, Security-Classified
       Correspondence, RG165, Entry 418
War Department Records, War Plans Division, RG165, Entry 281

Naval Historical Center, Washington, D.C.

Strategic Plans Division Records, Series III

Franklin D. Roosevelt Presidential Library, Hyde Park

Adolf Berle Papers
Harry Hopkins Papers
Henry Morgenthau Jr. Papers and Presidential Diaries
Franklin Delano Roosevelt Papers, Map Room Files
Franklin Delano Roosevelt Papers, Official Files
Franklin Delano Roosevelt Papers, President's Personal Files
Franklin Delano Roosevelt Papers, President's Secretary's File
Sumner Welles Papers

United States Air Force Academy Library, Colorado Springs

William Mitchell Papers

United States Army Military History Institute, Carlisle Barracks

Army War College Curriculum Records
Guy V. Henry Papers

University of Virginia Archives, Charlottesville

Edward R. Stettinius Papers

Sterling Memorial Library, Yale University, New Haven

Henry L. Stimson Papers

2. Published Documents

A. AUSTRALIA

Hudson, W.J., and Jane North, eds., *My Dear P.M.: Letters to S.M. Bruce, 1924–1929*.
       Canberra: Australian Government Publishing Service, 1980.
Martin, A.W., and Patsy Hardy, eds., *Dark and Hurrying Days: Menzies' 1941 Diary*.
       Canberra: National Library of Australia, 1993.

B. CANADA

Christie, Loring, "The Anglo-Japanese Alliance," *External Affairs*, vol. 18, September 1966, pp. 402–13.

Hilliker, John F., ed., *Documents on Canadian External Relations: Volume 9. 1942–1943.* Ottawa: Department of External Affairs, 1980.

Inglis, Alex I., ed., *Documents on Canadian External Relations: Volume 5. 1931–1935.* Ottawa: Department of External Affairs, 1973.

Munro, John, ed., *Documents on Canadian External Relations: Volume 6. 1936–1939.* Ottawa: Department of External Affairs, 1972.

Murray, David R., ed., *Documents on Canadian External Relations: 1939–1941, Part II. Volume 8.* Ottawa: Department of External Affairs, 1976.

Riddell, Walter A., ed., *Documents on Canadian Foreign Policy 1917–1939.* Toronto: Oxford University Press, 1962.

Stacey, C.P., *Historical Documents of Canada. Volume V: The Arts of War and Peace, 1914–1945.* Toronto: Macmillan, 1972.

C. GREAT BRITAIN

Adams, D.K., ed., *British Documents on Foreign Affairs: Reports and Papers from the Foreign Office Confidential Print. Part II. Series C, North America, 1919–1939. Volume 20. Annual Reports 1928–1932.* Bethesda: University Publications of America, 1995.

D. UNITED STATES

Berle, Beatrice Bishop and Travis Beal Jacobs, eds., *Navigating the Rapids 1918–1971: From the Papers of Adolf A. Berle.* New York: Harcourt Brace Jovanovich, 1973.

Bland, Larry I., ed., *The Papers of George Catlett Marshall. Volume 1: "The Soldierly Spirit," December 1880–June 1939.* Baltimore: The Johns Hopkins University Press, 1981.

Bland, Larry I., ed., *The Papers of George Catlett Marshall. Volume 2: "We Cannot Delay," July 1, 1939–December 6, 1941.* Baltimore: The Johns Hopkins University Press, 1986.

Boorstin, Daniel J., ed., *An American Primer.* Chicago: The University of Chicago Press, 1966.

Complete Press Conferences of Franklin D. Roosevelt, Volumes 3 and 12. NewYork: Da Capo Press, 1972.

Ickes, Harold L., *The Secret Diary of Harold L. Ickes. Volume II: The Inside Struggle 1936–1939.* New York: Simon and Schuster, 1954.

Kimball, Warren F., ed., *Churchill & Roosevelt: The Complete Correspondence. II. Alliance Forged November 1942–February 1944.* Princeton: Princeton University Press, 1984.

McLellan, David S., and David C. Acheson, eds., *Among Friends: Personal Letters of Dean Acheson.* New York: Dodd, Mead & Company, 1980.

Nixon, Edgar B., ed., *Franklin D. Roosevelt and Foreign Affairs. Volume II: March 1934–August 1935.* Cambridge: Belknap Press of Harvard University Press, 1969.

Roosevelt, Elliot, ed., *F.D.R.: His Personal Letters 1928–1945 Volume I.* New York: Duell, Sloan and Pearce, 1950.

Rosenman, Samuel I., ed., *The Public Papers and Addresses of Franklin D. Roosevelt. Volume 6: The Continuing Struggle for Liberalism*. New York: Macmillan, 1941.
State Department, *Papers Relating to the Foreign Relations of the United States*. Washington, D.C.: Government Printing Office, 1893.
State Department, *Peace and War: United States Foreign Policy, 1931–1941*. Washington, D.C.: Government Printing Office, 1943.

3. Legislative Records

A. CANADA

Debate, House of Commons.

B. UNITED STATES

Congressional Record.
Hearings before the Committee on Military Affairs House of Representatives Sev enty–Fourth Congress, First Session, on H.R. 6621 and H.R. 4130, February 11–13 1935. Washington, D.C.: Government Printing Office, 1935.

SECONDARY SOURCES

1. Monographs

Arnold, H.H., *Global Mission*. New York: Harper & Brothers, 1949.
Beard, Charles A., *American Foreign Policy in the Making, 1932–1940*. New Haven: Yale University Press, 1946.
Bennett, Edward M., *Franklin D. Roosevelt and the Search for Security: American-Soviet Relations, 1933–1939*. Wilmington: Scholarly Resources Inc., 1985.
Bland, Larry, ed., *George C. Marshall Interviews and Reminiscences for Forrest C. Pogue*. Lexington: George C. Marshall Foundation, 1991.
Bothwell, Robert, *Canada and the United States: The Politics of Partnership*. New York: Twayne Publishers, 1992.
Bothwell, Robert, and William Kilbourn, *C.D. Howe: A Biography*. Toronto: McClelland and Stewart, 1979.
Breslin, Major Charles B., *World War II in the Aleutians: The Fundamentals of Joint Campaigns*. Newport: Naval War College, 1994.
Burns, James MacGregor, *Roosevelt: The Lion and the Fox*. New York: Harcourt, Brace and Company, 1956.
Callcott, Wilfrid Hardy, *The Western Hemisphere: Its Influence on United States Policies to the End of World War II*. Austin: University of Texas Press, 1968.
Callahan, James Morton, *American Foreign Policy in Canadian Relations*. New York: Macmillan, 1937.
Charmley, John, *Chamberlain and the Lost Peace*. London: Hodder & Stoughton, 1989.
———, *Churchill's Grand Alliance: The Anglo-American Special Relationship 1940–57*. San Diego: Harcourt Brace & Company, 1995.
Chase, James, and Caleb Carr, *America Invulnerable: The Quest for Absolute Security from 1812 to Star Wars*. New York: Summit Books, 1988.
Churchill, Winston, *The Second World War: Their Finest Hour. Volume 2*. Boston:

Houghton Mifflin, 1949.

Cline, Ray S., *Washington Command Post: The Operations Division*, 2nd edition. Washington, D.C.: Center for Military History, 1985.

Cloe, John Haile, and Michael F. Monoghan, *Top Cover for America: The Air Force in Alaska 1920–1983*. Missoula: Pictorial Histories, 1984.

Coates, K.S., and W.R. Morrison, *The Alaska Highway in World War II: The U.S. Army of Occupation in Canada's Northwest*. Toronto: University of Toronto Press, 1992.

Cole, Wayne S., *Roosevelt & the Isolationists, 1932–45*. Lincoln: University of Nebraska Press, 1983.

Conn, Stetson, and Byron Fairchild, *The Framework of Hemisphere Defense*. Washington, D.C.: Department of the Army, 1960.

Crabb, Cecil V., Jr., and Kevin V. Mulcahy, *Presidents and Foreign Policy Making: From FDR to Reagan*. Baton Rouge: Louisiana State University Press, 1986.

Creighton, Donald, *The Forked Road: Canada 1939–1957*. Toronto: McClelland and Stewart, 1976.

Cuff, R.D., and J.L. Granatstein, *Canadian-American Relations in Wartime: From the Great War to the Cold War*. Toronto: Hakkert, 1975.

Dallek, Robert, *Franklin D. Roosevelt and American Foreign Policy, 1932–1945*. New York: Oxford University Press, 1979.

Danchev, Alex, *Very Special Relationship: Field-Marshal Sir John Dill and the Anglo-American Alliance 1941–44*. London: Brassey's Defence Publishers, 1986.

Davis, Kenneth S., *FDR: The New Deal Years 1933–1937*. New York: Random House, 1979.

Dewitt, David B., and John Kirton, *Canada as a Principal Power: A Study in Foreign Policy and International Relations*. Toronto: Wiley, 1983.

Dziuban, Colonel Stanley W., *Military Relations between the United States and Canada 1939–1945*. Washington, D.C.: Department of the Army, 1959.

Eayrs, James, *In Defence of Canada: From the Great War to the Great Depression*. Toronto: University of Toronto Press, 1964.

———, *In Defence of Canada: Appeasement and Rearmament*. Toronto: University of Toronto Press, 1965.

English, John, *Shadow of Heaven: The Life of Lester Pearson. Volume One: 1897–1948*. Toronto: Lester & Orpen Dennys, 1989.

Fogelson, Nancy, *Arctic Exploration & International Relations 1900–1932*. Fairbanks: University of Alaska Press, 1992.

Freidel, Frank, *Franklin D. Roosevelt: A Rendezvous with Destiny*. Boston: Little, Brown and Company, 1990.

Gellman, Irwin F., *Secret Affairs: Franklin D. Roosevelt, Cordell Hull, and Sumner Welles*. Baltimore: The Johns Hopkins University Press, 1995.

Granatstein, J.L., *Canada's War: The Politics of the Mackenzie King Government, 1939–1945*. Toronto: Oxford University Press, 1975.

———, *Mackenzie King: His Life and His World*. Toronto: McGraw-Hill Ryerson, 1977.

———, *The Ottawa Men: The Civil Service Mandarins, 1935–1957*. Toronto: Oxford University Press, 1982.

———, *How Britain's Weakness Forced Canada into the Arms of the United States*. Toronto: University of Toronto Press, 1989.

———, *The Generals: The Canadian Army's Senior Commanders in the Second World War*. Toronto: Stoddart, 1993.

———, *Yankee Go Home? Canadians and Anti-Americanism*. Toronto: HarperCollins,

1996.

Grant, George, *Lament for a Nation: The Defeat of Canadian Nationalism*. Toronto: McClelland and Stewart, 1965.

Grant, Shelagh D., *Sovereignty or Security? Government Policy in the Canadian North 1936–1950*. Vancouver: University of British Columbia Press, 1988.

Greenfield, Kent Roberts, *American Strategy in World War II: A Reconsideration*. Baltimore: The Johns Hopkins University Press, 1963.

Haglund, David, *Latin America and the Transformation of U.S. Strategic Thought, 1936–1940*. Albuquerque: University of New Mexico Press, 1984.

Harper, John Lamberton, *American Visions of Europe: Franklin D. Roosevelt, George F. Kennan, and Dean G. Acheson*. Cambridge: Cambridge University Press, 1994.

Harris, Stephen J., *Canadian Brass: The Making of a Professional Army 1860–1939*. Toronto: University of Toronto Press, 1988.

Heinrichs, Waldo, *Threshold of War: Franklin D. Roosevelt & American Entry into World War II*. New York: Oxford University Press, 1988.

Herwig, Holger H., *Politics of Frustration: The United States in German Naval Planning, 1889–1941*. Boston: Little, Brown and Company, 1976.

Hilliker, John, *Canada's Department of External Affairs. Volume I: The Early Years, 1909–1946*. Montreal: McGill-Queen's University Press, 1990.

Hofstadter, Richard, *The American Political Tradition and the Men Who Made It*. New York: Vintage Books, 1989.

Holmes, John W., *The Shaping of Peace: Canada and the Search for World Order 1943–1957. Volume 1*. Toronto: University of Toronto Press, 1979.

————, *Life with Uncle: The Canadian-American Relationship*. Toronto: University of Toronto Press, 1981.

Horner, D.M., *High Command: Australia & Allied Strategy 1939–1945*. Sydney: George Allen & Unwin, 1982.

Hull, Cordell, *The Memoirs of Cordell Hull. Volume II*. New York: Macmillan, 1948.

Hunt, Michael, *Ideology and U.S. Foreign Policy*. New Haven: Yale University Press, 1987.

Jockel, Joseph T., *No Boundaries Upstairs: Canada, the United States and the Origins of North American Air Defence, 1945–1958*. Vancouver: University of British Columbia Press, 1987.

Jonas, Manfred, *The United States and Germany: A Diplomatic History*. Ithaca: Cornell University Press, 1984.

Keenleyside, Hugh L., *Memoirs of Hugh L. Keenleyside. Volume 2: On the Bridge of Time*. Toronto: McClelland and Stewart, 1982.

Kimball, Warren F., *"The Most Unsordid Act" Lend-Lease, 1939–1941*. Baltimore: The Johns Hopkins University Press, 1969.

————, *The Juggler: Franklin Roosevelt as Wartime Statesman*. Princeton: Princeton University Press, 1991.

Kinsella, William E., Jr., *Leadership in Isolation: FDR and the Origins of the Second World War*. Cambridge: Schenkman Publishing, 1978.

Leuchtenburg, William E., *In the Shadow of FDR: From Harry Truman to Ronald Reagan*. Ithaca: Cornell University Press, 1985.

Levering, Ralph B., *The Public and American Foreign Policy, 1918–1978*. New York: William Morrow and Company, 1978.

Linn, Brian McAllister, *Guardians of Empire: The U.S. Army and the Pacific, 1902–1940*. Chapel Hill: University of North Carolina Press, 1997.

Lowenthal, Mark M., *Leadership and Indecision: American War Planning and Policy*

Process 1937–1942. New York: Garland Publishing, 1988.

Mackenzie, David, *Inside the Atlantic Triangle: Canada and the Entrance of Newfoundland into Confederation, 1939–1949.* Toronto: University of Toronto Press, 1986.

Marks, Frederick W., III, *Wind over Sand: The Diplomacy of Franklin Roosevelt.* Athens: The University of Georgia Press, 1988.

Martin, Lawrence, *The Presidents and the Prime Ministers. Washington and Ottawa Face to Face: The Myth of Bilateral Bliss 1867–1982.* Toronto: Doubleday, 1982.

McFarland, Keith D., *Harry H. Woodring: A Political Biography of FDR's Controversial Secretary of War.* Lawrence: The University Press of Kansas, 1975.

McIntyre, W. David, *The Rise and Fall of the Singapore Naval Base, 1919–1942.* London: Macmillan, 1979.

Merk, Frederick, *Manifest Destiny and Mission in American History: A Reinterpretation.* New York: Vintage Books, 1966.

Miller, Edward S., *War Plan Orange: The U.S. Strategy to Defeat Japan, 1897–1945.* Annapolis: Naval Institute Press, 1991.

Neatby, H. Blair, *William Lyon Mackenzie King. Volume Three, 1932–1939: The Prism of Unity.* Toronto: University of Toronto Press, 1976.

Nelsen, John T. II, *General George C. Marshall: Strategic Leadership and the Challenges of Reconstituting the Army, 1939–41.* Carlisle Barracks: Strategic Studies Institute, United States Army War College, February 1993.

Offner, Arnold A., *The Origins of the Second World War: American Foreign Policy and World Politics, 1917–1941.* New York: Holt, Rinehart, and Winston, 1975.

Overy, Richard, *Why the Allies Won.* London: Pimlico, 1995.

Paterson, Thomas G., J. Garry Clifford, and Kenneth J. Hagen, *American Foreign Policy: A History/1900 to Present.* 3rd edition. Lexington: D.C. Heath, 1991.

Perkins, Dexter, *The New Age of Franklin Roosevelt 1932–45.* Chicago: The University of Chicago Press, 1957.

Phillips, William, *Ventures in Diplomacy.* Boston: Beacon Press, 1953.

Pogue, Forrest C., *George C. Marshall: Ordeal and Hope, 1939–1942.* New York: Viking Press, 1966.

Pope, Maurice A., *Soldiers and Politicians: The Memoirs of Lt.-Gen. Maurice A. Pope.* Toronto: University of Toronto Press, 1962.

Preston, Richard A., *The Defence of the Undefended Border: Planning for War in North America 1867–1939.* Montreal: McGill-Queen's University Press, 1977.

Reynolds, David, *The Creation of the Anglo-American Alliance 1937–41: A Study in Competitive Co-operation.* Chapel Hill: The University of North Carolina Press, 1982.

Rock, William R., *Chamberlain and Roosevelt: British Foreign Policy and the United States, 1937–1940.* Columbus: Ohio University Press, 1988.

Rothstein, Robert, *Alliances and Small Powers.* New York: Columbia University Press, 1968.

Sarty, Roger, *The Maritime Defence of Canada.* Toronto: The Canadian Institute of Strategic Studies, 1996.

Schlesinger, Arthur M., Jr., *The Age of Roosevelt: The Crisis of the Old Order 1919–1933.* Boston: Houghton Mifflin, 1957.

——, *The Age of Roosevelt: The Coming of the New Deal.* Boston: Houghton Mifflin, 1959.

Sherry, Michael S., *In the Shadow of War: The United States since the 1930s.* New Haven: Yale University Press, 1995.

Sherwood, Robert E., *Roosevelt and Hopkins: An Intimate History*. New York: Harper & Brothers, 1948.

Shiner, John F., *Foulois and the U.S. Army Air Corps 1931–1935*. Washington, D.C.: Office of Air Force History, 1983.

Smith, Denis, *Diplomacy of Fear: Canada and the Cold War 1941–1948*. Toronto: University of Toronto Press, 1988.

Stacey, C.P., *Six Years of War: The Army in Canada, Britain and the Pacific*. Ottawa: Department of National Defence, 1955.

———, *Arms, Men and Governments: The War Policies of Canada 1939–1945*. Ottawa: Department of National Defence, 1970.

———, *Canada and the Age of Conflict: A History of Canadian External Policies. Volume 1: 1867–1921*. Toronto: University of Toronto Press, 1977.

———, *Canada and the Age of Conflict: A History of Canadian External Policies. Volume 2: 1921–1948. The Mackenzie King Era*. Toronto: University of Toronto Press, 1981.

Stimson, Henry L., and McGeorge Bundy, *On Active Service in Peace and War. Volume II*. New York: Harper & Brothers, 1948.

Stuart, Reginald, *United States Expansionism and British North America, 1775–1871*. Chapel Hill: The University of North Carolina Press, 1988.

Swanson, R.F., ed., *Canadian-American Summit Diplomacy, 1929–1973*. Toronto: McClelland and Stewart, 1975.

Taylor, Charles, *Six Journeys: A Canadian Pattern*. Toronto: Anansi, 1977.

Thompson, John Herd, and Stephen J. Randall., *Canada and the United States: Ambivalent Allies*. Montreal: McGill-Queen's University Press, 1994.

Walt, Stephen M., *The Origins of Alliances*. Ithaca: Cornell University Press, 1987.

Warnock, John W., *Partner to Behemoth: The Military Policy of Canada*. Toronto: New Press, 1970.

Watson, Mark Skinner, *Chief of Staff: Prewar Plans and Preparations*. Washington, D.C.: Department of the Army, 1950.

Watt, D.C., *Succeeding John Bull: America in Britain's Place 1900–1975*. Cambridge: Cambridge University Press, 1984.

———, *How War Came: The Immediate Origins of the Second World War*. New York: Pantheon Books, 1989.

Welles, Sumner, *The Time for Decision*. New York: Harper & Brothers, 1944.

———, *Seven Major Decisions*. London: Hamish Hamilton, 1951.

Wilson, Joan Hoff, *American Business and Foreign Policy, 1920–1933*. Boston: Beacon Press, 1973.

Wiltz, John E., *From Isolation to War, 1931–1941*. New York: Thomas Y. Crowell, 1968.

2. Articles

Beatty, David, "The 'Canadian Corollary' to the Monroe Doctrine and the Ogdensburg Agreement of 1940, " *The McNaughton Papers*, vol. 5, 1994, pp. 30–45.

Bezeau, M. V., "The Realities of Strategic Planning: The Decision to Build the Alaska Highway," in Kenneth Coates, ed., *The Alaska Highway: Papers of the 40th Anniversary Symposium*. Vancouver: University of British Columbia Press, pp. 25–35.

Borg, Dorothy, "Notes on Roosevelt's 'Quarantine Speech,'" *Political Science Quarterly*, vol. 72, September 1957, pp. 405–33.

Bothwell, Robert and John Kirton, "A Sweet Little Country," in Norman Hillmer, ed., *Partners Nevertheless: Canadian-American Relations in the Twentieth Century.* Toronto: Copp Clark Pitman, 1989, pp. 43–65.

Claxton, Brooke, "The Place of Canada in Post-War Organization," *Canadian Journal of Economics and Political Science*, vol. 10, November 1944, pp. 409–21.

Clifford, J. Garry, "Both Ends of the Telescope: New Perspectives on FDR and American Entry into World War II," *Diplomatic History*, vol. 13, Spring 1989, pp. 213–30.

Corbett, P.E., "Anti-Americanism," *Dalhousie Review*, vol. 10, October 1930, pp. 295–300.

Cuff, Robert, and J.L. Granatstein, "The Rise and Fall of Canadian-American Free Trade, 1947–8," *Canadian Historical Review*, vol. 58, December 1977, pp. 459–82.

Emme, Eugene M., "The American Dimension," in Alfred F. Hurley and Robert C. Ehrhrat, eds., *Air Power and Warfare: The Proceedings of the 8th Military History Symposium United States Air Force Academy 18–20 October 1978.* Washington, D.C.: Government Printing Office, 1979, pp. 56–82.

English, John Allan, "Not an Equilateral Triangle: Canada's Strategic Relationship with the United States and Great Britain, 1939–1945," in B.J.C. McKercher and Lawrence Aronsen, eds., *The North Atlantic Triangle in a Changing World: Anglo-American-Canadian Relations 1902–1956.* Toronto: University of Toronto Press, pp. 147–83.

Fenwick, C.G., "Canada and the Monroe Doctrine," *The American Journal of International Law*, vol. 32, October 1938, pp. 782–85.

Fisher, Robin, "T.D. Pattullo and the British Columbia to Alaska Highway," in Kenneth Coates, ed., *The Alaska Highway: Papers of the 40th Anniversary Symposium.* Vancouver: University of British Columbia Press, 1985, pp. 9–24.

Granatstein, J.L., "The Conservative Party and the Ogdensburg Agreement," *International Journal*, vol. 22, Winter 1966–67, pp. 73–76.

——, "Getting On with the Americans: Changing Canadian Perceptions of the United States, 1939–1945," *The Canadian Review of American Studies*, vol. 5, Spring 1974, pp. 3–17.

——, "Hume Wrong's Road to the Functional Principle," in Keith Neilson and Roy A. Prete, eds., *Coalition Warfare: An Uneasy Accord.* Waterloo: Wilfrid Laurier Press, 1983, pp. 55–77.

——, "Free Trade between Canada and the United States: The Issue That Will Not Go Away," in Denis Stairs and Gilbert R. Winham, eds., *The Politics of Canada's Economic Relationship with the United States.* Toronto: University of Toronto Press, 1985, pp. 11–54.

——, "Mackenzie King and Canada at Ogdensburg, August 1940," in Joel J. Sokolsky and Joseph T. Jockel, eds., *Fifty Years of Canada–United States Defense Cooperation: The Road From Ogdensburg.* Lewiston: The Edwin Mellen Press, 1992, pp. 9–29.

Granatstein, J.L., and Cuff, R.D., "The Hyde Park Declaration 1941: Origins and S i g n i f i cance," *Canadian Historical Review*, vol. 55, March 1974, pp.59–80.

Green, James Frederick, "Canada in World Affairs," *Foreign Policy Reports*, vol. 14, 1 July 1938, pp. 86–96.

Haglund, David G., "George C. Marshall and the Question of Military Aid to England, May–June 1940," *Journal of Contemporary History*, vol. 15, October 1980, pp. 745–60.

Hannigan, Robert, "Reciprocity 1911: Continentalism and American Weltpolitik," *Diplomatic History*, vol. 4, Winter 1980, pp. 1–18.

Harris, Stephen, "The Canadian General Staff and the Higher Organization of Defence,

1919–1939," in B.D. Hunt and R.G. Haycock, eds., *Canada's Defence: Perspectives on Policy in the Twentieth Century.* Toronto: Copp Clark Pitman, 1993, pp. 69–81.

Harrison, Richard A., "Testing the Water: A Secret Probe towards Anglo-American Co-operation in 1936," *The International History Review*, vol. 7, May 1985, pp. 214–34.

Haycock, R.G., "The 'Myth' of Imperial Defence: Australian-Canadian Bilateral Military Co-operation, 1942," *War & Society*, vol. 2, May 1984, pp. 65–84.

Hillmer, Norman, "The Anglo-Canadian Neurosis: The Case of O.D. Skelton," in Peter Lyon, ed., *Britain and Canada: A Survey of a Changing Relationship.* London: Frank Cass, 1976, pp. 61–84.

————,"Defence and Ideology: The Anglo-Canadian Military 'Alliance' in the 1930s," in B.D. Hunt and R.G. Haycock, eds., *Canada's Defence: Perspectives on Policy in the Twentieth Century.* Toronto: Copp Clark Pitman, 1993, pp. 82–97.

Hillmer, Norman, and J.L. Granatstein, "Historians Rank the Best and Worst Canadian Prime Ministers," *Maclean's*, vol. 110, 21 April 1997, pp. 34–38.

Jacob, Philip E., "Influences of World Events on U.S. 'Neutrality' Policy," *Public Opinion Quarterly*, vol. 4, March 1940, pp. 48–65.

Kasurak, Peter, "American Foreign Policy Officials and Canada, 1927–1941: A Look through Bureaucratic Glasses," *International Journal*, vol. 32, Summer 1977, pp. 544–58.

Keegan, John, "A Generation of Victors," *New York Times Book Review*, 16 August 1987, p. 10.

Kennedy, Greg C., "Strategy and Supply in the North Atlantic Triangle, 1914–1918," in B.J.C. McKercher and Lawrence Aronsen, eds., *The North Atlantic Triangle in a Changing World: Anglo-American-Canadian Relations, 1902–1956.* Toronto: University of Toronto Press, 1996, pp. 48–80.

Kottman, Richard N., "Hoover and Canada Diplomatic Appointments," *Canadian Historical Review*, vol. 51, September 1970, pp. 292–309.

————, "The Hoover-Bennett Meeting of 1931: Mismanaged Summitry," *Annals of Iowa*, vol. 42, Winter 1974, pp. 205–21.

Krauskopf, Robert W., "The Army and the Strategic Bomber, 1930–1939," *Military Affairs*, vol. 22, Summer 1958, pp. 83–94.

Lowenthal, Mark M., "Roosevelt and the Coming of the War: The Search for United States Policy 1937–42," in Walter Laqueur, ed., *The Second World War: Essays in Military and Political History.* London: Sage Publications, 1982, pp. 50–76.

Lower, A.R.M., "Loring Christie and the Genesis of the Washington Conference of 1921–1922," *Canadian Historical Review*, vol. 47, March 1966, pp. 38–48.

Marsden, Paul, "The Costs of No Commitments: Canadian Economic Planning for War," in Norman Hillmer, Robert Bothwell, Roger Sarty, and Claude Beauregard, eds., *A Country of Limitations: Canada and the World in 1939.* Ottawa: Canadian Committee for the History of the Second World War, 1996, pp. 199–216.

McCoy, General Frank R. McCoy, Hanson W. Baldwin, and Major George Fielding Eliot, "War Planning," *Council of Foreign Relations Report No. A-B 35.* New York: Council of Foreign Relations, 15 December 1941, pp.1–5.

Miller, A.J., "The Functional Principle in Canada's External Relations," *International Journal*, vol. 35, Spring 1980, pp. 309–28.

Morton, Louis, "Inter-Service Co-operation and Political-Military Collaboration," in Harry L. Coles, ed., *Total War and Cold War: Problems in Civilian Control of the*

Military. Columbus: Ohio State University Press, 1962, pp. 131–60.

Morton, W.L., "Review of *William Lyon Mackenzie King. II. The Lonely Heights, 1924–1932*," in *Canadian Historical Review*, vol. 45, December 1964, pp. 320–21.

Perras, Galen Roger, "Once Bitten, Twice Shy: The Origins of the Canadian Army Pacific Force, 1944–1945," in Greg Donaghy, ed., *Uncertain Horizon: Canadians and Their World in 1945.* Ottawa: Canadian Committee for the History of the Second World War, 1997, pp. 77–99.

Pickersgill, J.W., "Mackenzie King's Political Attitudes and Public Policies: A Personal Impression," in John English and J.O. Stubbs, eds., *Mackenzie King: Widening the Debate.* Toronto: Macmillan, 1978, pp. 15–29.

Pollock, Fred E., "Roosevelt, the Ogdensburg Agreement, and the British Fleet: All Done with Mirrors," *Diplomatic History*, vol. 5, Summer 1981, pp. 203–19.

"R," "Neighbours, A Canadian View," *Foreign Affairs*, vol. X, April 1932, pp. 417–30.

Sarty, Roger, "Mr. King and the Armed Forces," in Norman Hillmer, Robert Bothwell, Roger Sarty, and Claude Beauregard, eds., *A Country of Limitations: Canada and the World in 1939.* Ottawa: Canadian Committee for the History of the Second World War, 1996, pp. 217–46.

Schlesinger, Arthur M., Jr., "Franklin D. Roosevelt's Internationalism," in Cornelis A. van Minnen and John F. Sears, eds., *FDR and His Contemporaries: Foreign Perceptions of an American President.* New York: St. Martin's Press, 1992, pp. 3–16.

Shiner, John F., "General Benjamin Foulois and the 1934 Air Mail Disaster," *Aerospace Historian*, vol. 25, December 1978, pp. 221–30.

———, "The Air Corps, the Navy, and Coast Defense, 1919–1941," *Military Affairs*, vol. 45, October 1981, pp. 113–20.

Stoler, Mark A., "From Continentalism to Globalism: General Stanley D. Embick, the Joint Strategic Survey Committee, and the Military View of American National Policy during the Second World War," *Diplomatic History*, vol. 6, Summer 1982, pp. 303–21.

3. Newspapers

Baltimore Sun
Boston Globe
Boston Post
Calgary Herald
Canadian Methodist Magazine, vol. 11, February 1880.
Christian Science Monitor
Cleveland Plain Dealer
London Daily Telegraph
Manchester Guardian
Montreal Daily Star
Montreal Gazette
Montreal Herald
Montreal Standard
New York Herald Tribune
New York Sunday News
New York Times

Ottawa Citizen
Ottawa (Morning) Journal
Providence Journal
Toronto Daily Star
Toronto Financial Post
Toronto Globe and Mail
Vancouver Daily Province
Vancouver Sun
Victoria Daily Colonist
Washington Herald
Washington Post
Winnipeg Free Press

4. Dissertations

Bothwell, Robert S., "Loring C. Christie and the Failure of Bureaucratic Imperialism," doctoral   dissertation, Harvard University, 1972.

Kasurak, Peter Charles, "The United States Legation at Ottawa, 1927–1941: An Institutional Study," doctoral dissertation, Duke University, Durham, 1976.

Mangusso, Mary Childers, "Anthony J. Dimond: A Political Biography," doctoral dissertation, Texas Tech University, 1978.

Perras, Galen Roger, "Stepping Stones on a Road to Nowhere? The United States, Canada, and the Aleutian Islands Campaign, 1942–1943," doctoral dissertation, University of Waterloo, 1995.

5. Unpublished Papers

McMannon, Timothy J., "Warren G. Magnusson and the Alaska Highway," paper presented to the symposium "'On Brotherly Terms': Canadian-American Relations West of the Rockies," University of Washington, Seattle, September 1996.

Perras, Galen Roger, "'The parties with whom we have been estranged so long can scarcely be brought into a close relationship at a moment's notice': Canada's Failure to Provide Military Aid to Australia, 1942–1945," paper presented at the annual meeting of the Australian Studies Association of North America, Vancouver, 7–9 March 1996.

Index

About the Author

GALEN ROGER PERRAS is a Post-Doctoral Fellow in the History Department at the University of Calgary. He holds an M.A. in War Studies from the Royal Military College of Canada and a Ph.D. in Canadian and American History from the University of Waterloo. The author of numerous articles, he has also worked as a strategic analyst for the Canadian Department of National Defence.

ISBN 0-275-95500-1

HARDCOVER BAR CODE